St Andrews

St Andrews

City by the Northern Sea

Raymond Lamont-Brown

BIRLINN

Published in 2006 by
Birlinn Limited
West Newington House
10 Newington Road
Edinburgh EH9 1QS

www.birlinn.co.uk

ISBN 10: 1 84158 450 9
ISBN 13: 978 1 84158 450 8

British Library Cataloguing-in-Publication Data
A catalogue record for this book is available from the British Library

Typeset by Iolaire Typesetting, Newtonmore
Printed and bound by GraphyCems, Spain

Contents

List of Illustrations

Acknowledgements

This book is the result of over two decades of residence in St Andrews and some thirty years in total studying the environs. It is dedicated to all who love the burgh and have its best interests at heart. The text forms a purely personal selection of the historical characters who played a role in the burgh's development and an individual choice of what to highlight for the historical perspective. Herein too, are aspects of history discussed in countless conversations with St Andreans from town and gown. I am grateful to the following who helped add colour to the text: the late Dr Ronald Gordon Cant and my old friend the late Alexander Brown Paterson MBE, with a thanks too, to Gordon Christie, Donald Macgregor, Margaret MacGregor, the Rev. Alan D. McDonald as well as my friends over the years in the St Andrews Preservation Trust and the University of St Andrews. A special thanks goes to my wife, Dr E. Moira Lamont-Brown, for her help and companionship in researching the St Andrews story.

Every effort has been made to trace the copyright holders of works quoted in the text, although the death of authors and reversion of rights often make this task difficult; each quote is sourced in the notes.

Historic St Andrews: A Chronology

c.8000 BC	Early inhabitants colonise the estuary fringe of the Eden.
4000–2500 BC	Neolithic activity in St Andrews area.
2400–700 BC	Bronze Age habitations appear.
500 BC	Celtic speaking settlements.
100 BC	St Andrews area within the territory of the tribesfolk, the *Venicones*.
79 AD	Roman legionaries first appear in St Andrews region; camps at Auchtermuchty, Carpow, Newburgh, Edenwood, by Cupar, and Bonnytown, by Boarhills.
400–850	Rise of Pictish St Andrews. Settlement within the Pictish province of Fib.
c.733	Bishop Acca of Hexham believed to carry relics of St Andrew to Kilrymont; beginning of the Cult of St Andrew. 6 Feb. celebrated as 'The Coming of St Andrew's Bones'.
746	Death of Abbot Tuathalan at Cennrigmonaid; placename rendered Kilrymont, later St Andrews.
877	Viking vessels off St Andrews; Battle of Inverdovat.
906	St Andrews the seat of the Bishop of Alba.
920	Culdees, a canonical body at St Andrews.
c.1050	Building of St Rule's Church developed; extended c.1130.
1140–50	Foundation of the burgh of St Andrews by Bishop Robert at David I's behest.

1144	Foundation and endowment of the Augustinian Priory of St Andrews.
1160	Malcolm IV confirms burgh status.
1162	New cathedral begun by Bishop Arnold.
c.1200	Bishop Roger de Beaumont orders building of the first castle at St Andrews.
1303–04	Edward I of England holds parliament at St Andrews, and gives offerings at the Shrine of St Andrew.
1318	5 July. Cathedral consecrated by Bishop William de Lamberton.
1350	Plague in St Andrews.
1362	Plague.
1410	11 May. *The Studium Generale Universitatis* founded at St Andrews as a 'school of higher studies'.
1412	28 Feb. Charter of Incorporation and Privileges granted to the University by Bishop Henry Wardlaw.
1413	28 Aug. University Charter confirmed and amplified by the papal *Bulla* of Pope Benedict XIII.
1414	Candlemas, Feb. The arrival in St Andrews and promulgation of the papal *Bulla* bringing the University of St Andrews into formal existence.
1419	Jan. Land acquired in South Street for a 'College of Theologians and Artists honouring Almighty God, the Blessed Virgin Mary, the Blessed John the Evangelist and All Saints.'
1433	23 July. Paul Crow burned at St Andrews Market Cross.
1450	27 Aug. St Salvator's College buildings inaugurated.
1457	James II's Act forbids the playing of golf.
1471	James III's Act forbids the playing of golf.
1472	13 Aug. Bishopric of St Andrews erected into an archepiscopal and metropolitan see by Pope Sixtus IV.

1491	James IVs Act forbids the playing of golf.
1502	James IV 'legitimation of golf'.
1512	20 Aug. St Leonards College founded.
1528	29 Feb. Patrick Hamilton burned at St Andrews.
1529	Plague.
1533	Henry Forrest burned at St Andrews.
1537	12 Feb. St Mary's College founded.
1538	June. James V marries Marie de Guise-Lorraine at St Andrews Cathedral.
1546	1 Mar. George Wishart strangled and burned at St Andrews. 29 May, Cardinal Archbishop David Beaton murdered at St Andrews Castle.
1546–47	St Andrews Castle besieged by the Regent, the Earl of Arran.
1552	25 Jan. Mary Queen of Scots ratifies burgh status. Charter for St Andrews Links.
1558	28 Apr. Walter Myln burned at St Andrews; the last heresy trial held in the cathedral.
1559	11 June. John Knox preaches in Holy Trinity. 14 June. St Andrews Cathedral attacked by rant-inspired, nobility stage-managed mob.
1560	24 Aug. Parliament abolishes Papal Authority in Scotland.
1561–65	Mary Queen of Scots makes individual visits to St Andrews.
1563	22 Feb. Execution of Pierre de Bocosel, Seigneur de Chastelard at St Andrews Market Cross.
1568	Plague.
1569	Execution of Nic Neville in St Andrews for witchcraft; William Stewart, Lord Lyon King of Arms hanged in St Andrews for 'necromancie'.
c.1570	Latin Grammar School founded.
1572	John Knox acts personally in St Andrews witch trial.

1585	Plague.
1598	Multiple witch executions in St Andrews.
1605	Plague.
1611	Archbishop Gledstane's golf charter.
1614	St Andrews made a Burgh of Regality under the Archbishop of St Andrews.
1617	11 July. James VI & I visits St Andrews.
1620	James VI & I elevates burgh into a Royal Burgh. Lammas market secured as a privilege.
1645	26 Nov. to 4 Feb. 1646 Parliament of Scotland meets at St Mary's College.
1646	17 Jan. Sir Robert Spottiswoode, Lord President of the Council and prominent Royalist beheaded at St Andrews Market Cross on a charge of High Treason.
1647	Plague.
1650	4–6 July. Charles II in St Andrews.
1665	Plague.
1667	Plague. Probable last indictment for witchcraft in St Andrews – Isobel Key imprisoned in Tolbooth.
1706	Daniel Defoe in St Andrews as government agent.
1747	24 June. Union of the College of St Salvator and St Leonard by sanction of parliament.
1754	14 May. 'The Society of St Andrews Golfers' instituted.
c.1755	English Grammar School founded.
1773	18–20 Aug. Dr Samuel Johnson and James Boswell in St Andrews.
1833	Opening of Madras College.
1834	King William IV becomes patron of The Society of St Andrews Golfers: becomes Royal & Ancient Golf Club.
1835	Manufacture of gas for public use begun in St Andrews.
1852	29 May. St Andrews–Guardbridge–Leuchars railway opened.

1854	Royal & Ancient Golf Club House opened.
1858–61	New Town hall built in Queens Gardens.
1870	Telegraph link to St Andrews.
1876	Sept. First royal visit to St Andrews for over 200 years by Prince Leopold, Duke of Albany.
1877	26 Oct. St Leonards School opened in Queens Gardens.
1885	First telephone link to St Andrews.
1905	Electric supply first switched on in St Andrews.
1912	Lord Lyon King of Arms matriculates St Andrews burgh ensigns.
1919	Foundation of the James Mackenzie Institute for Clinical Research, The Scores.
1922	Freedom of the Burgh conferred on the Prince of Wales, later King Edward VIII.
1933	Foundation of The Byre Theatre, Abbey St.
1937	Founding of the St Andrews Preservation Trust.
1939	20 Oct. First Air Raid warning in St Andrews.
1940	25 Oct. Town receives first bomb 'direct hits'.
1946	End of free golf in St Andrews.
1957	Opening of Langlands School.
1959	Opening of Greyfriars Roman Catholic School.
1964	Jan. St Andrews–Guardbridge–Leuchars rail link closed.
1971	Opening of Canongate School.
1974	Opening of Lawhead School.
1975	End of St Andrews Town Council.
1988	St. Andrews Swimming Pool opened at East Sands.
1989	Opening of Sea Life Centre.
1990	British Golf Museum Founded.
2001	Opening of New Byre Theatre.
2005	Merger of New Park School (1937) with St Leonards School.
2006	Merger of Langlands School with Canongate School.

Author's Preface

People, places, facts and faces, scenes and memories long forgotten – this book aims to conjure them up to present the familiar in the unfamiliar and delve into the heart of St Andrews past and present. The story of St Andrews never ends. For a thousand years the burgh has been in the cockpit of Scottish history, and many times the events in the burgh formed the core of Scottish history.

Many visitors to St Andrews ask when the name of the Apostle was first used for the burgh, and why there is no apostrophe giving Andrew 'possession' of his burgh. The charter memorandum citing Bishop Robert's foundation of the burgh between 1140 and 1150 gives first use of St Andrews as a placename in the phrase *apud Sanctum Andream in Scotia*. And it was Margaret, saint and queen's biographer, Turgot of Durham, who seems to have been the first Bishop of St Andrews see to have the Apostle's name in his title 1107–15. As to the lack of an apostrophe, it seems to have been a scribe's convention since medieval times.

King William IV was the last monarch to have the name of St Andrews in a title. His father George III had created him Duke of Clarence and St Andrews in 1789 and the title merged with the crown at William's accession in 1830. The use of the burgh in a royal title remained dormant until in October 1934 King George V created his fourth son HRH Prince George, Duke of Kent, the Earl of St Andrews on the occasion of his marriage to Princess Marina of Greece. The prince was a frequent visitor to St Andrews in the mid-1930s, to be honoured by the university in 1936 and to play-in as Captain of the Royal and Ancient Golf Club in 1937; Prince George's grandson,

George Philip Nicholas, born in 1962, holds the title today as a courtesy.

The earliest charter relating to St Andrews is that of Bishop Robert, who, with the permission of King David I, founded a 'bishop's burgh' here. Its title was *Carta Roberti Episcopi Sancti Andree de Burgo* and only exists as a sixteenth-century copy. When King Malcolm IV attended Bishop Arnold's consecration at St Andrew's Cathedral on 20 November 1160 he confirmed the burgh's status. The charters were ratified again by Mary, Queen of Scots, on 25 January 1552, and in 1614 St Andrews was made a Burgh of Regality under George Gledstanes, Archbishop of St Andrews, and King James VI made it into a Royal Burgh in 1620. The early charters and documents relating to the burgh have long vanished, but a summary of the burgh's status and ancient rights appeared in the *Great Register*, also known as the *Black Book of St Andrews*.

No single volume can tell the full story of St Andrews, its people, its visitors and friends. This book, which is dedicated to all who love St Andrews and wish to see it flourish, may serve as a taster for all who wish to learn more about the burgh and its ever-lasting story.

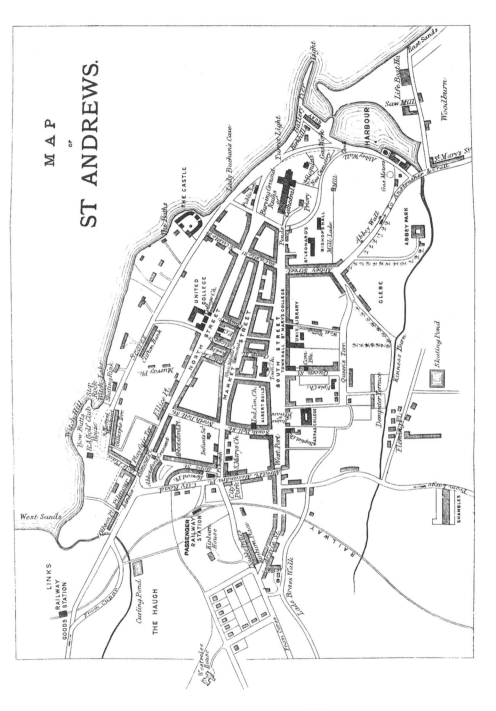

1. St Andrews street plan, 1887

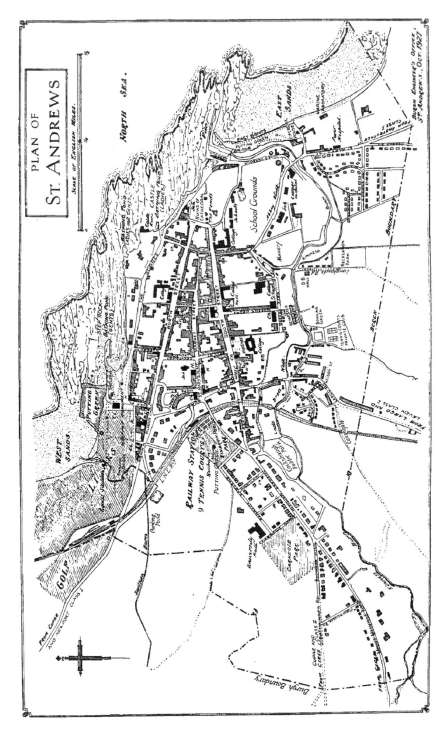

2. Burgh engineer's development of St Andrews by 1927

3. Escutcheon of the City of St Andrews showing the symbols of the boar and
the martyred saint on his Crux Decussata

CHAPTER I

They Came to St Andrews: Early Burgh History

I warmly welcome your eager desire to know something of
the doings and sayings of the great men of the past, and of
our nation, in particular.

The Venerable Bede (673–735)

Earliest Times

Stand on Kinkell Braes, where the cliffs descend to the Maiden's
Rock, and where the coastal path to Crail sweeps down to the
East Sands, and look across to the ruined towers of St Andrews
Cathedral. There on the triangle of land above the harbour
lay one of the holiest places in medieval Christendom, and
the birthplace of modern St Andrews. For a thousand years
pilgrims made their way to St Andrews to worship within the
largest cathedral in Scotland and to be spiritually refreshed in
the presence of the corporeal relics of the Holy Martyr and
Apostle Andrew of Bethsaida in Galilee, a man who the faithful
believed had walked and talked with Jesus. Yet long before the
medieval pilgrims had wandered their way across Fife, humans
had made homes in the acres that became St Andrews.

Some eighteen thousand years ago St Andrews shorelands
were locked up in sheets of ice which formed the Devensian, or
the last glaciation period. Slowly, around ten thousand years
ago, the coastline at what was to form the Firth of Tay and
St Andrews Bay began to appear, and by 5000 BC the sea level,
raised by melting ice, finally cut off Scotland from the mainland
of Continental Europe.

From ten thousand years ago, as the ice sheets melted and the
coastline was still miles away from St Andrews cliffs today,
plants began to colonise the land. This foliage was sought out
by grazing animals like wild pigs, roe deer and red deer, with

meat-eating predators including early man. Covering the period from 10,000 to 5,000 years ago, the Mesolithic (Middle Stone Age) era saw the coming of the early human inhabitants to the estuary fringes of the Tay and the Eden. These humans came from the south and across the North Sea from the North European plains, and following the sea coasts and river mouths penetrated the creeks and estuaries. The earliest form of transport on water being the hollowed-out oak, pine and elder log boats. Such a 26-foot example in oak was found in the River Tay at Errol in 1895, dating from around AD 500. Another and better preserved 30-foot oak log boat was discovered nearer to St Andrews at Carpow in 2002 and dates from the mid-Bronze Age at around 1220 BC. Its use shows these waters were used for fishing, wildfowling and transport.

Two important Mesolithic sites which evolved at Friarton, a mile south of Perth, and at Morton, once an island, but now on St Andrews' neighbour the Tentsmuir peninsula, give us clues as to the people who lived here during this period. Stratification levels at Morton of shell pits, deer horn, split cattle bone, fish bones and stone implements also revealed that these fishermen were also hunter-gatherers who supplemented their diet on birds, leaves, nuts and roots.

The earliest inhabitants of the St Andrews area then, were nomadic people who absorbed the knowledge of food production around 4500 BC from the people who moved east from Europe. These farmers began to transform the landscape around St Andrews by clearing woodland and building monuments and prehistory entered the Neolithic Age which lasted from around 4000 to 2500 BC. New innovations were also evolved including wheat and barley cultivation and pottery; little is known about the daily lives of the Neolithic folk hereabouts, but their monuments for the dead and ceremonial centres for tribal rituals offer archaeological clues. The struggle of the inhabitants around St Andrews shores to win a living against nature and the weather led them to invest supernatural powers to the flora and fauna around their dwellings. Those who lived by the shore were devotees of spirits associated with sea creatures and birds and the artefacts of fishing; while the dwellers in land worshipped hinterland animals and the tools of hunting and cultivation.[1] An important Neolithic site relevant to the area of early habitation around St Andrews is at Balfarg near Markinch with its stone circle and grave pit.[2]

The Bronze Age covers the period from around 2400 BC to around 700 BC, wherein the temperature range was slightly higher than today and rainfall greater. The stone circles and chamber tombs of the Neolithic Age now merged with a new tradition of cairns and barrows and the appearance of hill-forts. This was the era of the cult of chieftains and tribal leaders and the grave goods burials of the period show how distinctive beaker-shaped pots now appeared with the development of metalworking traditions in tin, copper, gold and bronze for everyday use as knives and tools as well as jewellery like lignite beads. People now lived in thatched round houses as the most common dwelling.

The final technological and cultural stage in which iron largely replaced bronze in implements and weapons, saw the interaction of the great states of the Mediterranean with the barbarian tribes of the north. It commences in the eighth century BC and events were played out over a period of eight centuries. By 500 BC Scotland was firmly in the Celtic-speaking area of the tribes known as the *Caledonii*. By the second century AD the Celtic peoples of Europe, like the Gauls, had been conquered, particularly by the Roman legions, but in Scotland they were able to maintain an independence.

By now wheat and barley were grown and farm animals were being reared; hunting had declined, but around the Firth of Tay and the mouth of the Eden the resources of the sea were exploited. By the late first century BC tribal kingdoms emerged and the land now forming St Andrews was in the territory of warrior-tribesfolk known as the *Venicones*. They lived in smaller palisaded settlements – defended farmsteads – so, around the Tay mouth environs there would be scattered farming hamlets centred upon a hill-fort.

What kind of people were the representatives of Celtic heathendom who inhabited the area that would become St Andrews? They were a people known as the Urnfield Celts, from their burial practices, whose kinsmen came to the west from the region of the Upper Danube. Their predominant physical appearance included their tall height, pale skin, fair wavy hair, blue eyes and a certain muscularity. Their hair was largely left uncut, to be smeared with lime wash, and they sported beards and drooping moustaches. These aspects we can gauge from classical sculptures, and such first-century writers as Diodorus Siculus who described the tribesmen's dress of trousers, checkered or striped cloth material garments, including tunics and cloaks.[3] A certain amount of gold, silver, bronze and electron jewellery survives from this period. As to the character of these folk, the geographer Strabo says:

> The whole race, which is now called Celtic or Galatic, is madly fond of war, high spirited and quick to battle, but otherwise straightforward and not of evil character. And so when they are stirred up they assemble in their bands for battle, quite openly and without forethought; so that they are easily handled by those who desire to outwit them. For at any time or place, and on whatever pretext you stir them up, you will have them ready to face danger, even if they have nothing on their side but their own strength and courage . . . To the frankness and high-spiritedness of their temperament must be added the traits of childish boastfulness and love of decoration.[4]

The most significant form of prehistoric monument left to us of early St Andrews settlement is the burial. During excavation in 1975–77 at Hallowhill, on the south side of St Andrews, some 140 graves were examined. Again during 1980 an area of Kirkhill, abutting the ruins of the cathedral, was excavated which revealed prehistoric burials.[5] Then in 1990 a large Late Bronze Age hoard was discovered, again south of the town, which contained a total of 150 artefacts from axeheads and knives to bronze tools and ornaments of amber and cannel coal. Importantly too, were traces of wool found adhering to the socket of an axe, exhibiting a plain weave used in clothing.

At first the early settlers on the St Andrews promontory

cremated their dead and placed the ashes with the grave goods in round or square cists. Between the fifth and the ninth centuries the long cist was the most popular type of burial. In this type the body was laid full-length in the graves wherein the sides, roof and floor were made of slabs. From the discoveries we can see that St Andrews headland was an early settlement area, probably as far as modern Market Street. The early settlers also colonised the banks of the Kinness Burn, for urns have been found at Lawhead, and when ground was levelled at Balnacarron in 1859 and 1907 more urns were discovered. Settlements were also to be found, surrounded by the swamp forests of oak, pine and beach at Dunork, Dunino and Drumcarrow.

The Romans

The first contacts between Rome and Britain was Julius Caesar's expeditions of 55 and 54 BC. His intent was to use diplomacy to keep the tribes of the south-east of Britain from crossing the *Oceanus Britannicus* (the Channel) to assist the warring tribes of Gaul. The Romans did not appear again until Emperor Claudius I's full-scale invasion with Aulus Plautius as commander in AD 43. It was not until the Roman governors Quintus Petillius Cerialis, AD 71–74, and then Gnaeus Julius Agricola, AD 77–83, advanced north that substantial territory gains were made in what is now called Scotland. The term 'Roman Scotland' covers roughly the periods AD 71–215, within the rules of the emperors Vespasian to Caracalla – who abandoned northern outposts in Scotland. It is likely that Roman soldiers first appeared in the St Andrews area as a consequence of Agricola's incursions to the north-east although the Roman *exploratores*, the reconnaisance units of several kinds, may have surveyed the lands of Tayside and north-east Fife by AD 79. At this time chronicler Tacitus, son-in-law of Agricola tells of the conquest of Lowland Scotland as far as the Highland Line. Scholars call this period Flavian I (AD 79–88) after the imperial Roman dynasty of Vespasian and his sons Titus and Domitian.

Further the Roman historian Cassius Dio tells us that a

confederation of Celtic tribesmen known as the *Maeatae* were
made up of the *Venicones* and the *Vacomagi*. The *Venicones*
predominated in the St Andrews area. The fact that there
were few permanent Roman installations on the eastern Angus
and Fife shores would suggest that the *Venicones* eventually
became philo-Roman. Nevertheless the *Venicones* who lived in
what is now the St Andrews area would be largely overawed by
the line of Roman frontier forts at Carpow, Bertha, Cargill,
Cardean, Oathlaw and Stracathro. Where St Andrews is
situated was just outside the territory occupied 142–63 known
as the Antonine Frontier Zone.

No permanent Roman occupation of the St Andrews area
was attempted, but the tribesfolk of the *Venicones*, who fished St
Andrews Bay and tilled the nearby hillsides were monitored in
their main local settlements of Clatchard Craig, above Newburgh, Fife, and at Dundee's Law Hill by the garrisons at
Carpow, Longforgan and the marching camp by Rosekinghall,
Muir of Lour.

In AD 209 the imperial task force of Emperor Septimus
Severus moved into Scotland to confront the *Maeatae* and their
northern neighbours the *Caledonii*, and the Romans began
construction of the 25-acre half-legionary vexillation fortress
at Carpow, near Newburgh. This fort would be used by the II
Augusta and VI Victrix legions. Called by the Romans *Horrea
Classis*, the camp acted as a base for the Roman fleet's activities
in the *Tava Fluvius* (River Tay) and adjacent coastlines. Here
there is evidence that a boat-like bridge (*traiectus*) stretched
across the expanse of soft tidal mud to the north shore of the
Tay. Carpow was abandoned some time around AD 215, and
the Romans did not return to the St Andrews area again.[6]
There was no Roman road to St Andrews, the nearest lying to
the west linking the fort at Ardoch, Perthshire, with the
legionary fortress of *Pinnata Castra* (Inchtuthil); instead the
legions used the extant prehistoric tracks. Three Roman forts
lie in a line showing the Roman penetration of Fife down the
River Eden; there is the 63-acre marching-camp at Auchter-
muchty; the encampment at Edenwood, Cupar; and the nearest to St Andrews is the 35-acre site at Bonnytown near the

junction of the Cameron and Kinaldy burns, west of Boarhills. All of these were temporary camps and may have been used by the *exploratores* and perhaps as monitoring bases (i.e. of the movements of the *Venicones*) by such as the men of Severus' II Parthica legion. Fife was probably an important local source of coal, salt and grain. Roman coins have been found in the St Andrews environs from time to time; in 1979 an *antoninianus* of M. Piavonius Victorinus was found in the grounds of St Leonards School.

The Picts

It was probably the Romans who gave the Picts their name from the Latin *picti*, painted or tattooed people, and they appear historically in classical reference in AD 297.[7] Nevertheless they do not come fully into historical focus until they were written about by the Venerable Bede (673–735).[8] The Picts were undoubtedly the same people as the Iron Age tribes of Roman Scotland, the *Maeatae* and the *Caledonii*. Caesar wrote that they were divided into three classes: *druids*, or priests; *equites*, or knights; and *plebs*, the common people. He described how they were a part of a paternalistic society under chiefs. The political centre of their area was that between the Forth and the Mounth, on the shoulder of Mount Keen, Aberdeenshire; Bede divided the Picts into two territorial groupings and the Taylands of Angus and Fife would be classified as being in Southern Pictland. Tradition puts St Andrews within *Fib* (from which we get Fife), one of the four provinces of the southern Picts. (Pictish St Andrews lasted until around 850.)

The most famous of the artefacts of the Picts were the metalworkings they decorated with symbols and the three classes of symbol stones of the fifth to ninth centuries.[9] A fine example of Dark Age art is seen in the St Andrews Sarcophagus, a stone bier-like box made up of slabs slotted into cornerposts, dating from the late eighth or early ninth centuries. The sarcophagus was found in a deep grave near St Rule's Tower in 1833. It bears vigorous high relief of a hunting scene and sculpture which scholars have linked with biblical references.[10]

It is worthwhile noting that St Andrews Cathedral museum, as well as displaying the sarcophagus, also carries pieces of early Christian sculptured stones all found within the ecclesiastical site which academics believe link St Andrews with eighth- to tenth-century Northumbria wherein St Andrews was the centre of an important school and workshop of Celtic–Anglian art and culture that faded away before the coming of the Norman prelates.

Christianity

Christianity first came to the land of the Picts around 565, when the abbot and confessor St Columba and his followers ventured from Ireland and settled in Iona. The Picts now followed the rule of the Celtic Church of Columba and were often at war with their southern neighbours the Northumbrians. By 634 Northumbria was evangelised by Celtic monks from Iona, invited to the wild, windswept eastern coastlands by the Northumbrian king. Here they met the opposition of the Roman Church which had been proselytised by St Augustine's Roman mission and at the Synod of Whitby, in 664, attended by St Wilfrid and St Colman in the Roman and Celtic interests respectively. So during 663–4 the Roman Church prevailed and the Celtic Church retreated to the west whence it came.

As the late seventh century developed, Pictish territory was being invaded by the Angles of Northumbria, but in 685 the Angles under Egfrith of Northumbria were routed by the Picts led by Brudei III son of Bili mac Nechtan, King of Strathclyde and the Picts, at Nechtanesmere, to the south of Dunnichen Hill, near Forfar. This certainly freed the area where St Andrews would be sited of possible Anglian warlike occupation.

Nechtan III, mac Derile, of the Picts, led a kingdom that was at its most powerful; he chanced his arm against the Northumbrians on the plain of Manaw in Lothian and his *Maeatae Picts* were slaughtered. A period of internal rebellion followed Nechtan's peace with Osred, king of Northumbria, and Nechtan, after he had put down internal disquiet, accepted the Christian faith. In 710 Nechtan took up the ritual of the Roman

Church, having sought advice of the abbot of St Peter's at Monkwearmouth, Northumbria and by 717 he had expelled the Celtic monks from his kingdom. There were fundamental differences between the Celtic Church and that of Rome – such as the date of Easter and the use of the tonsure by clerics – but the new rule of Rome was utilised in St Andrews and hence there came the link between St Andrews and the Northumbrian artistic culture. It can be said then that Nechtan's reign, which ended 728/9, saw the conversion of the Picts from a pagan hierarchy to a Christian people.

The religious site at St Andrews was now to see a denominational change. When the Columban communities decayed, their place was taken by the Celtic-speaking clergy known as the Culdees, who nominally conformed to Rome. The Culdees, a derivation of *céli dé* 'companions of God', were a loose assemblage of non-celebate individuals, whose earliest occurrences on record come from the first half of the ninth century. The Culdees patterned their life on such desert hermits as those of Syria and dwelt in *carcairs*, houses like boxes of stone, set round their church of timber and turf. These contemplative anchorites ceased to be hermits by the ninth century and evolved as an organised community, and by 921 they were a canonical body of thirteen persons at St Andrews. The period of ecclesiastical change in St Andrews was set against rumbustious times. By 794 the Norsemen (Vikings and Danes) had appeared in northern waters to be challenged by Constantine mac Fergus, King of the Dalriada Scots; the Scots and the Picts found themselves siding to face the common enemy. Viking vessels were certainly seen off St Andrews, for in 877 the battle of Inverdovat took place with the Vikings on the heights above modern Newport-on-Tay.

This was the year too, that a new church evolved at St Andrews on the extant ecclesiastical site. The church was built for the Culdees at St Andrews by Constantine I, king of the Picts and Scots just before his death in a battle against the Vikings at Crail. After he abdicated in 943, Constantine II, retired to the Culdee monastery at St Andrews, and died there in 952 almost certainly to be buried in its precincts. Was the

St Andrews Sarcophagus the bier of Constantine II? We shall
never know but we can be sure that at Constantine's death St
Andrews was a very sacred place for reasons that will be
revealed in Chapter 2. But the Culdees of whom Constantine
is said to have become abbot are worthy of further comment.
Tradition has it that their first church was set on Lady's Craig
Rock, at the end of the present pier, but tide and storm forced
the clerics to build a new church on the rocky headland above.
This church developed into that of the Blessed Mary of the
Rock; the twelfth-century nave and thirteenth-century choir,
with the footings of the altar, were re-discovered at Kirkhill in
1860.

The Culdees survived into St Andrews' development as a
medieval burgh.[11] In 1144 there were two bodies of clergy in
the burgh, the Culdees and the Augustinian Canons who came
to form the chapter of the cathedral. The Culdees survived the
provisions of king, pope and bishop, but slowly lost their
influence over the ecclesiastical administration of the site.
The Culdee clergy – who became less and less Celtic – were
presided over by a provost and evolved a collegiate church,
Collegium Sanctae Mariae Virginis in Rupe, one of the earliest in
Scotland and by the thirteenth century they were a Chapel
Royal. It lost its royal dignity by the end of the fifteenth
century. The Culdees nurtured several prominent medieval
clergy such as William Wishart, who became Archdeacon of
St Andrews, Chancellor of the Kingdom and Bishop of St
Andrews in 1272. In June 1559 the church was pulled down
by the Earl of Argyll and the Prior of St Andrews, afterwards
the Earl of Moray.[12]

This then was the early history of the triangular site overlooking the North Sea, which would become one of the most
important locations in Scottish history and the place to be given
greater prominence by one of the most significant men in
biblical history.

CHAPTER 2

A Saint's Bones: Links with the Apostle Andrew

> Now as He walked by the sea of Galilee, He saw Simon
> and Andrew his brother casting a net into the sea; for they
> were fishers. And Jesus said unto them, Come ye after me,
> and I will make you to become fishers of men. And
> straightway they forsook their nets and followed Him.
>
> The Gospel According to St Mark 1.16–18

In the scriptorium at the abbey of St Ciaran at Clonmacnois
(Cluain moccu Nois), Co. Offaly, Ireland, the eleventh-century
monk Tigernach wrote these significant words: *Mors Tuathalain
abbatis Cinnrighmonaid*. Thus he recorded the death of Tuatha-
lan, Abbot of Cennrigmonaid, the Gaelic placename for 'The
Head[land] of the King's Mount', under the date 746. The
words of this usually reliable chronicler are important for this is
the first date we can be sure about concerning St Andrews.
Cennrigmonaid is the first known name for the location that is
now St Andrews, and in the twelfth century this was rendered
in Latin as *Kilrymont*, when *Kil* (church) replaced *Kin* (headland).

The Cult of St Andrew

How did a humble Galilean fisherman, with the Greek personal
name of Andreas (Andrew), described in the Gospels of St
Mark and St Matthew as the brother of Simon Peter and a
disciple of St John the Baptist, come to be associated with
Cennrigmonaid? The evolution of a Cult of St Andrew at
Kilrymont/St Andrews is one fraught with historical controversy.[1] Although there are various versions of the foundation
legends of the establishment of a cult Church of St Andrew
at Kilrymont,[2] two main themes may be cited. Both were

recorded by Augustinian canons of different generations of the priory established at St Andrews in the twelfth century, and at least one was deemed to have been transcribed from old Pictish sources.[3]

The first version was rewritten some time in the reign of David I (1124–53) and tells how Angus (Oengus) I (729–61), ruler of the Picts and Dal Riada, raided into the Merse (modern Berwickshire), where he encountered hostile Northumbrians south of the Tweed. Walking with his earls, Angus then witnessed a flash of blinding light and heard the voice of the Apostle Andrew calling Angus to face the enemy bearing before his army the Cross of Christ. This, recorded the chronicler, Angus did and won the battle.

Meanwhile, continued the Augustinian writer, an angel was guiding from Constantinople, capital of the eastern Roman Empire, one of the guardians of the corpse of the Apostle to the safe anchorage at the summit of the king's hill 'that is Rigmund' (the name survives in the two farms of Easter and Wester Balrymonth – 'village of the king's hill' – to the south of modern St Andrews). This guardian was identified as a monk called St Rule, or St Regulus, who met Angus at the gate of the king's encampment, probably the site of the later castle. To further celebrate his victory over his enemies, Angus pledged the 30-acre site of Cennrigmonaid to the Glory of God and the Apostle St Andrew. It is recorded too, that, led by St Rule, bearing the hold relics of St Andrew on his head, the royal party made a circuit of Kirkhill whereon they erected twelve consecrated crosses to mark out the holy ground.[4]

The second cited version, dates from around 1279, putting it in the reign of Alexander III (1249–86). This also identifies St Rule and makes him a bishop, bringing him from Patras in Achaia, Greece, where St Andrew had been martyred on the distinctive cross called a *crux decussata* which has entered Scottish heraldry as the patriotic Saltire. St Andrew was martyred some time during the reign of Emperor L. Domitius Claudius Nero and because the grandson of Emperor Constantine the Great was bent on taking the cadaver of St Andrew to Constantinople, Bishop Rule was commanded by an angel to extract a tooth, a kneecap, an upper-arm bone and three fingers of the saint's right hand and secrete them for holy purposes. In this the Augustinian chronicler was mirroring the corporeal relics that were said to be held in St Andrews cathedral of the time.

Then Angus is introduced again; this time he is recorded as being encamped near the mouth of the Tyne to take on 'the Saxon King' Athelstane. Before the pitched battle Angus had a vision of St Andrew who subsequently gave him victory over superior odds. The angel who had commanded Rule to secure the relics of Andrew, now sent him to 'the utmost part of the world' with the relics. Thus, Rule and his companions set off with their sacred trust and journeyed west for eighteen months, landing in the midst of a storm at the place called Muckross, 'the headland of the boars', soon to be called Kilrymont. Rule and his followers waded ashore and erected a cross to defy the demons of the place. Soon after Rule was met by Angus who endowed the bishop with land and twelve crosses were set up at Kilrymont round a dedicated precinct that was to be the focus of a reliquary site for St Andrew. For good measure the chronicler notes that seven churches – probably wattle and daub buildings – were erected at St Andrews: one to St Rule as leader; St Aneglas the Deacon; St Michael the Leader of the Heavenly Host (for it is said that Rule stepped ashore on 29 September, the 'Night of St Michael'); also to the Blessed Virgin; St Damian, the Martyr; St Bridget, founder of the Abbey of Kildare; and one to the Virgin Muren, daughter of King Angus and Queen Finchem. Interestingly, an old legend recounts how Muren was born while St Rule was in Scotland. Again it says Muren was the first holy person to be buried at Kilrymont and that her church was the focus of a nunnery of women of royal blood. Thereafter the area was established as a place of pilgrimage.[5]

These versions of the coming of St Andrew's bones to Kilrymont/St Andrews, were tweaked and regurgitated to suit monastic purposes and to them can be added the *Breviarium Romanum* and Scotland's own *Breviarium Aberdonense* sponsored by Bishop William Elphinstone, both developing the St

Andrew story.[6] Then there is the conundrum of Acca, saint and bishop, c.660–742.

The church and Anglo-Saxon abbey of Hexham, Northumberland, was founded around 674 by St Wilfred, Bishop of York, out of a grant of land endowed by Ethelreda, queen of Ecgfrid, King of Northumbria. Hexham Abbey was dedicated to St Andrew following Wilfred's visit to Rome and return with certain relics of the Apostle which were kept in the crypt reliquary chamber. Prior Richard of Hexham takes up the story of these relics and Wilfred's successor, Acca.

A disciple and companion of Wilfrid, Acca was appointed abbot of Hexham by his patron and succeeded Wilfrid as bishop in 709. Acca also visited Rome and is said to have carried back relics of saints including some of St Andrew. Acca was driven from his bishopric in 732 and is purported to have removed some of the relics of St Andrew from the crypt at Hexham. It is likely that any such relics were *brandea* – pieces from garments – as any corporeal relics would have been guarded day and night by the Hexham monks. However, Richard of Hexham asserted that Acca fled northwards to the land of the Picts and was received by Angus.[7]

Did Acca encourage Angus to institute a cult of St Andrew at Kilrymont/St Andrews? It is a story far more plausible than the foundation versions promoted by the later Augustinian canons. After all King Nechtan III mac Derile (706–29) encouraged a cult of St Peter around 710,[8] and maybe Angus wished to have his own cult at Kilrymont. We shall never know for sure, but we can say that Acca and Angus were real people, although they became part of the religious propaganda of the Augustinian canons who wished to establish St Andrews as a site which predated Canterbury, Iona and Whithorn. But what of St Rule in the St Andrews story?

Scholars have speculated as to who Rule was, and such as the late Professor Douglas Young (1913–73), of St Andrews, averred that he was possibly the first Bishop of Senlis in the French *département* of Oise, who was born in fourth-century Greece and was called St Rieul by the French.[9] Certainly dedications to St Rule, bynamed St Regulus, are scanty, at least in the east of Scotland, and such a name could have been confused with that of the Irish cleric St Riaguil of Muicinsi (Lochderg). Again it should be remembered that the tower in the cathedral precinct today called St Rule's, or St Regulus's, was recorded as St Andrew's [Church] in the fifteenth century.[10]

Whether or not St Rule was an invention of the monastic scriptorium, or an amalgam of other clerics, St Rule is firmly fixed in St Andrews lore. St Rule's Cave, abutting the east Scores, was long pointed out as a holy place, but it is certainly an eighteenth century romantic invention launched into immortality by St Walter Scott (who loved such tushery about hermits) for he mentions the saint in his *Marmion*:

> To fair St Andrews bound,
> Within the ocean-cave to pray
> Where good Saint Rule his holy lay,
> From midnight to the dawn of day,
> Sung to the billow's sound.
>
> ('The Castle', Canto I, verse 29)

4. The seals and coins of Alexander I (1107–24). During his reign Turgot the first Norman Bishop of St Andrews was consecrated

Just as the Culdees held important land rights in nearby Kinkell, Lambieletham and Kingask, traditional land endowment of the early monastery founded at Kilrymont included the famous *Cursus Apri Regalis*, the run of the royal wild boar. This tract of land stretched from the southern boundaries of modern St Andrews to the village of Boarhills, then westwards to include Cameron and Kemback and the land south of the River Eden to within a mile or two of Cupar. When Alexander I regranted the *Cursus Apri Regalis* in the twelfth century he presented to the then monastery a set of 16-inch boar's tusks which were fixed by silver chains to the altar of St Andrews. Thus was a Pictish fetish firmly placed within the relics of the monastery offering a continuum of devotion on the site. Importantly this fetish was reflected in the arms of the burgh and King Angus was deemed to lay an important foundation in the history of Scottish chivalry. The extant arms of the burgh of St Andrews are a rearrangement of the device on the reverse of an old burgh seal of 1357 and are described thus in the *Lyon Register* (1912):

> Parted per pale Azure and Argent: in the dexter, on a mount in base the figure of St Andrew Proper, bearing his cross in front of him Argent; in the sinister, growing out of a mount in base an oak tree Proper, fructed Or, in front of the trunk of a boar passant Sable, langued Gules, armed Or.

Above the shield is set 'a mural crown in an Escrol below the shield' the modern motto *Dum Spiro Spero* ('While I breathe, I hope').

Writing in his *Cosmography*, the ecclesiastical writer Peter Heylyn (1600–62) tells how King Angus established 'The Order of St Andrew as the 'principal order of knighthood' in the kingdom. Heylyn goes on: 'The knights did wear about their necks a Collar laced with Thistles, with the picture of St Andrew appendant to it; the motto *Nemo me impune lacessit* ('No one provokes me with impunity') – the motto and precursor of The Most Ancient and Most Noble Order of the Thistle founded in 1687.

During the ninth and tenth centuries the enclave at Kilrymont/St Andrews was set in a sea of threats and alarms. By 834 the shadowy Alpin, King of the Dal Riada Scots enters legend rather than history. Historians like Henry Maule of Melgund, by Brechin, tell how Alpin's army faced the forces of Brude VI macFerat of the Picts and was slain 'in the county of Horrestia (Angus) . . . some thirteen or fourteen leagues from Alectum (Dundee)'. Dundee historian James Thomson adds that Alpin's headquarters was on the Dundee Law, visible from St Andrews, and that Alpin was slain at Pitalpy, which he identifies as Pitalpin ('Grave of Alpin') on the road between Dundee and Coupar-Angus.[11] By 970 the Kingdom of the Scots was established with a major royal-aristocratic centre at Scone, and the preservation of its unity was pursued by Kenneth II during his reign 971–95. Little is recorded of Kenneth's successor, Constantine III 'The Bold', 995–97, who conspired in Kenneth's death at Finella Castle, near Fettercairn, or of Kenneth III 957–1005, and his co-ruler Giric II, who were both killed at Monzievaird, near Lochearn by Kenneth II's son Malcolm. Malcolm II now engaged in the pursuit of invading Danes in sight of St Andrews. In 1010 he defeated Camus, leader of the Danes at Barry, Angus, across the Tay from St Andrews.[12] At this time then, Kilrymont/St Andrews would be in a state of high alert as the Danish vessels lay off the estuary. With the coming of Malcolm II, though, the fogs of history begin to lift and the settlement that would be St Andrews and its environs began to take on a more recognisable shape.

In 906 St Andrews became the seat of the Bishop of Alba, and by 975 the diocese of St Andrews was expanded by the inclusion of lands from Forth to Tweed wherein the Bishop of St Andrews was *primus inter pares* (the senior bishop amongst equals): indeed the alternative title of Bishop of St Andrews until the thirteenth century was *episcopus Scottorum*. The first name we have for a Bishop of St Andrews is Cellach, Bishop of Alba, during the reign of Constantine II. At Scone in 906 Cellach 'vowed' with Constantine to 'preserve christian laws and disciplines and protect the rights of churches and gospels'.[13] It is said that the fifth known early bishop, Cellach II (971–96), son of Ferdlag, was the first Scottish bishop to travel to Rome to have his episcopate confirmed.

During the episcopate of Fothad II (1059–93), two important events happened which were to change the whole aspect of
the holy enclave of Kilrymont; first, there was the coming of the
Normans, and, second, a new church was built probably near
the site of an older church. This new church is known to us
today as St Rule's or St Regulus's (Tower). In medieval records
this church is called 'the old church', but the Dundee-born
historian Hector Boece (c.1465–1536), referred to it as *diui
Reguli templum*, the Church of St Rule, from which its modern
name derives.

Norman Rule

Norman rule came to Scotland peacefully, for William I,
bynamed The Conqueror, did not attempt to conquer Scotland, instead he was content to establish a loose overlordship.
In 1072 William went north to Abernethy, where King
Malcolm III (1058–93) submitted to him as vassal at a ceremony in the shadow of the round tower at Abernethy; and there
Malcolm handed over his eldest son Duncan as a hostage.

A few years before the Abernethy fealty Malcolm III, nick-
named Canmore (Great Head), had married for his second
wife, Margaret, granddaughter of Edmund II of England.
Margaret had fled to Scotland with her mother Agatha, sister
Christina and brother Edgar Atheling, as refugees of the Norman invasion. A devoted churchwoman, Margaret set about
introducing more refined fashions to the somewhat brutish
Scottish court and with her husband's acquiescence enthusiastically overhauled religious practice in Scotland, instituting the
use of the Roman rite in worship, clerical celibacy, the keeping
of Lent, the Easter mass and the observance of Sunday,
amongst other things. From her confessor and biographer, in
Vita S.Margarete, Turgot, Prior of Durham, we learn that she
patronised Scotland's existing religious houses. By the twelfth
century, incidentally, Fife is being described as a 'region'
governed firmly by a sub-king as the Kingdom of Fife.

Margaret corresponded with Lanfranc, Archbishop of Canterbury, and brought Benedictine monks to Dunfermline to

build a church in honour of the Holy Trinity, to which a priory was established. Importantly for St Andrews, Margaret is believed to have persuaded Malcolm to concede the ecclesiastical overlordship of the Archbishop of York and Bishop Fothad II of St Andrews professed submission to the archbishop. Thus the Scottish Church was given over to Norman bishops and Fothad was the last of what might be called the Celtic bishops of St Andrews. Margaret was the catalyst that gave modern St Andrews its birth and the Normans brought their own clergy, a thorough ecclesiastical reorganisation and monastic settlement. By August 1107 Turgot became the first Norman Bishop of St Andrews to be consecrated by Archbishop Thomas of York at the command of Henry I of England and at the request of Henry's brother-in-law the new Scots king Alexander I (1107–24). Turgot held his episcopate until his death on 31 August 1115 at Durham where he was buried, rather than at the seat of his bishopric.[14] Until 1238 the See of St Andrews was the largest and wealthiest in Scotland, containing the most important burghs of the kingdom and governed by a very remarkable succession of Norman bishops. By the twelfth century then St Andrews was the centrepiece of the merging of the old Scottish culture with the new Anglo-Norman world.

St Rule's tower stands out today as an important landmark in the St Andrews story. The first Church of St Rule can be dated from the later eleventh century and was intended basically as a 'reliquary church' for Scotland's most important bishop. It had a small chapel (26 feet × 20 feet) and a 14½-foot square tower rising to 108 feet; it became a prominent marker to guide pilgrims to the heart of the cult of Scotland's patron saint. Within the chapel, and probably set upon its main altar, would be the relics of the Apostle. As we shall see, this church was greatly altered by Bishop Robert who set in motion the ecclesiastical site that gave birth to modern St Andrews.

5. Western elevation of St Rule's tower (right), thought to have been the first reliquary chapel for the relics of St Andrew [Historic Scotland]

6. South elevation of St Rule's Tower; with early work of mid-eleventh-century fabric, the finest example of a tower-choir edifice [Author's collection]

CHAPTER 3

A Glimpse of Heaven on Earth: Religious Foundations

> All the principal streets of St Andrews lead to the Cathedral. Portions of it may be seen from nearly the whole length of South Street. On entering the ruin by the west door – the 'golden gate' it has been called – the great size of the church becomes at once apparent.
>
> James Maitland Anderson, University Librarian, 1911

They lived in a green and unspoilt countryside, waking to the sounds of waves lapping the shores and the cry of sea birds. Soon after daybreak the murmurs of prayer gave way to the sounds of masons' tools, the rattle of carts and the bustle of daily life at the enclave of infant St Andrews. As people converged on the holy triangle of land, the garb of the clergy contrasted with the natural vegetable-dye sack-like tunics with leggings of the workers, who, upon a saint's day, might be tricked out in red, green and yellow rough surcoats, fastened with clasps, brooches and thongs. Life could be short and brutal; to be aged fifty was venerable, and teenage girls married older men. Yet it was an age of faith. The power of saints' bones gave life to the living community of early medieval St Andrews. And into that community came, one after the other, two men each with a mission. One was called Robert, the other Arnold. In his dreams Robert saw himself founding a church in whose walls the faithful might have a glimpse of heaven on earth; but it was Arnold who would breathe life into the building that became a 'wonder of Christendom'.

Eadmer, a monk of Canterbury, succeeded Turgot as Bishop of St Andrews after a five-year interregnum, 1115–20, in which the affairs of St Andrews had been administered by William, a monk of Bury St Edmunds, on behalf of Alexander I. But, Eadmer's rule was so undermined by the king that he returned to Canterbury to be replaced by Robert, the Anglo-Norman Augustinian Prior of Scone.[1]

When Robert came to St Andrews, St Rule's Church was deemed inadequate for the development of the new ecclesiastical plans for the site. Robert (d.1159), was nominated bishop by Alexander I before 1124 and he was consecrated by Thurston, Archbishop of York in 1127, by which time Robert was resident at St Andrews.[2] St Rule's Church was to be the cathedral of Robert's see and acted as a priory church for the new ecclesiastical order which was to dwell in its shadow. The church was extended to include a nave of some 60 feet by 27 feet and its new form took in a central tower, nave, choir and sanctuary with a total length of 125 feet.

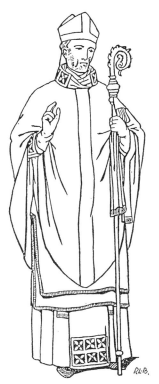

The work on the new extensions was probably carried out by a Yorkshire mason from St Oswald's Augustinian Priory at Nostell, West Yorkshire. Bishop Robert had originated there and Alexander I had brought Augustinians from Nostell to Scone at the encouragement of his friend Prior Adelward of Nostell.[3] St Rule's tower today leaves some clues as to its development. One the eastern face of the tower can be seen the three raggles of the roof. It is thought that the top raggle is that of a thirteenth-century roof and the bottom one of the roof built by Prior William de Lothian (1340–54). The south doorway and the staircase is considered to have been built in the sixteenth century. The choir was repaired in

7. Robert, Prior of Scone, became 'Bishop of the Scots', 1123/4. He died 1158/9. Here seen in full pontificals – mitre, alb, stole, maniple, tunicle, dalmatic and chasuble, with personal crosier which would go with him to the tomb.

1780 by local mason R. Thomson at the expense of HM Exchequer.

Just a little to the north-west of St Rule's, perhaps on the site of one of the defunct Celtic chapels, was sited the Church of the Holy Trinity which served as a parish church for Kilrymont's parishioners and of Bishop Robert's nascent 'burgh of St Andrew'. While the work was being done by the Yorkshire masons, the clergy would probably live in timber conventual buildings around St Rule's.

These days the ecclesiastical site which the visitor sees includes St Rule's Tower, the ruined cathedral and the equally ruined priory and their associated buildings. As the cathedral was administered by the priory and had its birth amongst the canons who were to care for it, it is perhaps best that visitors examine the site from the priory.

The Priory and Cathedral

The priory

St Andrews Cathedral became the central building of an important diocese, but it did not stand alone, for immediately to the south of its nave stood the cloister and conventual buildings of the priory of the Augustinian canons which was established by Bishop Robert. This was founded and endowed by 1144 and he gave to it such lands as those of Strathkinness; soon after its foundation David I (r.1124–43) visited the site.

The priory grew rapidly in influence; in 1147 Pope Eugenius III gave the rights of electing the bishop of the See to the priory and its clergy instead of the Culdees.[4] For it had been Bishop Robert's earnest resolve to eject the extant Culdees from the ancient site as they were secular and married men who could not (and would not) conform with sincerity to the self-denying ordinances of his Augustinian clergy.

The clergy at St Andrews priory followed the rule of St Augustine (354–430), Bishop of Hippo, a Roman from the province of Numidia (modern Algeria) who served as public orator at Milan. He was baptised by St Ambrose, Bishop of Milan, into Catholic Christianity, and became an intellectual

8. West-facing elevation of St Andrews cathedral showing the priory precincts running left from the nave [Historic Scotland]

genius who was to dominate Latin theology for centuries. His great works are his *Confessions* and *The City of God*. Surviving the barbarian hordes, towards the end of the eleventh century communities of Augustinians began to evolve. Bishop Robert's clergy at St Andrews were known as Augustinian Canons Regular and what made them different from cloistered monks was that they observed more freedom for active work in the community than was set down in the more formal Rule of St Benedict. Thus Robert's clergy were more worldly than monks, and left their priory to minister to the people in parish churches and carried out important church business in the diocese. Of the Augustinians the thirteenth-century musician-turned-monk, Guyot de Provins said: 'Augustine's rule is more courteous than Benedict's. Among them, one is well shod, well clothed, well fed. They go out when they like, mix with the world, and talk at table.' By 1418 the Prior of St Andrews enjoyed the use of the *pontificalia* – the wearing of a mitre – and James V described the priory in his *Letters* as 'the first and most famous monastic house in Scotland'.

The priory ruins that visitors see today are remnants of the work of Prior John White, and of his successor John de Haddington, covering the period 1236–58. The precinct was improved by Prior William de Lothian around the middle of the fourteenth century. The priory buildings were set around a square made by the cloister which was linked to the church by east and west processional doorways. A place designed to catch maximum sunlight, the cloister was an area of tranquility and seculsion from daily life and as a rule conversation was forbidden within its walls. Here walks might be taken and literary study indulged. Four covered walkways with roofs supported by open arches formed the perimeters of the cloisters, with the arches probably glazed by the fifteenth century. The central cloister garth was sown with grass, or maybe with horticultural specimens. It is likely that the cloister would be used for the teaching of novices and as a *scriptorium*; book recesses can still be seen in the northeastern part of the cloister. On the floor tiles of the cloister straw, hay or mats, would be strewn for warmth and quietness.

The south transept gable of the cathedral abuts the east range of the priory, divided from the gable by a slype (passage) leading to the priory cemetery and probably the now vanished infirmary and *misericord* (usually for the terminally sick); the slype also acted as an inner parlour (or, place of conversation) and had a bench along its wall; its gutter still remains. The chapter house, with its doorway dating from 1160–c.1200, is the main building of the east range; the chapter house was extended eastwards during 1313–21 at the expense of Bishop Lamberton and Prior John of Forfar; the stone benches where the clergy sat to discuss everyday affairs can still be seen. The floor of the chapter house was used as a burial area for the senior clergy and stone coffins may still be examined in situ.

Here in the chapter house the Augustinian canons would meet, ranged in order of seniority, the youngest nearest the door. A chapter meeting was held weekly at which commemorations of benefactors, past priors and martyrs took place and *obits* and a *requiescant in pace*. It was a place of business and news, and discipline was administered to any erring canons after a confession of fault or an accusation. Punishment was meted out for 'light faults' such as separation from the common table, or a lower place in the chapter or choir and reduction of food. For grave faults, the greatest humiliation was prostration at the church door where every canon going into the choir would step over the culprit's body. Corporal punishment was not unknown.

A chamber is sited next to the chapter house which was probably used as a vestry and maybe the prior's lodging before a separate house was built to the east; the south wall of this vestry was next to the day-stair which led up to the *dorter* (dormitory) which linked across the chapter house to the night-stair into the south transept of the cathedral. Hay was put on the floor of the *dorter* and beds were of straw; probably the sub-priors had beds of oak near the door, but all had no more than a mat by the bed, a woollen covering, and a woollen cloth under a hard pillow. Beyond the day-stair is the *calefactorium* (warming house) with its access doors to the cloister and the *necessarium* (latrine) which would probably be linked by a covered way. The warming house contained the only fireplace common to the community. The *Cloacina Maxima* (great drain) of the *necessarium*, also called the rere-dorter, can still be seen to the south of the site.

Only the sub-croft remains within the south range of the cloister, above which was the frater or *refectorium* (dining hall) and this was reconstructed at the end of the nineteenth century. Herein would be a high table, probably on a dais, where sat the senior clergy and perhaps important guests. There was no fireplace in the frater, but maybe a brazier was allowed in winter. At the beginning of a meal a *skilla*, or gong, would be struck and a grace said by the precentor. During the meals the canons would be read to from a pulpit.

Today the western range of the cloister is only represented by a barrel-vaulted cellar on the site of the Senzie (Synod) House. This building was used as a council-hall after the Reformation but during the time of the canons it became the sub-prior's residence. It gave its name to the medieval Senzie Fair, an event held for a fortnight after Easter. Scots, Flemings,

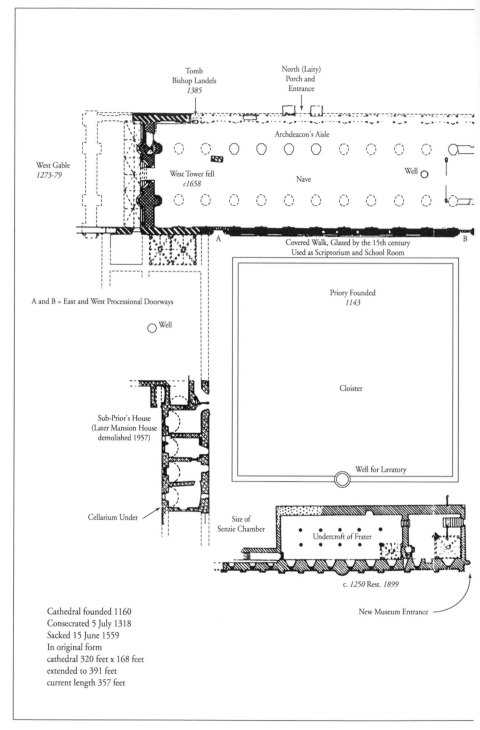

Tomb
Bishop Landels
1385

North (Laity)
Porch and
Entrance

Archdeacon's Aisle

West Gable
1273-79

West Tower fell
c1658

Nave

Well

A and B = East and West Processional Doorways

A

B

Covered Walk, Glazed by the 15th century
Used as Scriptorium and School Room

Well

Priory Founded
1143

Cloister

Sub-Prior's House
(Later Mansion House
demolished 1957)

Well for Lavatory

Cellarium Under

Site of
Senzie Chamber

Undercroft of Frater

c. *1250* Rest. *1899*

New Museum Entrance

Cathedral founded 1160
Consecrated 5 July 1318
Sacked 15 June 1559
In original form
cathedral 320 feet x 168 feet
extended to 391 feet
current length 357 feet

9. Plan of cathedral

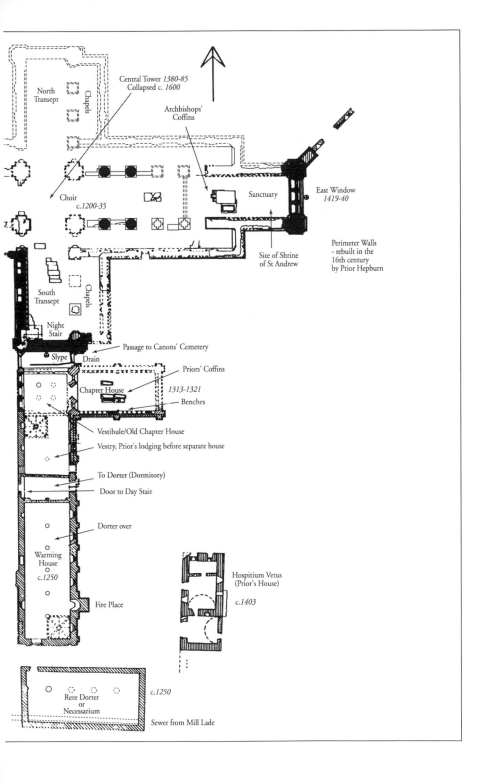

North
Transept

Chapels

Central Tower *1380-85*
Collapsed c. *1600*

Archbishops'
Coffins

Choir

c.1200-35

Sanctuary

East Window
1419-40

Site of Shrine
of St Andrew

Perimeter Walls
- rebuilt in the
16th century
by Prior Hepburn

South
Transept

Chapels

Night
Stair

Slype

Passage to Canons' Cemetery

Drain

Priors' Coffins

Chapter House

1313-1321

Benches

Vestibule/Old Chapter House

Vestry, Prior's lodging before separate house

To Dorter (Dormitory)

Door to Day Stair

Dorter over

Warming
House
c.1250

Fire Place

Hospitium Vetus
(Prior's House)

c.1403

Rere Dorter
or
Necessarium

c.1250

Sewer from Mill Lade

10. Relic twelfth-century vestibule doorway of the Chapter House looking east; the slype runs along the foot of the extant wall of the South Transept. [Historic Scotland]

Frenchmen and Englishmen all came to buy wools, skins, salmon and beasts, and sell linen, silks, tapestries, carpets, spices, wine, olive oil, armour, gold and silver ware and cutlery. Under the Senzie House may have been the *cellarium*, or place for stores. A mansion house was constructed above in 1802 by General

Campbell and the cloister was used as a garden, with green-houses set against the south wall of the nave. (The mansion was demolished in 1957.) The cloister was served by two deep wells and the one within the south cloister walk was the well of the *lavatorium* where the clergy washed before entering the *frater*; nearby would be a cupboard of oak for clean towels.

This priory had a dual function. It was the home of the community of Augustinian Canons Regular, and it was the administration centre of the Cathedral Chapter of the Diocese. Under usual circumstances the bishop (thence the archbishop) of the diocese was their superior and chose their prior with their agreement; but in reality the canons conducted and controlled their own affairs. It was the duty of the canons to supervise maintenance work on the cathedral and its precincts and conduct services; as priests – rather than monks – the majority of the clerics here would be ordained and would be expected to say mass once a day at one of the many altars in the cathedral. From their ranks came the officers of the cathedral.

The head of the chapter, that is an assembly of the canons of the cathedral, was the prior, who would also act as dean of the cathedral, and as vicar-general when the bishop was absent or unable to do his duties. We know that clergy retired to the priory precincts and the diocese seems to have had a suffragan from time to time when the bishop was away on state affairs. One such was Edward Stewart, Bishop of Orkney, who retired to St Andrews; another was William Gibson, Bishop of Libaria, who was suffragan to Cardinal Archbishop David Beaton. The prior's assistants were the sub-prior and the *tertius prior*.

The chronicles of the priory reveal the canons who were in charge of the daily running of the community.[5] The *sacristan* had charge of the church fabric, the holy vessels of the altar, the valuable linen, embroidered robes and the banners for the procession on saints' days; the *chamberlain* was responsible for the day-to-day clothes of the clerics as well as organising the statutory four baths a year. The *sacristan* also saw that the cathedral church was clean and looked after the lighting; he probably employed a layman to keep the warning sea light lit on the precinct wall. His assistant, the *sub-sacristan*, saw to the ringing of the bells for services and to the supply of 'live coals' in iron dishes for services to warm the hands in winter of the priests ministering at the altars. The infirmarian acted as physician, barber and keeper of the *herbarium* within the gardens to the south of the priory precinct where the St Leonards girls' school playing fields are today. The *precentor*, or *armarius*, acted as librarian and the almoner dealt with succour for the needy. The *cellarer*, kitchener and *pittancer* looked after food supplies and cooking and the latter looked after extra rations, 'pittances' on feast days and special occasions. The *refectorian* tended to the arrangements for serving meals and for the hygiene of the *lavatorium*. The grainger was in charge of the grain supplies for the *pistrinum* (bakehouse) and *bracium* (brew-house) and the collection of 'teinds' (Tithes) for the *granarium*.

The priory at St Andrews also had a *bedellus*, a messenger, a compiler of the brevaries and a canon skilled in calligraphy and miniature illumination. The university still retains the position of 'bedellus', an archbeadle who is the principal macebearer and executive agent of the university. Most of the canons of the priory would be craftsmen in their own right and some of them would be men of great academic distinction. One of the canons would also have charge of the *novices* coming into the order. There were probably no more than forty canons resident at the priory at any one time.

Daily life at St Andrews cathedral and priory was strictly regulated by time. The *Canonicae Horae* – Canonical Hours – were the times for daily prayers and were laid down in the church brevaries which regulated the divine services appointed to be recited at these hours. The canons' day was divided into seven hourly periods as defined in Psalm 119.164: '*Septies in die laudem dixi tibi*', 'Seven times in the day I have given praise to Thee'. These hourly divisions varied from winter to summer, but usually the St Andrews canons' day was fourteen hours long as set out in this timetable:

A typical day for canons

2.00 a.m.   Arise. The sub-prior checked the time and rang the bell in the dormitory. Throughout the waking hours gongs would be struck in

	accord with the practice of *tabula sonatilla*– striking to remind the canons of their passage through the earthly state.
2.15/2.30 a.m.	Prayers; psalms. Soft 'night bell' would be rung in church. A bell preceded each service. *Matins* (first service of the day). *Lauds*. Return to sleep.
Dawn.	*Prime*. Great bell summons servants and laity to early mass. Reading in the cloister.
8.00 a.m.	Wash; *mixtum* (light breakfast). *Tierce*. Morrow mass.
9.00 a.m.	Meeting in the chapter house. Work. Reading.
Noon.	*Sext*. High mass. *None*. Dine.
2.30 p.m.	Reading. Work.
5.00 p.m.	*Vespers*. Supper.
6.00 p.m.	*Compline* (the last service of the day).
7.00 p.m.	Retire.

11. Daily life at St Andrews cathedral and priory was strictly regulated by time. Here a cleric contemplates the passage of time for the monastic day in the presence of the Blessed Virgin.

Two canons would be expected to keep watch on the passage of time by consulting the *horologium,* under the supervision of the sub-prior. By the sixteenth century the priory and cathedral would have had clocks gifted to them such as the monastic alarm clocks approved in fifteenth-century Europe, bracket clocks, buttress clocks, pillar clocks and wisdom clocks (with their 24-hour dials). The now-vanished priory and cathedral clocks were easily purloined at the Reformation, and sundials were fine additions to a laird's garden.

The liturgy used by the canons in the cathedral of St Andrews would be the Sarum Rite adapted for the metropolitan church, and the canonical hours would be interspersed when necessary with the special needs of the feast days or the canons' individual masses, or such tasks as the blessing of the water at the altar of Our Lady for the *asperges* (a short service introductory to mass) and the blessing of candles at Candlemas (2 February, one of the old Quarter Days in Scotland). The cathedral also had a great musical tradition in which the canons would be involved. St Andrews Cathedral had its own composers like Patrick Hamilton, who wrote a nine-part mass of St Michael and Canon David Peebles (1530) who prepared a four-part arrangement of the Magnificat antiphon for first Vespers of Whitsunday, the *Si quis diligit me*; the priory sponsored a song school.

St Andrews Augustinian priory had three dependent religious houses: Portmoak, sometimes called Loch Leven Priory, was a land grant of David I in 1152, later endowed to his canons by Bishop Robert, and after the Reformation the priory of St Serf at Portmoak was granted to St Leonards College; Pittenweem, once a Benedictine foundation on the Isle of May was founded on the mainland before 1318; and Monymusk, founded by Gilchrist, Earl of Mar before 1245.[6] Canons of the priory administered these benefices and the Prior of Portmoak probably acted as *tertius prior* at St Andrews cathedral.

The Augustinian Priory of St Andrews included important subsidiary buildings. Known ones include: the Prior's House of 1403, the granary, demolished in 1655, the two Teinds Barns, the Abbey Mill, with brewhouse nearby, disused by 1861 and

12. St Andrews Augustinians had a dependent religious house at
Pittenweem

on the site of the sanatorium of St Leonards School. The Royal
Tennis Courts were located within the priory precincts, abutting the later gasometer of 1903. Of prime importance too, was
the *Novum Hospitium*, or New Inns, which was later used as a
royal residence by the Earl of Moray as Commendator and by
James VI in 1580, and as a home of the post-Reformation
archbishops. It was sited near the 1894 hospice of St Leonard's
School. The *Novum Hospitium* is believed to have been the last
building erected in connection with the priory before the
Reformation. The gateway to the *Novum Hospitium* of 1537
was restored in 1845 and 1894 and realigned down Pends
Road as an entrance to the school hospice. The gate bears
the arms of Prior John Hepburn and the Royal Arms of
Scotland. The priory guest house (*magna aula hospitium*) of
c.1350 was sited between the modern frontages of the buildings
of St Leonards School known as Bishopshall and St Rule's;
probably the guest house was on the site of a much earlier
building; a portion of the wall and fireplace are to be seen
within the boarding house quads.

The whole of the priory precinct was enclosed by a wall. It

remains the longest extent of early walling in Scotland, with a circuit that is almost complete. The extant wall is of the early sixteenth century and is the work of the priorate of John Hepburn (d.1522), son of Patrick, Lord Hailes, whose heraldic panels proclaim him at different places as the builder, Hepburn's walls were reconstructions of earlier walls, as the precinct is known to have been enclosed since the fourteenth century. The walls enclose an area of around 30 acres, rise to 20 feet and are 3 feet thick. The walls were fortified by attached round and square towers equipped with gun-loops and embellished with canopied niches for sacred statues and heraldic panels. Thirteen towers remain.[7]

Visitors and residents alike can enjoy a pleasant circuit of the walls to follow a journey through history. Start from the cathedral where Hepburn's walls begin at the late twelfth century east gable. There is a gateway displaying the Hepburn arms (on a chevron, two lions combatant rending a rose, with pastoral staff behind and 'AD VITA[M]' 'for life', from the old legal maxim referring to property conveyance '*ad vitam aut*

13. Priory walls remain as the longest extant, early medieval walling in Scotland

culpam' 'for life or until a misdeed'). Next to the gateway is a round tower where a 'Turret Light' was fixed and where the 'White Light' was erected in 1849 serviced from a stair within.

The walls now run along the line of the cliffs, known hereabouts as 'Dane's Wark', to the so-called gun-holed, 'Haunted Tower', which comprised a watch-room of sorts, a short stair and a vault below. After the Reformation, the tower room was appropriated as a mausoleum by such as the Martines, Lairds of Denbrae, which, when filled, was sealed. Two niches on the outside of the wall probably contained statues of the Blessed Virgin, one in her form of 'St Mary of the Rock' (in honour of the chapel built on the cliff nearby) and the other with the infant Christ. In line with the niches is a panel with the Hepburn arms, surmounted by a pot of lilies to represent the beauty and purity of the Blessed Virgin. The tower's upper rooms were opened in 1868 and a plethora of coffins and numerous bodies were uncovered. The tower was opened again in 1888 when an iron grille was set in the long built-up doorway.

Pause here for a moment, for the opening of the tower in 1868 led to the local historian David Hay Fleming (1849–1931) to recount that one body was of 'a lovely young woman, beautifully dressed, a scarf round her head from which fell long, black hair. On her hands were long gloves of leather.' Some have identified her as Mrs Katherine Clephane of Denbrae, who died when plague struck Scotland in 1605.[8] More fantastically the event inspired Dean of Guild William T. Linskill (d.1929) to formulate a ghost story around this 'Haunted Tower' which has passed into St Andrews folklore. Said Linskill: 'People used to run for their lives when passing this tower at night; and the older fisher folk have told me some hair-raising uncanny stories of awesome sounds and sights that have been heard and seen by many at that Tower'.[9] Thus was the story of the St Andrews 'White Lady' born.

Go on now to the next tower; it is round and obscured on the inside by the sepulchral monument to the Playfair family. At this point the wall veers towards the harbour and at the actual turn a tower was removed, it seems, around 1880. The whole of this section of the wall was obscured by the Burgh Gasworks in 1835, and was only cleared in 1964. Here is to be found the round 'Inscription Tower' indicating that the wall was extended and adorned by John Hepburn's nephew, Patrick Hepburn, Bishop of Moray, one of the most immoral of the pre-Reformation prelates. The inscription on the tower reads: '[P]RECESSORI[S] OP[VS] POR[RO]HIC PAT[RICVS] HEPBVRN EXCOLIT EGREBIVS ORBE SALVT[I- FERO]' – 'Here the excellent Patrick Hepburn in his turn embellishes the work of his predecessors with a tower of defence.'

Known in pre-Reformation times as the Sea Yett, fronting the Inner Harbour and the East Bents stands the Mill Port. It once had flanking towers and openings for the pouring of pitch on enemies assailing the gateway; here too were the Hepburn arms. To the right of the gateway's front stood the Shore Mill of c.1518 a few yards away from the outlet of the *Cloacina Maxima*. This mill was reconstructed in the seventeenth century and renovated 1964–66. A series of blocked-up doors and windows can still be seen along the shore wall from the Mill Port; it is likely that they served offices set behind the wall as the canons had seaborne goods to administer and store and probably fish taxes to collect.

At the end of the Shore road the Doocot Tower stands at an angle and it probably had a conical roof and pigeon holes. The triangle of land by the Doocot Tower marks the site of the East Toll House, which was demolished in 1933; Abbey Cottage of c.1815 abuts the wall, but it had to be rebuilt after a fire of 1914. Next up Abbey Walk is the Teinds Yett of 1516–30, which stood adjacent to the great Teinds Barn; the gateway has a large aperture for wagons and a smaller one for pedestrians. This was the grand exit and entry to the south through which came the wagons with the 'teynd sheaves' at harvest time. The teinds were the Scottish equivalent of the English tithes due to the church. Marie de Guise-Lorraine entered the priory precincts in 1538 through this gateway on her way to her marriage with James V in the cathedral.

Hepburn arms appear in three places along the Abbey Wall

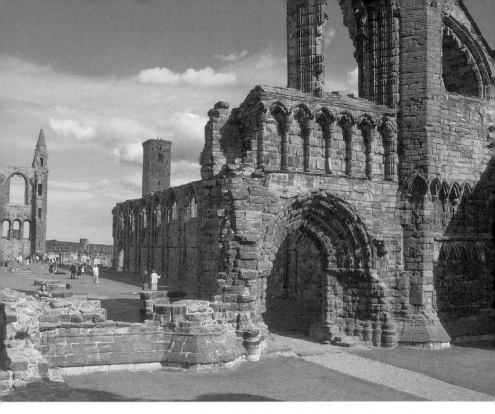

14. Late-thirteenth-century west door of St Andrews Cathedral, leading to the nave, choir and sanctuary [Historic Scotland]

section of the wall whose lower courses date from c.1350 and its upper section is contemporary with the Teinds Yett. Probably there was a tower opposite the old burgh school and the remaining tower (opposite St Nicholas's residence, St Leonards School) marked where the old priory wall swung sharply north to join with the gateway near St Leonard's Chapel that bears the Lennox arms. The remainder of the wall (St Leonard's Wall) is much later than Prior Hepburn's work.

The gateway of the Priory, colloquially called 'The Pends', is set at the end of South Street and linked with the precinct walls. Today only the outer shell of the gateway remains with its wall springers to show where the upper floor began; the roadway is at a higher level than the medieval way through. The Pends dates from c.1350 and its central arch was removed 1837–8. The Pends road probably followed an old track and was the main entrance into the domestic range of the priory; it was not opened as a public right of way until the nineteenth century. Some 67 feet by 21 feet, the gateway had a porter's room by the great wooden entrance door and a side entrance where visitors would make enquiries is still in place.

Outwith the precincts, and at a distance of about one mile near the sea (where the current swimming pool complex of 1988 now stands and the old site of St Nicholas farm and the modern housing development) stood a foundation connected with the priory. The lazar, or leper Hospital of the Blessed Nicholas of St Andrews and is one of the earliest leper hospitals in Scotland. In those days the term leprosy described any skin disease from lupus (tuberculosis of the skin) to erysipelas (St Anthony's Fire). Between 1188 and 1202 Bishop Roger de Beaumont of St Andrews gave to the hospital the lands of Peekie (then Putekin) and William the Lion confirmed the hospital's charters and gave the administrators a team of horses to bring their own brushwood from Kingsmuir (Crail). The lepers were allowed to beg at their own gate on the St Andrews–Crail road, and the Third Lateran Council allowed for lepers to have

15. The Pends is the ancient gateway into the priory precinct and dates from the fourteenth century [Author's collection]

their separate places of worship. Thus the enclave at St Nicholas would probably have living quarters, a chapel, a churchyard and its own clergy. As the disease began to die out, the inmates at St Nicholas would dwindle and as it was described in 1438 as 'a poor's hospital' it may have become a place of sanctuary for the infirm poor. The later uses of the buildings are obscure, but its endowments, revenues and clergy were absorbed by the Dominican Friars at their house in South Street by 1529 and it remained some kind of poorhouse until 1583.

The cathedral

Thus the Augustinian Priory of St Andrews was founded and endowed by Bishop Robert who, before he died in 1153, had in mind to build a great new cathedral at St Andrews to better house the sacred relics of the Apostle. This would not happen though until the episcopacy of his successor Bishop Arnold. Elevated to be second abbot of the Tironesian abbey of St Mary at Calkou (Kelso, Roxburghshire) Arnold was consecrated Bishop of St Andrews by William, Bishop of Moray, Legate of the Apostolic See, and in the presence of King Malcolm IV (r.1153–65), bynamed 'The Maiden'.[10]

By this time the old designation of Kilrymont was being replaced by the name of the Apostle to identify bishopric, burgh, precinct and church. As with the priory, the cathedral church of St Andrews had a dual purpose; it was the church of the diocese of St Andrews and it was the church of the Augustinian Canons. Until modern times it was the largest edifice ever constructed in Scotland and probably contained the most extensive collection of medieval art ever gathered together in Scotland.

The relic cathedral of today is the work of many centuries. In its first form it ran to over 320 feet long and 168 feet across its transepts which formed the crosspiece of its cruciform shape. In time it was to exceed 391 feet in length and have fourteen bays. Its length today is 357 feet. Today the visitor can get some idea of the height for the extant south nave wall – a mixture of architecture from 1160–1279 – rises to its full original height.

Building began at the east end and the outer walls of the

choir, the transepts and ten nave bays would be completed in one building phase. The stone probably came from the Strath-kinness area, but masons used stonework culled from the Celtic sites around as seen in identified fragments in the east gable (the only major twelfth-century gable to survive in Scotland). Phase one of the work was completed around 1190.

Bishop Arnold died in 1163 and was buried, as Bishop Robert had been, in St Rule's Church, But the building went on. Eleven successive prelates continued the work, and although they had a direct hand in keeping the work going the actual administration and construction decisions were carried out by the canon-appointed sacrist – he was also known as 'master of the fabric'. The building would be usable as a cathedral and priory church around 1230; records show that in 1238 Bishop Malvoisine, the last of the Anglo-Norman bishops, was buried in the south aisle of the choir which had been constructed during his episcopate.

The masons who worked on the cathedral are but shadowy figures today. Yet we know that the master masons worked alongside a huge workforce of suppliers of materials, the quarry-workers, lime burners, mortar mixers, joiners, iron workers, timber scaffolders, hoist operators, plankers, tem-plate-makers, carters and hewers. The illiterate masons worked not from plans but hands-on experience. Yet, one name comes down to us as a master mason at St Andrews. On the west wall of the south transept of St Mary's Cistercian Abbey at Melrose there is a plaque set as a posthumous testimonial to one John Morow (or Morvo) who worked on St Andrews Cathedral:

> John Morow sum tym callit was I,
> And born in Parysse certainly,
> And had in kepyng and mason werk
> Of santandroys ye hye kirk
> Of Glasgo, Melros, and Paslay
> Of Nyddysdall and of Galway
> I pray to God, Mari bathe
> & swete Sanct John, to kepe
> This haly kirk fra skathe.[11]

Another inscription at Melrose, again in the south transept above the doorway leading into the stair turret, gives us a clue that the masons who worked on St Andrews Cathedral formed perhaps the earliest masons' guild in Scotland:

> So gays ye compass evene about
> So truth and laute [loyalty] do but doubte
> Behold, to ye hende; quath John Morow.

Work on the cathedral construction continued at a steady rate and by the episcopate of Bishop William Wishart (1271–79) the cathedral was well on towards its conclusion. Hardly had the

Labourers

Craftsman

Pilgrim

16. Labourers, craftsmen and pilgrims mixed together as the cathedral was being built [Sankey, Hudson & Co.]

west gable been completed than it was blown down in a gale. It was decided to rebuild the new gable two bays shorter than the old one, thus reducing the nave by 34 feet, and this allowed room for a *narthex* (a porch) also called a Galilee for the great west door, an unusual innovation in Scotland. The whole building was now available for use and consisted of a nave, the choir with its wooden seats for the clergy and the sanctuary under the great east window. The north and south transepts shared the choir. The nave would be empty of seats, the pilgrims or parishioners kneeling or standing, but along its north and south walls would be low stone seats for the infirm to rest – from these seats we have our proverb 'the weakest go to the wall'. In Prior John Haldenstone's day the nave itself contained 18 of the cathedral's 31 altars, but in its earliest form it would be empty. The nave ended at the choir screen.

The north aisle of the nave, called the Archdeacon's Aisle, had a small projection called the Consistory House, where administrative discussions took place, probably with an altar to St John the Evangelist by its door. At the north-west corner of the nave stood the chapel of St John the Baptist with the baptismal font nearby; and in the south-west corner, the *aspersorium*, the holy water stoup into which the pilgrims dipped their fingers to cross themselves. At the east end of the nave the cathedral well is still to be found, out of which water was drawn for the liturgical ceremonies, for washing and so on; it was probably first used as a source of water for the building of the cathedral. In medieval times the well would probably have an ornate cover. It is likely too that there would be a clock of some kind in the nave, and succeeding bishops and priors added to the furniture of the whole cathedral.[12]

Of prime importance amongst the holy areas of the cathedral, the choir was located at the east end of the church in front of the high altar. Two aisles divided the choir stalls from the outer walls and herein were the tombs of bishops Trail, Lamberton, Gamelin, Malvoisine, de Gullane and Wishart. To the right and left of the choir door probably stood altars to the saints Peter and Paul. Above the western entrance to the choir stood the Holy Rood (the Cross of Christ Crucified), a gift of Margaret, Queen of Malcolm III, set on its beam and flanked by figures of the Blessed Virgin and St John, representing the attendant church. The Rood Loft was where the Gospel was read at mass. By the Altar of the Rood was kept the Rood Light, the next most important light in the cathedral to the Sanctuary Light (indicating Christ's presence in the tabernacle). The choir also contained the choir lectern in centre and the bishop/archbishop's chair. In front of the entrance to the choir was the huge choir screen to protect the sacred areas. The floor of the choir was paved with large tiles of black and brown, and yellow and green, laid diagonally; most of these were made locally at the priory kiln and the more ornate were probably imported from the Low Countries. A set of tiles has been reconstructed *in situ* in the north part of the choir. Besides the choir, tiled areas of the east end would include the altar of the Blessed Virgin, in the north aisle, and the altar to St Andrew in the south. It was Prior James Haldenstone who established the importance of the Chapel of the Blessed Virgin (the Lady Chapel), in the north side of the choir aisle by promoting at its altar a solemn mass at which he celebrated in full *pontificalia* wearing the mitre which his office had been granted; here too Bishop James Kennedy founded a daily mass for his soul and that of his mother Mariota Stewart, in 1465.

The lofty central tower of the cathedral was begun around 1230 and took several decades to complete; yet the lead roofing of the cathedral was stripped away in 1304 by Edward I for use in munitions for the siege of Stirling – during the Scottish Wars of Independence. At last Bishop William de Lamberton (1297–1328) consecrated the cathedral on 5 July 1318; the special consecration crosses can still be seen on the exterior of the choir and south transept. When the cathedral was all of a piece there would be twelve consecration crosses, one for each article of the Creed; these were anointed with holy oil as badges of Christ, stamping the building with His mark. Already in place too, would be the insignia of the priory (a crowned St Andrews cross) and that of the Order of the Augustiniana (a Heart pierced with Crowned Arrows). The dedication of the cathedral at St Andrews was a symbolic act of the highest national importance. Robert I, The Bruce (r.1306–29),was master of the realm, the English-held town of Berwick-upon-Tweed had fallen the same year, and Bruce's brother Edward was King of Ireland; again, it was the seal on Bruce's restored prestige and the seal of Lamberton's restored position in the diocese – he had been Edward I's erstwhile prisoner in the castle of Winchester. Nevertheless all these things were soon to be threatened.

Now St Andrews Cathedral was all of a piece with its high altar and sanctuary the focal point. The altar was set against a screen (which enclosed the Chapel of the Relics) and was to have a fine mid-fifteenth century altarpiece, provided by Prior

David Ramsay (1462–69). On the altar sat a *textus* (Gospel book), a gift of Bishop Fothad, velvet cushions used as book rests, a fine crucifix, silver cruets and the silver *aspersorium*; other items would appear too during feast days when a huge red carpet was laid down in the sanctuary. The cathedral's silver and gold plates were the gifts of benefactors down the decades. Before the high altar was said the high mass, but it was also a place where important meetings were held on legal matters. To the right and left of the high altar stood the lifesize statues of the Blessed Virgin and St Andrew, in the cathedral since at least 1318 and long associated with the Douglas family; indeed the Virgin's statue was known as 'Le Douglas Lady'. Votive lights would always be burning at the feet of these statues.

Beyond the screen which made up the reredos of the high altar was the Chapel of the Relics of the Apostle Andrew entered by doors to each side of the altar. In the centre of this chapel was the reliquary containing the bones of St Andrew which would be elevated so as to be seen above the reredos by those sitting in the choir. Herein too would be the cathedral's other main relics and treasures. Very few people were allowed in this area to see the silver-encrusted spear shaft of Alexander I (which was made into a processional cross), the crystal cross carried on the field of Bannockburn (June 1314) and the reliquary of Margaret, queen and saint.

All of these relics were an enormous security risk and the safety of them was the duty of the sacrist and sub-sacrist, one of whom would always sleep in church. The choir and sanctuary would be protected by iron railings and gates, and stout locked doors, and a close watch was kept for potential thefts; even so there is evidence of some pilgrims opportunistically stealing precious stones and plate from the images and altars whenever they could. Fire was another hazard which had to be monitored by the sacrist and his deputy, particularly on feast days when the cathedral was flooded with light from candles and the cresset lights (a stone with one or more hollows which contained oil and floating wicks). The sacrist and his assistant probably overlooked the sacred areas from a watch-chamber above the choir screen.

Within the south and north transepts were six altars set within their own bays. The three altars in the south transept were probably dedicated to St Margaret of Scotland, St Michael and St Lawrence the Deacon and Martyr of Rome during the persecution of Valerian. It is possible too, that the north transept contained the altars of two saints dear to Scotland's clerics, St Thomas Becket the Martyr of Canterbury and St Martin, Bishop of Tours in the fifth century.

The whole of the cathedral pavements were crammed with the tomb slabs of clerics, aristocrats, famous commoners and unknowns, and the tombs of bishops and archbishops would be the most striking feature of the cathedral after the altars. Many prelates – most of whom would prepare their own tombs years before their deaths – had altar-tombs where prayers could be said for their souls, and the most popular place for their burials was the cathedral chancel (the choir and sanctuary). Some of the tombs would bear effigies, picked out in bright colours of red, blue, green and gold.

Heart burials too were popular in medieval times and St Andrews Cathedral contained examples; the heart of Bishop William Frazer (who died in Paris in 1297 a refugee from Edward I) was buried in the choir wall beside the tombs of bishops Gamelin and Lamberton. It is curious that although St Andrews Cathedral was the most important church in Scotland it had little royal patronage. No kings or queens were interred within St Andrews Cathedral, yet one royal personage did have a tomb here.

He was James Stewart (c.1479–1504), Duke of Ross and Archishop of St Andrews, the latter appointment procured (the young archbishop was actually well under the canonical age of appointment of 30) for him by his royal elder brother James IV. In the *Ledger* of Prior Andrew Halyburton we learn that James Stewart's tomb cost £31 8s 2d (*guldins*). 'The gret stan' of the tomb can still be seen before the site of the Altar of the Relics, almost 11 feet long by 5 feet, also over 5 inches thick; set in its upper face was a huge monumental brass with the incised figure of the archbishop. The stone was cleared of rubble in 1826 and shows the level of the cathedral floor in medieval times. The

Rev. C.J. Lyon notes that near to the coffin of James Stewart 'was found a skeleton with a deep cut on the skull as if caused by the heavy blow of a broadsword; and this might be young Archbishop A[lexander] Stewart, who received his death-wound at Flodden (September 1513), and whose remains would, in all probability, be conveyed for interment to his own cathedral church, and buried among his predecessors.'[13] Born around 1493, the illegitimate son of James IV and Marion Boyd, Alexander was only eleven when appointed archbishop.

All the tombs of the clergy were despoiled and looted at the Reformation, John Knox's inflamed rabble rightly presuming that the archbishops, bishops and priors would be buried in full canonicals with personal mass sets of gold and silver, and croziers, jewelled mitres and episcopal rings. Two graves, however, may still contain (the stripped) cadavers of their founders, that of Archbishop William Schevez (1478–96) in the choir and that of William Bell, bishop elect of St Andrews (1332–42) in the south choir aisle.

17. The seal of William Schevez (1478–96), Archbishop of St Andrews; scholars believe that he may still be buried in the choir of the cathedral [National Museums of Scotland]

A great fire consumed the cathedral during the end of the episcopate of William de Landells (1342–85), in 1378, necessitating repair to the choir and transepts. During the episcopates of Walter Trail (1385–1401), Henry Wardlaw (1403–40) and

James Kennedy (1440–65), when the university was being founded and state affairs were developing in complexity, the cathedral repairs and maintenance fell heavily on the shoulders of the priors, particularly Prior James Bissett (1396–1416). The repairs went on for several years; in 1409 the south transept was thrown down in a great storm, adding complications. Thereafter the work was finished in the days of Prior James Haldenstone (1419–43) who supplied glass lamps, altars and furnishings. There do not seem to be many structural changes to the cathedral after the days of Prior Haldenstone except those of Prior John Hepburn (1482–1522), even taking into consideration that the See of St Andrews was elevated into an archbishopric on 13 August 1472 by Pope Sixtus IV.

Pilgrims

Each day pilgrims would arrive at St Andrews bringing with them wealth and income for the cathedral chapter and a lucrative bed and board trade to the citizens, although some pilgrims would camp in the 'square' outside the cathedral west door, or stay – if they were prominent enough – at the hostel of St Leonard provided for the purpose. St Andrews was the only

Nobility   *Work in the Scriptorium*

18. Nobility came from all over Europe to worship at and give gifts to the shrine of St Andrew; some endowed altars and subsidised the work done in the scriptorium [Sankey, Hudson & Co.]

place outside continental Europe to boast corporeal relics of an Apostle and the draw was great. The pilgrims were socially both high and low, from barons and knights to labourers and the infirm seeking solace from the cares of life and disease within the aura of the bones of *Sancti Apostoli Andreae*; clerics came too, to refresh their faith. One such early visitor was Guderic the Pirate, who became St Godric (d.1170) and whose hermitage became the Benedictine priory of Finchale, Co. Durham.[14]

Although there were four main pilgrim routes to St Andrews, the main one was the East Coast route, linking with the pilgrim trails to and from the Shrine of St Cuthbert at Durham. From East Lothian the pilgrim route crossed from North Berwick to Ardross (northeast of modern Elie), Fife, via the *passagium comitis* ('the Earl's ferry') founded in the twelfth century by Duncan, 4th Earl of Fife; hostels for the pilgrims were established at North Berwick and Ardross and the ferry and hostels were run by the Cistercian nuns of the hospital and convent of North Berwick.[15]

From the west pilgrims crossed the Forth by the *passagium reginae* ('the Queen's ferry') founded by Queen Margaret and were succoured at the hostels at each side, and made their way by the King's Road to Cupar and Guardbridge. At the wooden *gair* bridge (replaced in 1419 by a stone bridge by Bishop Wardlaw) they gathered at the neighbouring *statio*, or halting place by the River Eden to travel on to St Andrews in a group under armed guard through the outlaw territory of Kincaple and Strathtyrum marshlands. From the north-east they crossed the Tay by the Ferry of the Loaf from Broughty Ferry to Ferry-Port-on-Craig or to the ferries at Woodhaven, or Balmerino, run by the monks of Arbroath Abbey and Balmerino Abbey respectively. Those coming from Perth and Scone Abbey crossed the Tay where the River Earn meets the Firth by Port Aran, and if they were not going to Balmerino Abbey, they would likely skirt Cupar and cross by the Church of the Holy Trinity at Moonzie, to Pitbladdo and Foodieash and via Dairsie Castle to Guardbridge. The pilgrims were of all nationalities, from Germany and France, Scandinavia and Spain, all mingling with pilgrims from all over Scotland and local pilgrims from Fife towns and villages all seeking pardons for sins or relief from physical suffering.

The visitor standing in the ruins of the cathedral today finds it hard to picture the throng in the nave in medieval times. They would be doubtless repelled and sickened by the cluster of wretched cripples writhing down the nave to be as close as they could to the Chapel of the Relics. Had they been there they would retch at the stench of poverty and disease and stop the ears against the screams of the insane fettered in chains and cords to the pillars; and all around attention would be distracted for us by the pious noisily mouthing their prayers and offering coins, marked in the saint's name, mingled with the sounds of the sick vomiting and the dying groaning. On the altar steps, or on a table placed in the nave, the pilgrims would pile their silver, wood and wax images, and a strange collection of gifts – a model arm to be healed, a replica leg that was palsied, a worm that a pilgrim had vomited and piles of home-made candles of thread and animal fat.

The focus of the pilgrim's devotions was the Shrine of the Relics of St Andrew, but few but the mighty would be able to see the relics in their Great Reliquary of Celtic workmanship called the *Morbrac*.[16] Prior James Haldenstone identified the corporeal relics of the Apostle in the *Copiale Prioratus Sanctiandree* as being:

> brachium dextrum beati Andree apostoli ab humero usque ad cubitum, et tres digiti manus eius dextre, et patella de genu eius dextro, cum uno dente et alio osse de capite eius glorioso.[17]

Herein Haldenstone recorded 'the right humerus, three finger bones of the right hand, the right knee-cap, one tooth and a bone from the saint's head.' The arm of St Andrew was particularly venerated; during 13 and 19 March 1303–4 Edward I of England and his queen, Margaret, each offered a jewel to embellish the bone.[18]

At certain times, like the Feast of St Andrew (20 November) and the Coming of the Relics (6 February), the reliquary would be set on its *feretory* (bier) by the 'dewar' or keeper of the reliquary, and under a canopy it would be processed round the streets of St Andrews after high mass had been said in its presence at the high altar. Down South Street and up North Street the *Morbrac* would be carried, preceded by masters and scholars from the colleges carrying flowers and leafed branches, while members of the town's guilds would enact their religious tableaux and pageants. Around the *Morbrac* the clergy processed in fine vestments and sang hymns to suit the occasion.

The relics were normally kept under lock and key. A constant watch was kept over them in their own chapel. Sometimes they left St Andrews, particularly in time of national emergency. Such a time was in 1543 when Henry VIII threatened to 'spoyle and turne upset downe the cardinalles town of St Andrews' as a part of his 'rough wooing' of Mary, Queen of Scots; this time the relics went for safe keeping to the Douglas family at Lochleven castle prominent devotees of the St Andrew cult.

What happened to the relics at the Reformation is not known, but it is hardly credible that the canons of the cathedral would not know that the reforming mob were approaching the cathedral with despoliation in their hearts, John Knox had given them enough warning with his hysterical bluster. After all the St Andrew relics were amongst the most important in Christendom. So, did the canons secrete the relics in some place? Or, were they spirited out of the country to be returned to Rome? Reputed relics of St Andrew still remain in Scotland. In 1879 the Archbishop of Amalfi, Italy – reputed site of the 'apostle's tomb' – gave a large portion of the shoulder blade of St Andrew to the Roman Catholic cathedral of St Mary, Edinburgh, and in 1969, Pope Paul VI gave another corporeal relic to Cardinal Gray while on a visit to Rome, this too is in St Mary's cathedral.[19] A small portion of bone from Amalfi is also lodged in a reliquary at the Roman Catholic Church of St James at St Andrews.

Most pilgrims to St Andrews Cathedral would wish to have their own holy souvenir of the visit. There they could buy a pilgrim's badge. These badges showed the Crucifixion of St

Andrew at Patras on his X-shaped cross – to wear such a badge, the devout believed, would gain them protection from the saint against evil and were proof of pilgrimage. Each badge had four stitch-eyelets so that they could be sewn onto coats, tunics or hats. A few extant examples have an A for Andrew, usually between the saint's feet, while others bear the letters 'MAR-TY[R]'. Badges were generally cheaply cast from a tin-lead alloy, and those who wore them might obtain free passage on the ferries on their way to St Andrews. Examples of the badges have been found at sites from Canterbury to Perth; one was discovered in St Andrews and is known as the 'Castlecliff Badge'.

Royalty and heresy

The cathedral was the location for many important occasions and meetings. One of the most colourful occurred in 1538. Here in June of that year the widowed James V married his third cousin Marie de Guise–Lorraine, widow of Louis, Duc de Longueville. They had been married by proxy on 9 May at the castle of Châteaudun, thereafter Marie journeyed to Scotland landing in Fife at Balcomie Castle. Her splendid cavalcade made their way through Kingsbarns and Boarhills and thence through The Tiends gateway to the *Novum Hospitium*. Formal marriage took place before the high altar of the cathedral, and amongst the marriage portions James V conferred the Earldom of Fife upon his bride. Forty days of revelry took place at St Andrews and a welcoming masque was devised by Fife poet Sir David Lyndsay, Lord Lyon.[20]

Diocesan synods, presided over sometimes by the archbishop, or the vicar-general or substituting commissary, were also held in the cathedral. The synod covered all aspects of ecclesiastical life in the diocese/archdiocese. Business of the synod was held in the Senzie (Synod) Hall after mass and a sermon. There was at this time receipt of the parochial dues and the accepting of gifts to the church.

Most of the heresy trials of the diocese were held in the cathedral: on 23 July 1433, Paul Kraver (Craw) was burned at St Andrews after his trial in the cathedral and during February

19. James V (1513–42); King of Scots, married Marie de Guise-Lorriane at St Andrews cathedral in 1538; they had already been married by proxy on 9 May at the castle of Châteaudun, France

1527 Patrick Hamilton was arraigned and at his trial the preacher was Alexander Campbell, Prior of the Blackfriars. Sentence was read by James Beaton in the presence of a great multitude of clergy. In 1533 Henry Forrest was burned at the north side of the cathedral so that the people of Forfarshire (modern Angus) could see the flames as a deadly warning and George Wishart was tried in the cathedral before Cardinal Archbishop David Beaton. On 20 April 1558, Walter Myln was tried before Archbishop John Hamilton and the preacher was Simon Maltman, warden of the Greyfriars; this was the last trial in the cathedral. The trials were looked upon as social occasions, and within the cathedral, probably before the chancel screen, the clergy sat in a specially erected wooden grandstand (*magna scala*); alongside was a pulpit for the red-hooded 'accuser' and the accused person spoke from a rostum. The ordinary folk filled the nave to hear the proceedings.

The end of the cathedral

The end of the cathedral came when new religious thought was asserted out of the fresh theological opinions from the Continent. Yet, there was more to it than that. First there was growing opposition in Scotland to the French influence brought about by the marriage of the Dauphin Francis with Mary, Queen of Scots in 1558. The nobility began to work against this alliance, and to avoid being classed as traitorious rebels and potential regicides they invited the exiled John Knox to return to Scotland and they tied in their political cause with his 'godly work'. Then, reform offered an opportunity to work off old family scores and line pockets with the wealth of the church properties. Cardinal Beaton was murdered in retaliation for the execution of Protestant martyr George Wishart and the whole thing escalated into a national crisis in which many of the academic clergy, in particular, saw advantage.

Thus, undermined by its own clergy, the death knell of the cathedral was to be rung on Sunday, 11 June 1559. With the town occupied by the Protestant lords, James, Argyll, Ruthven, Erskine of Dun, Wishart of Pittarrow and others, John Knox preached at Holy Trinity Church and continued his rantings for three days, whereupon the work of destruction began on Wednesday, 14 June. Hardly had Knox finished speaking about Christ's expulsion of the merchants from the temple than the mob, orchestrated by the Protestant lords, sacks at the ready to carry off the booty, made for the cathedral 'to purge the kirk and break down the altars and images and all kinds of idolatrie' as the *Historie of the Estate of Scotland* said.[21]

The wooden statues were piled in a heap where Myln had been martyred and burned by the followers of the Protestant lords and at their direction. Knox was just whitewashing the acts of vandalism when he said that the cathedral was raped by the St Andreans themselves and with the agreement of the magistrates. Altars, images, tombs, statues were all broken up and the

20. John Knox (1505–72), Scottish reformer and historian. He was to be the nemesis of the religious life of the medieval church. He had been taken prisoner at St Andrew's Castle and sent to France in 1548.

dead robbed of their funeral goods. The buildings of the cathedral were left intact, but on that day four hundred years of continuous worship came to an end . . . the dream inspired by Bishop Robert to offer his flock a 'Glimpse of Heaven on Earth' was shattered.

Without a doubt, the crypto-Protestant clergy did make off with moveable plate and valuables from the cathedral before the mob came. James Stewart, Earl of Moray, and prior, certainly feathered his own nest with cathedral booty, and the cathedral bells, brass lairs, lead, timber, slates and other usable building material would be systematically filched by all who could carry it away. The cathedral was used as a quarry right into the eighteenth century.[22]

After the Reformation, the chapter of St Andrews remained, as about half of the clergy began to serve the new religion and up to at least 1570 twice-annual meetings were held to discuss the upkeep of the priory and the needs of the 'new clergy'. By 1565 James Stewart, Earl of Moray, as prior, was living in the priory house and the canons dwelt in their buildings, although there are tales of brutality and intimidation towards them and they were expected to wear secular clothes.

John Hamilton was the last of the medieval Archbishops of St Andrews and he was driven from his See in 1559; Hamilton was executed in 1571 for the alleged part he played in the assassination of the Regent Moray and the archbishopric was assigned to John Douglas, Principal of St Mary's College. The position of archbishop remained under attack and was considered irrelevant under Presbyterianism, but episcopacy was not abandoned and the title persisted until the appointment of the last Protestant archbishop Arthur Rose, whose title died with him in 1704. The name of St Andrews disappeared as an ecclesiastical title until 1842 when it was restored as the Bishopric of St Andrews, Dunkeld and Dunblane and still exists as such within the Episcopal Church in Scotland. When the Roman Catholic hierarchy was restored in 1878 it was decided to utilise St Andrews and Edinburgh in the title of one of the two new Scottish Roman Catholic archbishops and so it remains.

21. Shattered head of Christ. The cathedral of St Andrews was despoiled by the mob on Wednesday, 14 June 1559, stage-managed by rapacious members of the aristocracy. [National Museums of Scotland]

22. James Stewart, Earl of Moray (1531–70). Known as 'the Good Regent', he was the illegitimate son of James V by Margaret Erskine, wife of Robert Douglas of Lochleven. He became Commendator of St Andrews Priory in 1538 and there hosted his half-sister Mary, Queen of Scots.

During 1826 the ruins of the cathedral were taken over by the Barons of the Exchequer and excavated, and in 1946 the priory was given over to the then Ministry of Works. The immediate environs to the north and east of the cathedral were used extensively as burial areas and it is known that interments continued in the cathedral nave until 1834. The Chapter House was excavated during 1904–05 and a large amount of coloured window glass was found in the north transept. The markings of the original sites of the pillars of the cathedral nave and the lines of the demolished walls were cut out in the turf in 1888, and in 1988 the long-sealed south processional doorway, from cloister to nave, was reopened.

The cathedral museum is housed in what was the thirteenth-century undercroft of the frater, now linked by the museum entrance walkway to the warming house; both buildings house the main museum displays. It may be noted that in the 1890s John Patrick Crichton-Stuart, 3rd Marquess of Bute (1847–1900), commenced an ambitious restoration of the undercroft. His work in red sandstone (cf. the original medieval stone) remained incomplete when the Crichton-Stuarts handed over the site to the Ministry of Works in 1946.

Artefacts from the cathedral excavations were once housed in the United College with the St Andrews Literary and Philosophical Society and the University Court as custodians.[23] In 1904 a museum was established at the cathedral site in accordance with a lease from the then heritor

23. John Patrick Crichton-Stuart, 3rd Marquess of the County of Bute (1847–1900). Lord Rector of St Andrews in 1892 and 1898, he commenced an ambitious restoration of the undercroft of the cathedral priory, but the work was never finished.

Lord Norman Edward Crichton-Stuart. In 1991 the museum was re-established to include a visitor centre. The museum displays a fine collection of Celtic monuments – including the re-displayed St Andrews Sarcophagus – medieval tombstones, moulded and sculpted stones from the site, a fine set of casts of ecclesiastical seals and various domestic range and church artefacts. One particular highlight, too, is the speculative reconstruction of the tomb of Bishop Henry Wardlaw (episcopate 1403–40), who died in St Andrews Castle. In 2005 a new education centre was established on the site of the Prior's House.

CHAPTER 4

A Precipice Fortified: St Andrews Castle

Syre Andrew Murray cast it down
For there he found a garrysoun
Of English men intil that place.

Andrew of Wyntoun,
Augustinian Canon (c.1355–1422)

Around 6 a.m. on the morning of Saturday 29 March 1546, a group of men followed a lumbering wagon down Castle Street and made for the main entrance to St Andrews Castle. Armed and cloaked, the men were well known figures in the burgh. Norman Leslie, eldest son of the Earl of Rothes, walked with William Kirkcaldy, son of Sir James Kirkcaldy of Grange, his uncle John Leslie of Parkhill, John Melville of Carnbee, Peter Carmichael, a kinsman of the laird of Balmaddie and others, all dissenting gentlemen and each with a grudge against the man they had gathered to conspire against and were now about to kill.

Even at that early hour, St Andrews Castle was bustling; a hundred masons and labourers were at work repairing the castle frontage, and porter of the outer gate, Ambrose Stirling, had ordered the drawbridge to be lowered to allow passage for wagons of building materials. On the wall-tops a handful of guards lolled and yawned in the morning light, their watchfulness somewhat lax in the absence that forenoon of John Beaton of Balfour, captain of the castle.

Under cover of the wagon, Norman Leslie and his companions entered the castle to be met by John Poll, gunner, who for a purse of coin would assure the gathering assassins an easy passage through the castle's corridors and stairs. At first, porter Ambrose Stirling had an unremarkable conversation with William Kirkcaldy, but on seeing the others present became alarmed; as he attempted to lower the drawbridge he was

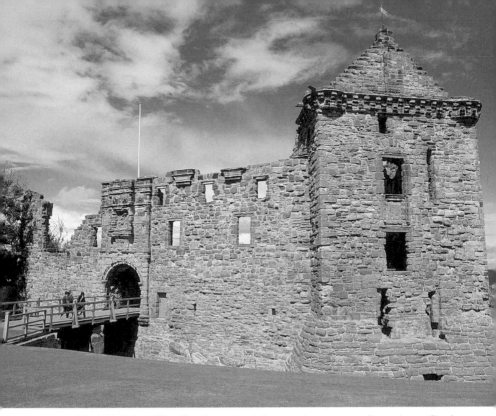

24. Archbishop Hamilton's entrance front and gateway to St Andrews Castle surmounted by his five-pointed star badge. The fourteenth-century Fore Tower rises to the right, to join Hamilton's late-sixteenth-century work. [Historic Scotland]

clubbed to the ground, his keys snatched and his inert body thrown into the moat. Servants, guards and attendants scattered as the armed men showed aggression. Aroused by the commotion the man they had come to assassinate appeared at the window of his chamber in the east blockhouse.

Down below someone shouted that Norman Leslie had taken the castle, and David Beaton watching the milling crowd below his window knew that he was the next prize. Unable to escape as William Kirkcaldy and others now held the postern gate – from which Beaton's mistress Marian Ogilvy had lately exited unaware of the events about to unfold – and the other blockhouse doors were now guarded by Leslie's men. David Beaton barricaded the door of his chamber with the help of his bodyservant Amand Guthrie. Hardly had heavy furniture been placed against the portal than John Leslie, James Melville and Peter Carmichael began to batter the oak planks. Beaton tried to use his diplomatic skills as he shouted to the men through the door to parlay. To no avail; the door would not budge so Leslie called for a brazier of hot coals to burn an entry. Fearing incineration, David Beaton had the door unblocked and the three men gained access.

25. David Beaton, Bishop of Mirepoix, France, and Presbyter Cardinal of St Stephen on the Caelian, Archbishop of St Andrews (1538). He was assassinated at St Andrews Castle, Saturday, 29 May, 1546.

David Beaton admonished them for invading the privacy of a prince of the church and argued for his non-molestation. He was ignored and fired with hatred James Melville stabbed Beaton to be followed by Peter Carmichael. The erstwhile most powerful courtier in Scotland lay dead at their feet.

Soon news of the murder spread like wildfire through St Andrews. Sir James Learmonth of Dairsie, provost of St Andrews, appeared at the castle gate with a posse; citizens ran to the castle from all sides. On the castle walls an elated Norman Leslie shouted that the hated Beaton was dead. To prove to the crowd that what he said was true, Beaton's naked body was slung from the (now vanished) blockhouse in bedsheets.[1]

In time David Beaton's body was cut down and pickled in salt and sealed in a kist and placed within the Bottle Dungeon; eventually the cadaver was secretly buried by his relatives in the chapel of the Blackfriars in South Street.[2] What had precipitated this violent murder?

David Beaton, Abbot of Arbroath, Bishop of Mirepoix, France, Archbishop of St Andrews, Papal Legate *a latere*, and Presbyter Cardinal of St Stephen on the Caelian, was born around 1494, the son of John Beaton of Balfour and his wife Elizabeth Monypenny and succeeded his uncle James Beaton as archbishop, 1538–39.[3] Beaton was the pillar of the pro-French faction in James V's Scotland and an opposer of the wiles of Henry VIII of England. Beaton refused to ratify the marriage contract which Henry had proposed between his son Edward and the infant Mary, daughter of James V. To persuade the Scots of the desirability of this match Henry conducted the 'rough wooing' and his armies invaded Scotland from 1543. During that time, in 1546, when Beaton was strengthening the castle against a threatened attack, events were brewing that were to lose his faction the castle and Beaton his life. To understand the outcome we must introduce George Wishart.

To thwart Beaton, Henry VIII had begun to treat with various lords and gentry who were in dispute with the cardinal, and many of whom like the Earls of Cassilis and Glencairn were known as the 'English Faction'. An intimate associate of this faction was the Angus-born (c.1513) Protestant preacher George Wishart, who loathed Beaton and the medieval (i.e., Roman Catholic) Church. While a schoolmaster in Montrose Grammar School, Wishart taught the New Testament in Greek and was charged with heresy and at length spent some time in Switzerland, to settle at Corpus Christi College, Cambridge. He continued to preach what was deemed heresy and returned to Scotland in the train of the English envoys who came to urge the royal marriage. Wishart's disciple, by the by, was John Knox of Haddington whose name is also intertwined in the St Andrews Story.

Henry VIII saw Beaton as an enemy of his policies, and therefore England, and encouraged plots to assassinate the cardinal. Whether or not Wishart was involved in these plots is not certain, but Beaton soon recognised Wishart as a man dangerous to the medieval Church's authority and a demagogue capable of whipping up violence against its officers. Wishart was arrested while preaching at Haddington and was brought to St Andrews, where after four weeks of imprisonment he was tried for heresy on 28 February 1546 on the formal accusation of John Wynram, sub-Prior of St Andrews. Wishart was sentenced to death, and was strangled and burned in front of St Andrews Castle on 1 March 1546. A pupil of Wishart's at Cambridge, Emery Tilney, left a description of how Wishart would appear to the people of St Andrews:

[He was] a man of tall stature, polled-headed, and on the same a round French cap of the best; judged to be of melancholy complexion by his physiognomy; black-haired, long bearded, comely of personage, well spoken after his country of Scotland, courteous, lowly, lovely, glad to teach, desirous to learn, and was well travelled; having on him for his habit or clothing never but a mantle or frieze gown to the shoes, a black [Milan] fustian doublet, and plain black hosen, coarse new canvas for his shirts, and white falling bands and cuffs at his hands – all the which apparel he gave to the poor, some weekly, some monthly, some quarterly, as he liked, saving his French cap, which he kept the whole year of my being with him . . . His charity had never end, night noon, or day . . . infinitely studying how to do good unto all, and hurt to none.[4]

Today Wishart's initials are spelled out in granite blocks on the site of the execution; the setts were placed here in 1946 on the 400th anniversary of his 'martyrdom'. Did Wishart already know that Beaton's days were numbered? Tradition has it that Wishart looked up at the window of the new blockhouse tower which Beaton was having built and caught the eye of the cardinal and his guest Gavin Dunbar, Archbishop of Glasgow, who were watching the immolation begin and said: 'He who in such state, from that high place, feedeth his eyes with my torments, within a few days shall be hanged out at the same window, to be seen with as much ignominy, as he now leaneth there in pride.' If this tradition has substance, then even Wishart was compliant in the murder of Beaton.

St Andrews Castle was the scene of many bloody events. The rumbustious nature of Scottish medieval politics made it necessary that the bishops of St Andrews have a fortified residence. Until the development of St Andrews Castle as a fortress, prison and archepiscopal palace, the bishops had resided first within the old Celtic enclave and then the Augustinian priory. Records show that Bishop Roger de Beaumont, Chancellor of Scotland and erstwhile Abbot of Melrose, who was the son of Robert, Earl of Leicester and cousin of William I, The Lion, built the first castle here shortly before his death in 1202.[5] It is likely though that the site was some sort of earthen fortification long before Roger's time, set on the pentagonal mini-headland, with its beetling cliffs rising sheer from the Hind Lake. Probably Bishop William Malvoisine (d.1238) finished off Roger's work; the only part of the latter's castle remaining is the rear section of the Fore Tower (and original entrance to the castle) overlooking the courtyard.

The political jockeyings of the Wars of Independence and Sir William Wallace too, caused St Andrews Castle much spoilation. It changed hands several times between the Scots and the English over the next few years. In 1303–4 Edward I of

England held his parliament in St Andrews and was using the castle as a royal residence. Shortly after Bannockburn, 23–4 June 1314, it was occupied and repaired by Edward's stubborn opponent Bishop William de Lamberton (d.1328). It was taken again by the English in 1332 during the resistance of David II to the warlike episodes of the pretender to the Scottish throne, John Balliol, on behalf of Edward III, and Bishop James Ben (d.1332) was expelled. The castle was rebuilt in 1336 by the English noblemen Henry de Beaumont and Henry Ferrers, who, it is said, also rebuilt the Norman castle of the de Quincys at Leuchars. Sir Andrew Moray, besieged St Andrews Castle in 1337 and, reported Wyntoun, 'erd syn dang it doun' as a part of Bruce's scorched earth policy. On this occasion the Scots were aided in their siege through the use of the 'Boustour'; this was a great stone-throwing machine, the trebuchet, which also helped the Scots assail the stronghold of Bothwell Castle.[6]

Until 1385 St Andrews Castle lay neglected and ruined when it was rebuilt from its foundations by the Avignon anti-pope

26. Eastern elevation of St Andrews Castle [Historic Scotland]

Clement VII's ambassador or *referendarius*, Bishop Walter Trail
(d.1401). The castle we see today is mainly of Bishop Trail's
period for his foundations were basic for all future construction.[7] By Trail's day the castle assumed its irregular pentagon
shape, with five towers at the five main angles. During periods
of reconstruction the bishops probably resided at the priory or
at their Boarhills palace of Inchmurtach.

The early layout of the castle, 1200–1400, consisted of the
bishop's own apartments, to the front with its chapel of 1386;
below the chapel were probably the rooms and library of the
chaplain with a loggia on the north facing wall. Two towers
were built over the northern cliffs: The Sea Tower (the donjon
to the north-west) was the residence of the castle's constable
who oversaw the bishop's household and was in charge of the
defences, remembering, of course, that artillery was a crown
monopoly and the castle probably had no guns of its own in
time of peace. The office of constable was an important perk
handed out by the bishop and several prominent Fife families
held the position, like the de Wemysses of Kilmany appointed
by Bishop Wardlaw. The Kitchen Tower and its allied chambers dealt with the necessary sustenance of the garrison. The
tower was linked to a now vanished east range hall (it fell into
the sea in 1801) where food was served, with the hall linked to
private accommodation for the bishop's guests; storage cellars
were on the ground floor. Next to the Kitchen Tower was the
Seagate with a slipway down to the sea; all round the landward
side of the castle, to west and south would be the beginnings of a
moat.

The Sea Tower, built in Trail's day, contains a medical
garderobe (privy) and various levels of prison accommodation.
Prisoners of noble birth probably used the upper chambers with
a small prison cell underneath; here it is though George
Wishart was incarcerated before his execution in 1546. Here
too, was imprisoned James Ogilvy, 2nd Earl of Airlie. A
Royalist commander he was captured at the Battle of Philiphaugh, 13 September 1645 and condemned to death by the
parliament at St Andrews. Leading from an unlit vault is the
famous bottle dungeon. Hollowed out of the solid sandstone,

the 24-foot-deep dungeon is shaped like a bottle with a 'neck' some 5 feet in diameter and within its damp depths, said John Knox, 'many of God's children were imprisoned'. Perhaps one of the dungeon's first occupants was Canon Thomas Plater, who had murdered Prior Robert of Montrose in 1393. There are those academics who discard the 'dungeon' classification and argue that the pit was no more than a grain store excavated for Trail's vital supplies.

While royal personages like David, Duke of Rothesay, the eldest son and heir of Robert III (r.1390–1406), was imprisoned here on the orders of his uncle the Duke of Albany in 1402, his brother James I (r.1406–37) had a more comfortable life in the castle under the tutorial eye of Bishop Wardlaw. James later returned to the castle after his eighteen years of English incarceration and used it as a favourite residence. If we can believe the *Golden Charter* of James II (r.1437–60), his son James III (r.1460–88) was born here in 1452 and from James III's reign the castle was the palace and prison of Patrick Graham, first Archbishop of St Andrews, before he was removed to permanent confinement to the Isle of St Serf, Lochleven, where he died in 1478. The castle was visited often by Mary of Guelders, the cultivated and religious spouse of James II, who brought with her several of their eight children.

The violent death of Archbishop Alexander Stewart with his father James IV at Flodden Field in 1513, caused more alarms at the castle. No less than four contenders came forward for the vacant See. There was Gavin Douglas (c.1474–1522), the poet and ultimate Bishop of Dunkeld who seized the castle to cement his nomination. Prior John Hepburn was elected by his canons and drove Douglas from the castle, James Beaton, Archbishop of Glasgow, was also nominated as was Andrew Foreman, Bishop of Moray, the Pope's nominee who was duly elected. The castle, however, remained in the hands of the Hepburns for a while and Foreman resided at Dunfermline.

After the murder of Archbishop James Beaton's nephew Cardinal David Beaton, the Protestants held the castle and with the help of Henry VIII they retained it for a year. In due time the castle was besieged by the Regent, the 2nd Earl of

27. James I (r.1406–37), King of Scots, was tutored at St Andrews castle by Bishop Henry Wardlaw

Arran, who, supplemented by a French fleet and arms under the command of Leon Strozzi, Prior of Capua, succeeded in capturing the castle which was greatly damaged from cannon mounted on the cathedral tower and on the tower of St Salvator's Church in North Street. Still to be seen is a military relic of this siege in the mine and countermine, rediscovered in 1879. During Arran's siege in 1546 he ordered a passageway to

be cut through the rock (the entrance is beneath the house at
the corner of Castle Wynd at the north end of North Castle
Street) with the intent of breaching the castle's foundations and
thereby gaining entry. The defenders, however, cut an inter-
cepting countermine to thwart this exercise. Today's visitors
can clamber through this rare example of the medieval sapper's
work. These mines gave rise to many a Victorian 'secret
passage' story, and Dean of Guild Linskill was a keen promoter
of them.

The castle is known to have been rebuilt by Cardinal
Beaton's successor Archbishop John Hamilton (archepiscopate
1547–71), illegitimate son of the 1st Earl of Arran, and Bishop
of Dunkeld. Hamilton's armorial cinquefoil (a five-pointed
star) is seen above the present (in fact fourth) entrance gateway; his heraldic panel is also to be seen on the front wall of the
Fore Tower between two windows. By Hamilton's day the
buildings of the castle were complete; from the entrance with its
vaulted guard rooms and postern door the frontage runs west to
lead to the west blockhouse of 1544. A suite of four rooms
comprised the frontage, the west elevation overlooking the
bishop's garden (a part of the grounds of Castlecliff, 1877);
joining the curtain wall at the Sea Tower and the Kitchen
Tower were the 'gentlemens' appartments' where the Great
Hall joined the chapel to the east blockhouse.

Towards the end of 1559 the castle was in the hands of the
Protestant Reformers, who would cleanse it of 'idolaterie' and
vestiges of the medieval churchmen who lived there. The in-
ventory of 1565 shows that it was very scantily furnished by that
date. In 1583 James VI escaped from capture by the Ruthvens of
Huntingtower – the Gowrie Plot – and took shelter in the castle,
and in 1587 the castle passed, through the Act of Annexation,
and along with other Church property, to the Crown.

Effectively the castle was still connected with the archbishopric, but in 1606 James VI (now James I of England) granted
it to George Home, later Earl of Dunbar, who had been its
constable since James had disappeared down the road to
England with his court after 1603. By 1612 the castle reverted
to the archbishopric and it was repaired by the (Episcopal

St Andrews

Church) Archbishop George Gledstanes (1604–15). His successor Archbishop John Spottiswoode (archepiscopate 1615–39) complained that the castle was ruinous in 1629 and he removed his headquarters to the *Hospitium Novum*, in 1635. By then the office of constable had fallen into desuetude. Parliament ordered the St Andrews Town Council to repair the castle in 1645 and it was used as a state prison a year later. In 1654 the Town Council ordered that part of the castle stone work be used to repair the harbour and in 1656 castle slate and timber were sold to defray the expense of repairing the Long Pier.

The environs of the castle have changed greatly since the seventeenth century; writing in 1693, George Martine states that in his time people remembered how bowls were played on the level ground to the east and north of the castle (an area now reclaimed by the sea).[8] The antiquary Captain Francis Grose (1731–91) quoted old sources to say that the proprietor of the neighbourhood estate 'had the privilege of driving his cattle and goods on the east side of the castle'.[9] During the period 1724 to 1808 the castle 'close' was rented to various individuals and in 1802 Principal James Playfair of United College made an appeal for restoration of the castle, the tenant of the courtyard having closed the castle gate and 'ploughed up the area and planted potatoes on several parts of the ruins'. A keeper was first appointed in 1810. In 1857 the castle well was rediscovered and in 1864–65 the moat was cleared out. The walls abutting the sea were given protection supports in 1884–86, 1892 and 1903 and by 1904 the Castle Beach bathing pond was established, although the beach hereabouts had been used for bathing for some considerable time. In 1911 the castle was taken into government custody and guardianship as an ancient monument.

When in residence in St Andrews, the bishops' and archbishops' households were very large; the archbishops, for instance, ruled a realm within a realm from Kincardine to Lothian and the English border, and had command over the spiritual and secular lives of around 80,000 souls in medieval times. To run the archdiocese from St Andrews Castle they had hundreds of staff from clerks to masons, gunners to cooks, musicians to brewers, bodyservants to tailors and apothecaries to men-at-arms. Thus at all times the castle frothed with human activity. The archbishop's representatives were all seeing and had no doors closed to them. Many of the plum jobs on the bishops' and archbishops' staff were secured through nepotism, but the princes of the Church employed a wide range of local people from the Fife lairds to the artisans of the burgh.

One of the unusual functions of a Scottish bishop was to act as coiner. Probably because of his education at the court of his brother-in-law Henry I of England (r.1100–35), Beauclerc, David I (r.1124–53) was aware how English Norman boroughs minted coins. Hence it is likely that he too saw a link between Scots burghs' commerce and the national economic interest. We now know that coins were minted in St Andrews from David's reign, early examples showing that they were struck by Mainard the Fleming, the *praefectus* (cf. provost) of Bishop Robert of St Andrews.[10]

Coins too, were minted in St Andrews in Alexander III's (r.1249–86) time as Augustinian Canon Andrew of Wyntoun tells us in his *Orygynale Cronikil of Scotland*:

> Alexandre oure king
> That Scotland had in governyng
> Came in till his ryalte
> Till Sanctandrois the cite
>   And standard in the kirk rycht there
> Devotly forouth the hie altare
> In presens of all that stude by
> He grantit and gaif there frely
> To God and to St Androis he
> Grantit the stryking of the money
> As frely and as fulely
> As ony bischop before gane by
> In thare times had sic thyng
> In the time, or his faders the king
> Suffand the declaration
> Off the superscription
> And the feftment of that thing
> To remane ay with the king.

The bishop he granted this right to was William Fraser (elected 1279, d.1297), and examples are marked for Thomas the Minter. Fraser also supervised the St Andrews coinage for John Balliol (r.1292–96).

Bishop James Kennedy carried out his coining at St Andrews Castle, the safest place to keep the dies.[11] Kennedy had been granted by the charter of privilege of striking coins by James III (r.1437–60). Of the pennies coined at St Andrews for Kennedy the obverse bears an orb with a cross breaking through the legend to act as a mintmark. This is surrounded by royal titles: *Iacobus Dei Gra[tia]Rex* – 'James by the Grace of God King'. On the reverse a Latin cross in a tressure of four arcs appears the motto *Crux Pellit Omne Crimen* – 'the cross disperses all harm', the first line of the vesper hymn *Ante Somnum* by the Spanish-born fifth-century Latin Christian poet Marcus Aurelius Clemens Prudentius. Kennedy's St Andrews farthings were copied, numismatists state, from the 'black farthings' of James III, which had already appeared in the early, 1470s. The reverse design is quite original bearing a long cross pattée with six-pointed mullets and crowns in alternate angles; the reverse inscription read *Mone[ta] Paup[erum]*, for 'money for the poor'. The design of Kennedy's coins can compare closely with the work on the mace of St Salvator's College and knowledge of them dates back to 1919 when a 205-coin hoard of them was found in a drain at the Cluniac Abbey of Crossraguel, Ayrshire. Kennedy's coins had a wide circulation in the east of Scotland, and are a rare treasure for they form the only medieval coins of the whole of Great Britain not only to have been struck by the authority of a primate, but also bear his own arms. By the end of Kennedy's episcopate (1440–65) all coining ceased in St Andrews.

During the season 1988–89 excavations took place at the site of the west precincts of the castle. Clear evidence was found of outer courtyards wherein ancillary accommodation had been located to include stables, a tanner's yard, workshops, brew-houses, kilns, bakehouses and garden plots, flanking the Sea Tower and the west Blockhouse. The castle precincts were therefore seen to be much larger than had been supposed.

There was also evidence of Bronze Age activity at the castle site from around 2400–700 BC, proving a continuum of habitation of this site long before David I gave the acres as part of his *vil* (a feudal territorial unit) with its *clachan* to Bishop Robert to found as his new burgh. Where the archaeologists had worked a new visitor centre for the castle was built and opened in 1992, to house an audio-visual montage of castle–cathedral history.

CHAPTER 5

Bishop Robert's Burgh

It stands by the sea, laid out in parallel lines of roads, with
a noble surrounding of rich glebe, a place of lordly wealth;
while the old lustre of the pontiffs mitre remained, 'twas
here the pontiff's mitre gleamed . . . A town happy
beyond words.

Poemata, Professor John Johnstoun (1570–1612),
of St Mary's College

Burgh originally meant a fortified place, where people could
group to resist attack by an enemy, and as time went by two
main types of burgh developed in Scotland: Royal Burghs and
Burghs of Reality and Barony. The former were burghs directly
founded by the king, and the other those on the lands of a
subject superior, be they cleric or layman. David I gave
charters to twelve burghs, which he called *meo burgo* and
included St Andrews' neighbour Crail, while St Andrews itself
was in its origin a Bishop's Burgh. In 1614 St Andrews was
made a Burgh of Regality under the Archbishop of St Andrews,
and King James VI made it into a Royal Burgh in 1620.

The development of St Andrews as a burgh began some time
between 1140 and 1150, when it was raised into such status by
Bishop Robert with the active enthusiasm and permission of
David I. When his burgh was legally established Bishop Robert
looked south to Berwick-upon-Tweed for his first reeve (or,
steward). Berwick had been made a royal burgh around 1120
by David I and was one of the *Curia Quattuor Burgorum* (Court of
Four Burghs), and the See of St Andrews already had some
properties in Berwick and drew rent from burgages. Bishop
Robert chose the opulent wool merchant (*proprius burgensis*),
Mainard the Fleming, as his reeve.

We first met Mainard as Bishop Robert's coiner and it is

28. David I (r.1124–53), of the House of Atholl, sixth son of Malcolm III and (Saint) Margaret, as shown on his seal and coin. He enthusiastically gave permission to Bishop Robert to raise the settlement of St Andrews into Burgh status.

known that Mainard was granted 'three tofts' of land in the burgh by Bishop Robert.[1] These were situated *a vico burgendi usque ad rivum prioris* ('from the burgh street [South Street] down to the prior's stream [Lade]'.[2] It is probable that Mainard's tofts of house and cultivated land (riggs) lay down from the junction of modern South Street and Abbey Street. History proclaims Mainard as St Andrews' first *praepositus* (provost) but it should be remembered that he was first and formost the 'bishop's man'.

By the time of Bishop Richard (1163–78) we can see that the early heart of St Andrews was in that area including North Castle Street, South Castle Street (once Huckster's Wynd), part of the narrow end of Market Street and the site of no.s 19–21 North Street; probably the focal point of the secular St Andrews was the fortification that predated Bishop Roger's castle. Once the cathedral was established the second phase of the burgh development took place and by 1260 South Street as far as modern Bell Street would be laid out, with Market Street and North Street to approximately the New Picture House

29. Mainard the Fleming, first praepositus (provost) of St Andrews, c.1140 [Sankey, Hudson & Co.]

(1930), North Street being an extension of the route into the old Bishop's Burgh and South Street being a thoroughfare planned to lead directly into the cathedral precinct. The development of early housing at modern Gregory Place, Deans Court and the east end of South Street and Abbey Street would be within the barony of the priory and the archdeacon, outwith the original burgh.

By 1560 the burgh had developed to modern Murray Place, and the West Port. The area of Argyll Street to modern Alfred Place (once Cow Wynd) was a separate development, called Argyle, outwith the medieval burgh and had been a part of its neighbour Rathelpie, which stretched as far as Priory Acres. Rathelpie may have been a fortified Pictish settlement and the lands were ultimately in the endowment of the Hospital of St Leonard. Argyle – from *Earra Ghaidheal* 'borderland of the Gael' – where lived the folk called 'Pachlers', seems to have been a village of thatched houses for people who at first won their living from the land and became mostly stone masons in the summer and handloom weavers in the winter. The hamlet developed to have seven dairies and two bakehouses and a public house called the Thacket Inn owned by one Adam Dick whose sign said he 'Sells ale and whisky, But nae gin'.

Within Argyle too, was a chaplain's house and probably a residence of Gavin Dunbar, archdeacon of St Andrews 1504–19. On the northern boundary of Argyle is sited castellated Kinburn House, built for the Buddos in 1854–56 on the land bought in 1852 by Dr David Buddo of the Indian Medical Service. St Andrews Town Council acquired the house – named after a Russian fort captured by a Franco-British naval force during the Crimean War – in 1920 from the descendants of Provost John Paterson of St Andrews. The clock on the south-east tower was set up in 1948 as a memorial to Miss McLaren. Around the house today is a public park, bowling green and tennis courts. Since the 1990s Kinburn House has been the location of the St Andrews Museum.

The most important townsman in medieval St Andrews was the burgher, usually a family man, with perhaps, a dependant relative or two living under the same roof. Next in social rank under the burgher were the stallagers, the market stall holders who enjoyed fewer burgh privileges and paid fewer dues on property and trade; under them came the journeymen, the labourers and servants each with their own families. At the bottom of the social heap were the poor, the disabled and the chronically sick, the lepers and the beggars, all of whom looked to the religious orders for their aid.

The Medieval Burgh

The centre of medieval St Andrews burgh was the tolbooth where taxes were collected. When the old tolbooth was demolished in 1862 on its site in Market Street near to the modern location of the Whyte-Melville Memorial Fountain, it was noted that there had been four buildings on the site, with the first dating from soon after the granting of the burgh status of around 1144. The tolbooth, which developed as a two-storey building with an outside stone stair that was removed circa 1818, contained a police cell, a debtor's prison and a 'thief's hole' for the detention of petty criminals. Facing the east were the hustings where parliamentary candidates addressed their electors, and on the tolbooth wall were the jougs (removed around 1830), an instrument of punishment in the form of a collar to be placed around the miscreant's neck. The tolbooth was not used as a state prison as was the castle, although such as David Calderwood (1575–1651), the Presbyterian cleric and historian, was imprisoned in the tolbooth in 1617 prior to his banishment. Subscriptions for the upkeep of the tolbooth came from such as the Seven Incorporated Trades, the Royal Arch Masons, the Thistle and Rose Free Gardeners Lodge, and the Royal & Ancient Golf Club, which allowed these bodies to use the civic chambers for meetings. The tolbooth bell was recast in 1697 by John Meikle of Edinburgh and bore the inscription: 'CURA-IA-SMITH-MAG-ALEX-NAIRN-GEO RAYNER-IO-CRAIG-1697–BALNORVM-CIVITATIS-STI-ANDRAE-IN-CVRRARVM-SVM:REFVSVS-IO-MEIKLE-ME-FECIT-EDINBVRGH' – '[Erected] under the administration of James Smith, Mr Alexander Nairn, George Rayner, and John Craig, Bailies of the City of St Andrews, to be rung in all the Courts, 1697. Recast and manufactured by John Meikle at Edinburgh.' A new town hall containing this bell in the corner turret was built at St Andrews in the Scottish baronial style during 1858–61 at the top of Queens Gardens (then Queens Street) on the site of the shop belonging to Melville Fletcher & Sons, booksellers; the foundation stone for the town hall was laid with full masonic honours by Past Grand Master for Fife and Kinross John Whyte-Melville (1821–78); the town hall was reconstructed in 1968.

The Mercat Cross and the Public Weigh Beam, known as the Tron, stood in front of the tolbooth in a line with the entries to Church Street and College Street into the square. The Mercat Cross had six circular pyramidal steps with a 12-foot obelisk used as a pillory. At the Mercat Cross Paul Craw, the physician-cum-Hussite social revolutionary was burned at the stake in 1433 with a brass ball stuffed in his mouth to stop him addressing the crowd; Sir Robert Spottiswoode, Lord President of the Council and a son of John Spottiswoode, Archbishop of St Andrews, and three other royalists were beheaded here in 1646; and Samuel Rutherford (d.1661) Professor of Divinity at St Andrews, whose book *Lex Rex* of 1644 argued for the right of the people to depose their king, had his volume publicly burned here in 1660. The Mercat Cross was removed in 1768, but later, royal proclamations were read from a temporary rostrum on the site.

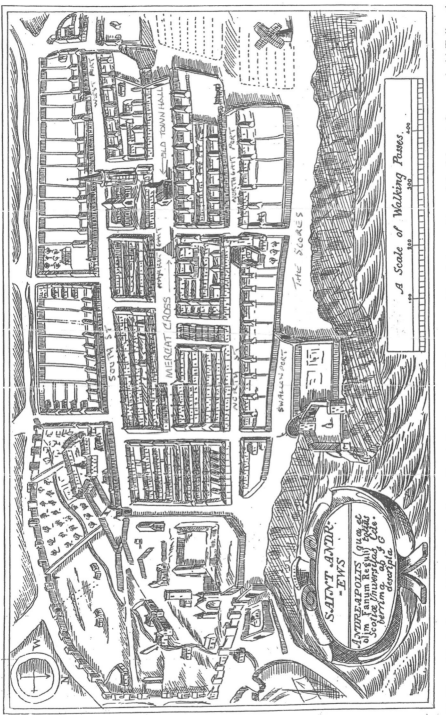

30. Plan of St Andrews, 1642, showing the medieval development of the street grid and the position of the Mercat Cross and old Tolbooth

At the Public Weigh Beam the weights and measures of the day were exhibited and used to assure fair play when commodities were being bought and sold. As with other parts of Scotland, St Andrews had a mixture of weights in the Middle Ages. *English pounds* (16 oz avoirdupois) were used for weighing flour, bread and pot-barley; *Dutch pounds* (17.5 oz avoirdupois) were used for animal meat and meal; while *Tron pounds* (22 oz avoirdupois) were used for wool, butter, flax, cheese, tallow, hides and hay. A *Scottish stone* always consisted of 16 lb and for many years the old Scots terms were widely used by the merchants, such as *boll* (8 stones), *firlot* (2 stones), *peck* (8 lb) and *lippie* (92 lb), for peas, beans and so on.

By the sixteenth century in St Andrews the two- to four-storey merchants' houses of stone predominated set on the site of two-storey stone and timber dwellings evolved by the twelfth century with their 'lang riggs', or long strip land holdings. The houses, set on the street front, ran back to the limits of the burgh. At the front of the house the *foreland* abutted the street and here the merchants carried on their trade; behind and reached by a *pend*, or passage, through the building were the courtyard of the house and the pleasure and kitchen gardens, the latter being known as the *kailyard*. A good place to see the line of the old 'lang riggs' is from the junction of Queens Terrace with Greenside Place. Number 49 South Street is a good example of a renovated Merchants House with its fine painted ceilings still intact; the property belonged to the Covenanter Robert Blair, one of those who signed the Solemn League and Covenant in 1638 and who preached at Charles II on his visit to the burgh; it is said that Charles actually visited the house.

As the burgh became more prosperous a higher density of population would be accommodated in the 'close developments' of the riggs and wynds which linked the old streets with crowded conditions in particular at Logie's Lane (once Coffin Row) and Baker Lane. At the 'back o'the toun', at the end of the lang-riggs, crofts would be built where farming went on at such sites as the Burgh Crofts (modern City Road and Pilmour Links) and Priory Acres. Nearly every one of St Andrews' medieval houses had its own well. Many of the street names in the old burgh date from mid-Victorian times, but even by then some streets had changed their names almost in each decade: East Burn Wynd or Prior's Wynd, for instance, became Abbey Street, and Foul Waste Union Street.[3]

In the sixteenth century the outer extremities of all the streets and wynds in St Andrews were closed by ports, or gates. There were also small gateways at Westburn Wynd, Abbey Wynd and Butts Wynd, with four main town gateways. On The Scores outside St Salvator's Hall are the remains of the buttress of the Swallowport of medieval Swallowgait, which was probably finally demolished in the storm of 1698. Northgait port stood just west of the New Picture House and was demolished in 1838; Northgait had stone balls set on the gateway pillars. Outside Northgait stood a large stone known as the 'Knocking Stone', where the handloom weavers of the 1840s 'knocked' their yarn.

Marketgait Port stood a few yards west of the junction of Greyfriars Garden and Bell Street and abutted the line of the garden of the Greyfriars monastery, and the Old Cow's Pool. The only remaining port of the burgh is the West Port. Called 'Argailles Port' in 1560 it was remodelled from an older gateway in 1589 and completely renovated in 1843 and 1950; its style was based on the now-vanished Netherbow Port at Edinburgh and it is one of the two remaining Scots town gateways.[4] In 1843 the gateway's two guard-houses were replaced by buttresses. The west panel on the gateway shows David I and was inserted in 1843 and is the work of local mason Balfour Simmers and cost £5 8s 6d (£5.42½p). At this gateway James VI was welcomed to the town on 11 July 1617 and was greeted by the public orator with a Latin address; the silver keys of the old burgh were delivered to Charles II in 1650, a ceremony not to be repeated until 1922 when the keys were offered to the then Prince of Wales (later Edward VIII), on the occasion when the freedom of the burgh was conferred on him. The original Southgait Port of twelfth century date probably was situated just east of Blackfriars.

The commercial life of medieval St Andrews was regulated by the trade guilds which set standards of quality of goods, terms of employments, mutual benefit privileges in time of

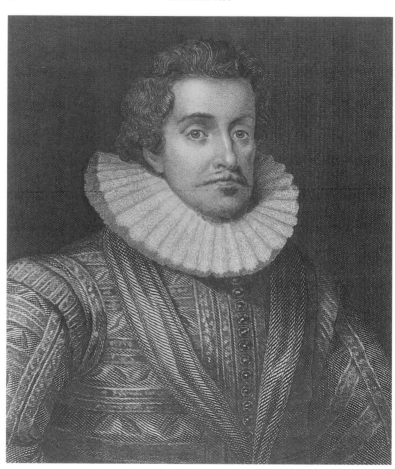

31. James VI, King of Scots and England (r.1567–1625), was welcomed into St Andrews in 1617 and conferred royal burgh status on the community in 1620.

sickness and so on. St Andrews had the famous Seven Trades of Baxters (Bakers), Fleshers (Butchers), Souters (Shoemakers), Smiths, Tailors, Weavers and Wrights and this was a sister organisation of the Guildry which was the medieval local government administration. The Seven Trades regulated the work of their members in the burgh and could effectively stop any 'outsiders' from setting up rival businesses. They also regulated the indenture of apprentices. For a fee of twenty pounds Scots (the Scots pound was a twelfth of a pound

32. HRH Edward, Prince of Wales (1894–1972), (King Edward VIII, 1936), was one of the few royals to receive the Freedom of the Burgh of St Andrews in 1922

sterling) each member of the Trades enjoyed the wide privileges of membership protection; the members wore gold medals to church on Sunday, sat in reserved pews in the burgh church and each had a livery for his trade which was worn on feast days and market days. The Trades owned land at Priory Acres, for instance, and existed as an entity until the first decades of Queen Victoria's reign.

The St Andrews Guild of Bakers had minutes of proceedings of their incorporation from their first meeting under Deacon James Brown on 3 June 1548 to 15 November 1861 when Deacon Thomas Smith presided over the conveyance of the old Abbey Mill.[5] They were the witnesses of all the main events in St Andrews and were part of the posse which assembled at the castle to investigate the murder of Cardinal Beaton in 1546; it was baker Andrew Honeyman who welcomed Charles II to St Andrews in 1650.[6]

The work of the Hammermen of St Andrews always attracted attention; this group included the town's armourers, saddlers, watchmakers, glovers, cutlers, pewterers and smiths. The hammermen were a well-established trade by 1394, the year that one of the guild brethren, William Plummer, was indentured by John Geddie, Abbot of Arbroath, to repair the abbey roof. The hammermen remained as an identifiable trade association until the late eighteenth century. The hammermen also included the gold and silversmiths. St Andrews hallmarked silver is very rare, yet examples are held at St Mary's College in the form of mazers (dish-like cups on a raised base) and the 'St Mary's College Capstan Salt' is marked PG (for maker Patrick Gairden) and the burgh hallmark of a Saltire within an oval.[7]

The Markets

The markets of St Andrews were the centre of economic life and on the town's market days the country folk would sell their produce and buy their own necessities. In time Mondays and Thursdays developed as St Andrews market days and the range of goods was wide to suit the medieval family, so on any one market day it would be possible to buy: barley, meat, spirits, flax, soap, candles,yarn, locks, hinges, starch, butter, bread, snuff, tobacco, ropes, nails, scythes and reaping-hooks, and arrange for funerals. Local coal was also sold. On 8 September 1785 a proposition was drawn up between Alexander Duncan of St Fort, Provost of St Andrews, William Landale, Dean of Guild *et al.*, to give permission to interested parties to mine coal at Pilmour Links and the North Haugh, but nothing came of the venture.

Outside the east gable of St Andrews tolbooth stood the Buttermarket where a weekly dairy products market was held up to the 1860s. The town had many dairy farms within its bounds at such places as Claybraes, Argyle Farm, Abbey Place, Westburn Lane, Kinnessburn Road and so on. The town's Linseed Market, 'once the greatest fair in the city, when every one had to sow their peck and spin their quantity', was active until 1870.[8] Lint and flax seed was grown locally and its byproducts were cattle food and oil, the flax itself being made into linen cloth.

Up to Victorian times Handsel Monday was still celebrated in St Andrews on the first Monday of the New Year, and formed a holiday for domestic servants and farm workers. Its name comes from the old Scots word for gift or tip and often took the form of a celebration meal subscribed for by employers. With its beginnings before the Reformation, when the priors gave gifts to the poor after Christmas, Handsel Monday's main attraction in St Andrews was a market selling candles and fruit.

Far more important than these markets were the five great annual fairs: Candlemas; the Easter Senzie Fair; Lammas; Martinmas; and St Andrews Day; by Victorian times only three of these fairs had survived.[9] St Andrews' only surviving fair is the Lammas Market and it is likely that this is the oldest surviving medieval market in Scotland. Lammas was the Lunasdal, the Celtic festival of autumn to honour the fruits of the soil. A delightful anachronism that clogs South Street and the middle of Market Street on the second Monday and Tuesday of August, Lammas Market was secured as a privilege for the burghers in 1620 by James VI & I and was confirmed by Act of Parliament under Charles I. Lammas, or loaf mass, Market was once a one-day hiring fair and an occasion of religious observance which brought a huge influx of people, and until 1800 or so it was the only place where people could buy ironmongery. By the 1870s it had been extended to include Tuesdays. The focal point of the fair was a beer tent at the corner of South Street and Queens Gardens where the hiring of farm workers took place for the ensuing year or half year. The

33. King Charles I (r.1625–49), secured the privileges for St Andrews to hold
a market at Lammas

Town Band played all day, with increasing visits to the beer
tent as the day progressed; the quality of their playing dete-
riorating in proportion to the beer imbibed. All the public
houses in St Andrews did a roaring trade and at the end of the
market the roads from the burgh became congested with a
rustic crowd bearing only too prominently evidence of the

riotous excess of pub and gin house. Today it is a colourful cacophony of multicultural street barkers and fairground features, electric generators taking over from the steam engines and horse power of Victorian times. Another bright occasion, St Andrews Horse Fair, was wound up after 1952.

The Knights

One very interesting group of medieval property owners in St Andrews were the Order of the Knights of the Hospital of St John of Jerusalem, a quasi-military religious order sworn to defend the pilgrim routes to the Holy Land and give succour to the Pilgrims, the sick and the poor. These knights first appeared in St Andrews around 1160, when a charter was witnessed by two of their number namely 'Richard of the Hospital of Jerusalem' and 'Richard, brother of the Temple'. Rather confusingly there were two groups of such knights, the Knights Templars and the Knights Hospitallers. The Templars had two headquarters in Scotland at Balantrodoch, Midlothian, and at Maryculter, Kincardine, while the Hospitallers had only one house, their

34. A Knight of the order of the Templars, a religious military order established during the Crusades. Property belonging to them was extant in St Andrews from around 1160. [Sankey, Hudson & Co.]

35. A Knight Hospitaller; when the Templars were disbanded/suppressed at the end of the thirteenth century their St Andrews properties fell to the Hospitallers.

Preceptory, at Torphichen in West Lothian. After the Templars were disbanded, or suppressed at the end of the thirteenth century their properties were absorbed by the Hospitallers.

These two groups of knights had tenements off and in North Street, one of which stretched back to Swallowgait, with the properties of nos 47, 49, 68–72 North Street and 45–53 Market Street. Numbers 67–71 South Street, abutting Baker Lane, belonged first to the Templars and then to the Knights of St John. Numbers 67–69 are now known as St John's and were bought by the university in 1970 for use as a graduate centre for advanced historical studies; the building is perhaps the oldest standing domestic building in St Andrews, its earliest phase dating from the fifteenth century on the site of medieval timber buildings. The knights were never resident in St Andrews; their premises were a source of revenue and their tenants paid their dues to the knights and then to secular landlords after the Reformation and these landlords received monies up to around 1820 when the town took over the superiority of the properties. By the sixteenth century the properties of St John's and no. 71 South Street (now the Department of Medieval History) were owned by Patrick Adamson, Archbishop of St Andrews (1575–92). By this time the castle was too dilapidated to be an archbishop's residence. Today the frontage of St John's displays the arrangement of former windows and doors.

Thus developed the burgh that Bishop Robert had inspired to take its important place in Scotland's history. Nevertheless the burgh offered a darker side.

CHAPTER 6

Plague, Witchcraft and the Headsman's Axe

> In 1563 the Scottish Parliament, by statute, for which
> John Knox was a chief agitator, formally constituted
> witchcraft and dealing with witches a capital offence.
>
> William Andrews, *Bygone Church Life in Scotland*, 1899

Plague

Fear of the plague drove out all normal human reason and sensibilities. The stricken were left to die like animals and those who survived could hardly cope with the piles of the dead disposed of in mass graves. Plague devastated St Andrews burgh from time to time, but the term is confusing as in medieval times it included everything from bacillary dysentery to the dreaded bubonic plague which spread from Asia to Europe during the fourteenth century. It arrived first in Sicily in 1347, and spread rapidly through Italy to the rest of Europe where its devastating effects earned it the name of the Black Death. The Black Death reached England in the summer of 1348 at Melcombe Regis (now a part of Weymouth, Devon), Southampton and London. By late May 1349 it had reached York and Durham by July. Plague crept up the pilgrim route to St Andrews and ecclesiastical records show that twenty-four canons of St Andrews Augustinian priory died of plague in 1350 and that in 1362 Bishop William de Landells (d.1385) and his senior clergy fled the burgh, the bishop going to Moray to escape the scourge. The exodus of cathedral officials undoubtedly sowed the seeds which led to the decline of the church's popularity in the burgh – together with the low standards of many of the newly appointed priests – and the fact that belief in God had signally failed to arrest the progress of the Black Death.

After the Black Deaths, plague was endemic in Britain for three hundred years. In 1529, 1568 and 1585 St Andrews was again wracked with plague, the severity of the 1585 epidemic causing the dispersal of students and contributing, because of its duration, to the increase in poverty in the burgh. In 1529 Edinburgh citizens were forbidden to travel to St Andrews lest the plague spread to the capital. There were four hundred deaths reported in St Andrews in 1585, and the state of sickness was much aggravated by the wet harvest that year. Plague came to the burgh again in 1605, 1647, 1665 and 1667; in 1647 the Principal of St Leonard's College died of the rat or flea-borne bacillus *Yersinia pestis*. The burgh's plague pits were almost certainly located just west of St James's Church on The Scores. Bones were discovered here in 1906, 1909 and in 1987 when rebuilding took place on the site.[1]

Witchcraft

Before the Reformation, witchcraft appears to have been noticed little in Scotland as the medieval Church had no Inquisition in the country. If any such cases appear on record culminating in execution of sorcerers the indictment was not for witchcraft *per se*, but for murder or attempted murder. Again up to the end of the fifteenth-century death sentences supposed to have been passed for witchcraft were really on an indictment of heresy for acts said to have been promulgated by magic. A few cases of supposed witchcraft mentioned in the old chronicles can be easily dismissed as a charge of witchcraft being used as a political tool, as in the case of the execution by burning of Jane, Lady Douglas, sister of the Earl of Angus, widow of John, Lord Glamis in 1537; she fell foul of the rapaciousness of James V.

When the Protestant Reformation came, however, the Scriptures were scoured for passages that backed up the politics of the new regime. The quote in Exodus, xxii, 18, 'Thou shalt not suffer a witch to live' gave the Presbyterian politicians the impetus to support the *Acta Parliamentorum Mariae* of 1563 which made witchcraft an illegal act and win for themselves an important legal lever against their enemies and helped confirm the ordinary folk in their credulity. Viewed today the use of witchcraft in propaganda as seen amongst the clerics of St Andrews and elsewhere is quite ludicrous. An example from the Presbyterian viewpoint 'declared that the [medieval and Episcopal] bishops were cloven-footed and had no shadows, and that the curates themselves were, many of them, little better than wizards'.[2] While those who supported the medieval Church proclaimed 'John Knox was deemed a skilful wizard . . . it was even said that in the churchyard of St Andrews he raised Satan himself, wearing a huge pair of horns on his head, at which blood-curdling sight Knox's secretary became insane and died'.[3]

36. Medieval St Andrews townsfolk were a mixture of shopkeepers, artisans and prosperous merchants [Sankey, Hudson & Co.]

Scotland had three great periods of witchcraft persecution, 1590–97, 1640–44 and 1660–63 and St Andrews burgh was the scene of some of the witch trials. There were few actual executions for witchcraft in St Andrews out of the 4000 or so capital indictments in Scotland during 1590–1680.[4] Here are several of the best-attested cases from the burgh.

In 1569 the sorceress Nic Neville was condemned and burned; but it shows how confused the texts can be for some sources call the accused Nick Niven and make the witch male.[5] In this year too the Regent James, Earl of Moray 'causit burne certane witches in Sanctandrois', and William Stewart, Lyon

King of Arms, was hanged for 'necromancie'. During 1572 a witch was personally condemned by John Knox and burned in the burghs, but the supposed witch Marjorie Smith was charged and accused by the Presbyterian Church Session of witchcraft but it is not known for sure whether or not she was consigned to the flames. Bessie Robertson was charged with witchcraft in 1581 as was Agnes Melville in 1588, but Melville survived until 1595 when she was executed along with Elspeth Gilchrist and Janet Locheguoir.

On 30 September 1613 a presentation was made to Archbishop George Gledstanes accusing Agnes Anstruther of witchcraft; nothing more is heard about witch accusation in St Andrews until 1630 which saw the trial of Margaret Callender. In 1644 one Bessie Mason 'a confessing witche' was interviewed by the Synod as was 'the woman called Sewis' in 1645. The last recorded case of witchcraft in St Andrews seems to be the accusation of Isobel Key in 1667 who was imprisoned in the tolbooth.[6] St Andrews historian Andrew Lang (1844–1912), first Gifford lecturer at the University (1888), noted:

> Some of the witches who suffered at Presbyterian hands were merely narrators of popular tales about the state of the dead. That she trafficked with the dead, and from a ghost won a medical recipe for the cure of Archbishop [Patrick] Adamson of St Andrews, was the charge against Alison Pearson . . . 'She was execut in Edinbruche for a witch'.[7]

Again the local historian David Hay Fleming talked of the 'last witch burned in St Andrews as being one Young in Market Street' around 1700. At the Step Rock (so named after 1835) the visitor can still look east along the cliffs towards St James's Church to the site of the Witch Lake where tradition has it witches were 'tested' (by water ordeal) until the late seventeenth century.

The Headsman's Axe

The Headsman's Axe, displayed at St Andrews Town Hall in Queens Gardens, reminds how the burgh saw a variety of executions; in 1622 a burgh execution cost £17 12s 0d (£17.60p). Yet one execution in particular perhaps links St Andrews' most famous sojourner to the darker side of the burgh's history.

Mary, Queen of Scots, whose intimacy with the headsman's axe in 1587 is internationally famous, visited St Andrews five times during 1561–65, her last visit being in the company of her husband, Henry Stuart, Lord Darnley, a short while before his murder at Kirk o'Field, Edinburgh. Wherever she went, the crowds acted with enthusiasm. Apart from anything else Mary made a striking figure in her rich, black dresses with their lace trimmings and billowing skirts. She was a fashion icon of her day and her collection of jewellery was breathtaking. Mary was every inch a queen, and she had inherited all of the legendary Stuart charm. The St Andrews crowds who gathered to see her witnessed her as a beautiful and enchanting woman first, and as a Roman Catholic queen second. One must remember that among the crowds gathered in St Andrews during her first visit on Tuesday, 10 March 1561, were agents provocateurs, John

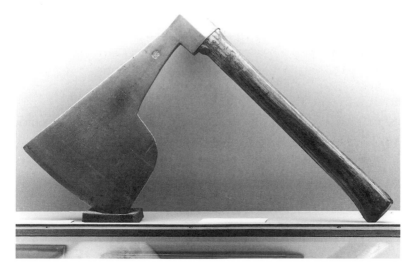

37. St Andrews headsman's axe used to execute commoner and aristocrat alike

38. Mary, Queen of Scots, (r.1542–67), executed 1587. Mary visited St Andrews on a number of occasions from 1561. Tradition has it she played golf and shot arrows at the butts in the town.

Knox's creatures, who watched Mary's every move and incited the crowds against her. That day, said the well-respected local historian David Hay Fleming, a priest was assassinated in St Andrews, as a chastening example of the new Protestant regime.[8]

39. Queen Mary's House, South Street, a fine example of a sixteenth-century Scottish town house

Mary's motives in coming to St Andrews were several. She was interested in a closer look at some of the ancient royal burghs in her kingdom, and she was keen to visit her half-brother the Lord James Stewart, Commendator of St Andrews priory. James Stewart, Earl of Moray, was the illegitimate son of Mary's father James V and Margaret Erskine. For the most part we have to rely on oral tradition as to where she stayed in St Andrews. During her visit in 1561 she is likely to have lodged with her half-brother who had apartments in the *Hospitium Novum*, or she may have stayed at the Prior's House. There are no written records to tell us if she stayed at the castle, and her subsequent main residence was the building we now know as Queen Mary's House, no. 4 South Street.

Queen Mary's House is a particularly fine example of a sixteenth-century Scottish town house. Although it has been greatly altered and extended by later owners much remains of the original structure, and the cellars have changed the least. The house was built by Alan Meldrum, Vicar of Leuchars and a Canon of the priory, in 1525, on land that was the property of the priory; this land had been inhabited from the twelfth

century as a part of Kilrymont' s policies and by the fourteenth
century it was a cultivated field, with a heather thatched timber
house of the early fifteenth century. In Meldrum's day there
was probably a wooden gallery projecting into South Street.
The west wing was built around 1575 by David Orme, Chamberlain to the Lord James. An East Wing (Priorsgate) dates
from around 1580 and was reconstructed around 1792.

During her visit of March to May 1562, Mary welcomed into
her presence the English ambassador to the Scottish Court, Sir
Thomas Randolph, and it is from his reports that we can build
up a picture of Mary's activities in St Andrews. We know for
certain that she took part in archery competitions at Smal-
month, the name of a nearby sward, and that she may have shot
at the butts too at 71 South Street. She also spent time riding
and she did some gardening. Her intellectual pursuits included
studying Livy under the tutorship of the Principal of St
Leonard's College, the Calvinst republican George Buchanan.
Sir Thomas Randolph, a former pupil of Buchanan at Paris,
was with the queen again in 1565, when he was waiting for
Mary's answer to the proposal that she marry the English
statesman Robert Dudley, Earl of Leicester, at the suggestion of
Elizabeth I. Sir Thomas wrote thus to his mistress Elizabeth I:

> Her grace lodged in a 'merchant's house', her train very few
> and small repair from any part. Her will was that I should
> dine and sup with her . . . Having thus spent Sunday,
> Monday and Tuesday I thought it time to utter to her grace
> your majesty's command [i.e., concerning the proposed,
> marriage candidate Leicester] . . . I had no sooner spoken
> these words but she said: 'I see now well that you are weary of
> this company and treatment: I sent for you to be merry and
> to see how like a bourgeois wife I live with my little troop' . . .
> very merrily she passed her time.[9]

Although the diocese still had an archbishop in John Hamilton,
he had no ecclesiastical authority in the realm and Mary had to
worship with discretion while in St Andrews. Mass had been
discontinued in all the town churches following the Act of 1560,

so she set up an Oratory at the South Street house to hear mass in private; her half-brother the Lord James had defied the new protestants in their bid to stop Mary worshipping according to the Roman rule.

Charles II lodged at Queen Mary's House when he visited the burgh during 4–6 July 1650, says local tradition, and at that

40. George Buchanan (1506–82), historian and scholar, Principal of St Leonard's College 1566–70. Mary, Queen of Scots, studied classics with him at St Andrews.

time the house seems to have belonged to Hugh Scrimgeour, servitor to John Spottiswoode, Archbishop of St Andrews. The house passed from church administrators to secular gentry families like James Lumisdaine of Rennyhill, who owned the property from the 1750s to 1785. The house and gardens were sold, in 1926, by the widow of the last private owner Captain Nunneley, to St Leonards School and rooms were laid out for a school library opened in October 1927 by the then Duchess of York (later HM Queen Elizabeth the Queen Mother), who returned in 1977 to open the junior library.[10]

It is thought that while in St Andrews Mary signed the death warrant that gave rise to a dramatic public execution in the burgh. The French poet and swaggering galliard Pierre de Bocosel, Seigneur de Chastelard came to Scotland from France in Mary's entourage in 1561. He was sent, it appears to Scotland by his employer Seigneur Montmorency d'Amville, for what purpose is not known. In time Chastelard acquired a deep infatuation for Mary and secreted himself on her bedchamber at Holyrood. He was discovered, and Mary hysterically demanded that her half-brother run the young man through; Lord James cautiously soothed the queen and Chastelard was admonished and told to leave court. Chastelard followed Mary on a trip to Fife in 1563 and when the queen paused at Rossend Castle, Burntisland, for the night, Chastelard again secreted himself in the queen's chamber. He said he had come to apologise when he was discovered once more.

This was serious *lèse majesté* and Chastelard was brought to trial and locked up in St Andrews Castle. He was condemned to death on 22 February 1563 and was taken to the scaffold, then sited in Market Street. He declined the consolation of the new Church of Scotland, and instead recited, says the chronicler Pierre de Bourdelle, Seigneur de Brântome, another of Mary's French entourage, some lines from the poet Pierre de Ronsard's 'Hymn to Death':

> *Je te salue, heureuse et profitable mort . . . puisqu'il faut mourir*
> *Donne-moi que soudain je te puisse encourir*
> *Ou pour l'honneur de Dieu, ou pour servir mon prince.*

[I salute you, happy and profitable Death . . . since I must die
Grant that I may suddenly encounter you
Either for the honour of God, or in the service of my prince.][11]

As the hangman put the noose around his neck Chastelard is
said to have shouted to the crowd: *Adieu, la princesse la plus belle
et la plus cruelle du monde*. [Adieu the most beautiful and most
cruel princess in the world]. It was a pretty harsh sentence for a
flirtatious adventure of a lovesick fool, but there are those who
believed that Chastelard may have been up to much more. Sir
Thomas Randolph reported to his royal mistress the whispers
that Chastelard was a part of a plot to assassinate Mary . . . but
the truth is never likely to be known.

St Andrews then witnessed the execution of both high and
low, but as the burgh waxed and waned visitors came from all
parts to savour its unique atmosphere.

CHAPTER 7

Visitors and Their Views

In June 1587 James [VI] came to St Andrews . . . The
King brought with him [Guillame de Salluste] du Bartes,
a French poet, then famous.

A.J.G. Mackay, *A History of Fife and Kinross*, 1896

Early Visitors

Royal visitors always created a stir in St Andrews, but many
commoners left interesting appraisals of what they saw. Among
the early visitors who left a written memory was Jaspar Laet de
Borchloen, who made this comment to Archbishop William
Schevez of St Andrews (archepiscopate 1478–97). He saw St
Andrews scholars as a 'crowd of learned men' who brought the
light of learning to a scholastic dark land and deemed the burgh
a 'cradle of learning'.[1]

In the sixteenth century the historian and scholastic divine
John Major (or, Mair, 1496–1550), who taught logic at St
Andrews (1522), defined for the world the 'threefold dignities'
of St Andrews – the relics of the Apostle, the primatial see and
the university – which 'brought . . . contact with the civilisa-
tion of Europe' to develop a place 'seemed destined for a fishing
village or haven for small craft'.[2]

Within his *Poemata Omnia* (1642), Arthur Johnston (1587–
1641), physician to Charles I and friend of Andrew Melville
(1545–1622), Principal of St Mary's College, showed how in
the seventeenth century two elements that would make the
burgh internationally famous – golf and the university. However, like all scholars of the time he addressed his continental
audience in Latin:

Nec fuit in toto sanctior orbe locus . . .

[In all the world was no holier place . . .]

Vestibus aequabant templorum marmora mystae . . .
[The attendant priests matched the temple's [i.e. the Shrine
  at Ephesus] marbles with their vestments . . .]

*Sacra tamen Musis urbs es, Phoebique ministris, nec major meritis
  est honor ille tuis . . .*
[Still you are a town sacred to the Muses and to Phoebus's
  votaries, and that is an honour no greater than you
  deserve . . .]

*Proximus est campus, studiis hic fessa juventus Se recreat, vires sumit
  et inde novas.*
[The links are close by; it is here Youth wearied with studies
  finds recreation, and gathers a new stock of strength.][3]

The heyday of St Andrews was undoubtedly the time when it
was a prosperous medieval burgh, the ecclesiastical capital of
Scotland. At the Reformation the whole focus of power, political and commercial, moved from St Andrews to Edinburgh
and Glasgow, and St Andrews never again achieved its former
prosperity.

From the jottings of visitors we begin to see something of the
declining city. In 1732 the philologist and antiquary John
Loveday (1742–1809), wrote this: 'The City of St Andrews
is only a shadow of what it has been. The streets show grass as
well as pavement.'[4] Again the traveller and naturalist Thomas
Pennant (1726–98) noted in 1772: 'St Andrews' numerous
towers and spires give it an air of vast magnificence . . . but
so grass-grown, and such a dreary solitude lay before us, that it
formed the perfect idea of having been laid waste by pesti-
lence'.[5] None of this, said Richard Pococke (1704–65), Bishop
of Ossery, then Meath, who was 'hospitably entertained by the
professors', kept students off their studies.[6]

Daniel Defoe and Samuel Johnson

Two visitors to St Andrews in the eighteenth century stand out.
Born in 1660, Londoner Daniel Defoe was destined for the

Presbyterian ministry and became a hosiery merchant instead. Service as a soldier in James, Duke of Monmouth's rebellion (1685) gave way to his establishment as a merchant and a seasoned traveller in England and the Continent. During 1697–1701, he served as secret agent to William III in England and Scotland. Across 1724–26 he produced a guide-book in three volumes entitled *A Tour Through the Whole Island of Great Britain* and recounted therein his visit to St Andrews:

> The city is not large, nor is it contemptibly small; there are some very good buildings in it, and the remains of many more. The colleges are handsome buildings, and well supplied with men of learning in all sciences, and who govern the youth they instruct with reputation; the students wear gowns of a scarlet-like colour, but not in grain, and are very numerous. The university is very ancient as well as the city; the foundation was settled, and the public buildings appointed at the beginning of the fifteenth century by King James I.[7]

Defoe goes on to describe the university colleges, the St Andrew legend, royal visits, Wishart's murder and that of Archbishop Sharp, noting its 'fine situation' amongst corn fields and saying that 'the famous physician Cardan esteemed it the healthiest town he ever lived in'.[8] Defoe considered St Andrews' delapidated harbour to be beyond redemption. He concluded with: 'The city of St Andrews is, notwithstanding its many disasters; such as the ruin of the great church, the demolition of its castle, and the archbishop's palace, and Oliver Cromwell's citadel; yet, I say, it is still a handsome city, and well built, the streets straight and large, being three streets parallel to one another, all opening to the sea.'[9]

Defoe's mention of 'Oliver Cromwell's citadel' is uncertain as to location but on 30 August 1651 St Andrew's surrendered to the Cromwellian army led by General George Monck, and was fined £500 sterling for putting up initial defiance. Thus St Andrews, as a prominent burgh became part of a conquered province of England and remained under military occupation until 1660.

41. Oliver Cromwell (1599–1658). St Andrews surrendered to the Cromwellian army of General George Monck on 30 August 1651.

The second cited visitor was Samuel Johnson (1709–84), the English writer, critic and lexicographer, who, accompanied by James Boswell (1740–95), the Scottish man-of-letters and Johnson's biographer, called at the town while on their tour of Scotland to the Hebrides. They arrived after 'a dreary drive in a dusky night' on Wednesday, 18 August 1773, and put up at 5 South Street, then known as 'Glass's Inn' (and so it remained

until around 1830).[10] After a good supper they visited St
Leonard's College, preceded by their landlord, Andrew Glass,
carrying a candle and a waiter a lantern. Johnson formed his
first impressions:

> St Andrews seems to be a place eminently adapted to study
> and education, being situated in a populous, yet cheap
> country, and exposing the minds and manners of young
> men neither to the levity and dissoluteness of a capital city,
> nor to the gross luxury of a town of commerce, places
> naturally unpropitious to learning; in one the desire of
> knowledge easily gives way to the love of pleasure, and in
> the other, is in danger of yielding to the love of money.[11]

Next day the curious couple were introduced to Robert Watson, Professor of Logic who had the previous year bought St
Leonard's and gardens; the introduction had come from their
erstwhile travelling companion from Leith, the advocate William Nairne (later Lord Dunsinane) who breakfasted in their
company. They visited the cathedral, St Rule's tower and the
castle and had dinner with a college of professors led by James
Murison, Rector of the university. Ever on the lookout to find
curiosities to intrigue his learned companion, Boswell drew
attention to 'two signposts'. One displayed the lettering 'James
Hood, White-Iron Smith' (tin-plate worker), while on the
other the same man was described as conducting 'The Art
of Fencing'. 'Upon this last', noted Boswell, 'were painted some
trees and two men fencing, one of whom had hit the other in the
eye.' Johnson declared, 'The Scotch are good fencers' and that
he would have signed up for lessons had he been a student.[12]
They next saw Holy Trinity Church and looked at St Salvator's
College and after tea they supped at Professor Watson's and
met the great-granddaughter of the murdered Archbishop
Sharp. Boswell complained of a lack of guide books of St
Andrews for the visitor 'such as we find in all the towns of
Italy and in some of the towns in England'.[13]

    On 20 August they breakfasted with Andrew Shaw, Professor
of Divinity, and visited the garden and grotto owned by the

Hon. Lt. Col. John Nairne, then tenant of Queen Mary's House. The grotto was made out of the ruined portico on the north side of St Leonard's chapel, and herein were displays of skulls, a 'wonderful large lobster claw', and relics of the cathedral tracery and vaulting. In the garden they viewed 'a fine old plane tree' concerning which Col. Nairne averred that there was only one more 'large tree in the country'. This allowed Johnson to score a sarcastic point: 'A tree might be a show in Scotland as a horse is in Venice'. The travelling pair left St Andrews at noon of the same day.

In 1806 Robert Forsyth wrote this:

> Travellers have often said that, on entering [St Andrews], they are in some degree impressed with similar feelings to those produced on entering the city of Rome . . . here, as in Rome, are to be seen the striking remains of ancient ecclesiastical magnificence; the magnitude and apparent grandeur of the buildings are evidently disproportioned to any business or active employment here carried on; and the town has the appearance of being too great for its present inhabitants, and of falling into ruin from the want of present wealth or energy.[14]

Sir Walter Scott

Sir Walter Scott (1771–1832) made three known visits to St Andrews in 1793, 1823 and 1827. During the 1793 visit he recorded in his *Diary* that he had gone up St Rule's tower and had carved the name of his then love, Williamina Belsches, on the turf beside the castle gate. The entry reads: The ruins [of the cathedral] have been lately cleared out. They had been chiefly magnificent for their size, not their richness in ornament'. This was an underestimation.

Scott's *Journal* for Saturday, 16 June 1827 records his third known visit to St Andrews with the Blair Adam Club; Scott and his friends had been staying at Charleton House, the home of the Anstruthers. Scott's biographer and son-in-law John Gibson Lockhart quoted Scott's own comment on the event:

I did not go up St Rule's tower, as on former occasions; this is a falling off, for when before did I remain sitting below when there was a steeple to be ascended? But rheumatism has begun to change that vein for some time past, though I think this is the first decided sign of acquiescence in my lot. I sate down on a gravestone, and recollected the first visit I made to St Andrews, now thirty-four years ago. What changes in my feelings and fortunes have since then taken place! – some for

42. Sir Walter Scott (1771–1832), visited St Andrews in 1793, 1823 and 1827. He was deemed 'ineligible' for the post of Rector of the University.

the better, many for the worse. I remembered the name I then carved in runic characters on the turf beside the castle-gate, and I asked why it should still agitate my heart. But my friends came down from the tower, and the foolish idea was chased away.[15]

The 'former occasions' mentioned included a visit by the Blair Adam Club on 13–16 June 1823; Scott was a member of that party which visited the East Neuk of Fife.[16] 'We visited St Andrews on this occasion' records the *Blair-Adam Estate* record books.

Over the years, Scott met several academics from St Andrews at various locations, houses and receptions. Writing from Abbotsford in 1826, he mentions one encounter which was to supply an acquaintance who was to be a character in an embarrassing future incident. The meeting was with Francis Nicoll (1770–1835), a noted Scottish divine who had had the parish of St Leonard's confirmed to him by the Prince Regent in 1819, the year he became Principal of the United Colleges of St Leonard's and St Salvator's; he became Rector in 1822.

In 1825 the Intrants of the Nations of the University of St Andrews 'made choice of Sir Walter Scott' as Rector; their choice was thwarted by the *Praeses* (President of Constituents, i.e., Principal Francis Nicoll), who declared that Scott was not eligible because he was 'unconnected' with the university (i.e., he was not one of their number).[17] Intrants wrote to Scott concerning the incident, and Scott replied graciously; he im-plies in his answer that he would not have accepted anyway. Nicoll also wrote to Scott to make his position clear (i.e., it was not his personal wish to debar Scott, only the university laws were against Scott's candidacy).[18]

In his novel *The Pirate* (1830) Scott makes use of his knowl-edge of a St Andrews location by having young Triptolemus Yellowly a student at St Andrews with the 'rector of St Leonard's' as his cicerone. In his introducton to the Border edition of *Guy Mannering* (1815), Andrew Lang refers to Scott making Dominie Abel Sampson an alumnus of St Andrews: 'I was boarded for twenty pence a week at Luckie Sour-kail's, in the High Street of St Andrews.' There is of course, no High Street in St Andrews and Lang avers that Scott was probably referring to South Street. Abel Sampson, herein, was further credited with 'a bursary in St Leonard's College'. By 1747 St Leonard's and St Salvator's had been amalgamated as United College. 'All this', adds Lang, 'is in direct contradition to the evidence in the novel, which makes the Dominie a Glasgow man'.

One further St Andrews association with Scott concerns Scott's friend Adam Ferguson (1723–1816), the philosopher and erstwhile Professor of Moral Philosophy at Edinburgh, retired to an estate at St Andrews. On his death he was buried at the cathedral cemetery and Scott wrote his epitaph.

As decade succeeded decade many other famous visitors came to St Andrews and left their written memories, or were inspired by its academic ambience and neighbouring landscape. One such was the advocate Sir John Skelton (1831–97), who wrote biographies of Mary Queen of Scots and Benjamin Disraeli. Skelton encouraged visitors to explore the 'ocean bay girt by green hills' at St Andrews and meet its neighbours after enjoying the 'outworks of a Scottish breakfast'.[19]

CHAPTER 8

Couthy Neighbours: The Surrounding Area

I wander on the Lade Braes, where I used to walk with you,
And purple are the woods of Mount Melville, budding new.

Robert F. Murray, *Poems* (1894)

Once the Kinkell Braes and Scoonie Hill, the ruined mills and
tranquil ponds of the Lade Braes brought the country to the
doorstep of medieval St Andrews. Now St Andrews' neighbours
seem less apart as developers grab huge tracts of hinterland.
Five neighbouring villages though developed their own indivi-
duality at Strathkinness, Kincaple, Denhead, Guardbridge and
Boarhills. Set three miles west of St Andrews, Strathkinness
comes into recorded history in 1144 when the burgh's founder
Bishop Robert gave the 'lands of Strathkinness' to the Augustinian Priory of St Andrews.[1] A civil settlement was established
by 1160 nearer to the modern B9939 than today.[2] This area was
used as agricultural land by the priory with adjacent grange,
and remained in ecclesiastical hands until the Reformation.
Around 1560 James Stewart, Earl of Moray, disposed a large
part of Strathkinness to one Michael Balfour.[3] Thereafter
various families were given title to the lands which developed
first as a long defunct hand-loom weaving hamlet then as an
agricultural community. The Younger family, who bought the
policies in 1900, built Mount Melville mansion house in 1903
and sold the grounds to Fife County Council in 1947; the
building is now a time-share complex (the estate forms a golfing
facility. The Duke's Course is owned by the Old Course Hotel).[4]
In recent decades Strathkinness has become a residential area
for those working in St Andrews, Dundee and elsewhere. As St
Andrews housing developments expand it is not beyond the
realms of logic that by the end of the twenty-first century the
village will conjoin with the ancient burgh.

Kincaple, just to the west of St Andrews, retains its status as a hamlet, now residential but with its eighteenth-century core of harled laird's house of 1789 and cottages, was once the home of workers in the local malt barns, brickworks and Guardbridge paper mill.[5] Denhead estate lies south of Strathkinness and passed through various ownerships. Once part of the barony of Claremont the estate owners included Sir William Murray, baronet of Nova Scotia, a prominent courtier of Charles I; here too, lived George Martine, secretary the the murdered Archbishop Sharp and local historian. The scattered houses are surrounded by old lime workings.[6]

Guardbridge is still dominated by its industrial ambience; a paper mill was established in 1872 on the site of the William Haig Seggie Distillery of 1810 where the Motray Water meets the River Eden. Here the early village began. In the thirteenth century the local landowner Seyer de Quincy, Earl of Winchester, moored his vessels here and in 1381 Robert II granted to the burgesses of Cupar 'a free port in the water of Motray'. The village developed as a homebase for the papermill workers from the 1880s to the 1930s. The six-arched bridge over the Eden was built by Henry Wardlaw, Bishop of St Andrews (1404–40) and in this area gathered the pilgrims of medieval times to be taken into St Andrews under armed guard through the wild lands of Kincaple.

Of all the neighbouring villages of St Andrews, in medieval times, Boarhills stands out as the most prominent.[7] This whole area was within the *Cursus Apri Regalis*, 'the run of the wild boar'; here prelate and noble hunted the local fauna. The modern village developed during 1815–67 from a medieval huddle of dwellings via a vernacular hamlet. Around the neighbourhood of Kenlygreen House (c.1790) are hillocks which may hide the remains of the vanished castle of Draffan, famous in local lore as a fortress of the Norsemen. Here too was located the episcopal country residence of the medieval bishops of St Andrews, who probably used it as a palace-cum-hunting lodge. Known as Inchmurdo (or, Inchmurtach), here died Bishop William Malvoisine in 1238 and Bishop Gamelin in 1271.[8] Some historians say that the present Kenly Green seventeenth-century doocot (restored 1987) was constructed from Inchmurdo stone after 1560.[9]

43. View of Guardbridge from the air of the 1940s, showing the paper mill and the site of the early medieval quays of St Andrews by the junction of the Eden and Motray waters [Mrs Hilda Kirkwood]

The arc of land set around the boundaries of St Andrews developed in its own way and from the twelfth century the territories were confirmed on the priory by papal bull. Local lore tells of a fortalice at Kinkell pre-1591; the Grange was a priory farmstead and Priest Den Parks recalls the ecclesiastical landlords. The Kinness Burn was spanned at the Shore Bridge of c.1789, set by Robert Balfour's House, and was forded at Greenside Place (a new bridge was built here in 1931) as was the Swilken Burn. The ford across the Kinness Burn at Bridge Street gave way in time to 'Maggie Murray's Bridge' at the foot of Melbourne Brae. Maggie Murray was the daughter of William Murray landowner at the Bassaguard (Bess Acre) from 1767 and of the land at Wal Wynde (Well Wynd Melbourne Place and Bridge Street), and had married Andrew Wallace, shipmaster. Maggie built the bridge at her own expense and in time the Murray properties hereabouts were purchased by William Gibson of Dunloch who built the Gibson Hospital and City Park.

By the twelfth century St Andrews had three noted mills. The mill at Kilrymont is likely to have developed as the later Abbey Mill (the Sanatorium of St Leonards School of 1899 is on the

44. Lumbo Farm. Once the lands around St Andrews were owned by the Augustinian Priory.

45. Melbourne Place was the medieval land of Wal Wynde, leading to the old ford over the Kinness Burn, replaced by the eighteenth-century Maggie Murray's Bridge.

site of the Abbey Mill and Brewhouse) which seems to have been disused as such by 1861; Putekin (Peekie) Mill was granted to the priory in 1144; and Nidie Mill on the Eden ceased to work in the late nineteenth century. Around 1240 Cairnsmill was given to the priory and Denbrae Mill was built by Prior Hepburn in the 1480s. Probably all of these mills were quite small and were driven by a paddle wheel. They were places of social intercourse for the townsfolk. The most famous of all St Andrews' mills was Lawmill which belonged to the priory, and was probably founded in the thirteenth century although we only have a sure record of it by the sixteenth century. By 1660 the mill was owned by the burgh, and by this time too it had the unusual feature of double grinding stones; after 1848 it was back in private hands. Four other mills were known within the burgh: New Mill – the Plash Mill – may be dated at least to 1550 when it was feud by the priory; it was bought by the town in 1696 and changed hands once or twice until 1866 when it was sold to the proprietors of New Park; it ceased to function as a mill after that. Craig Mill was built by Prior Hepburn after 1483 and seems to have been in ruins by

1606. Shore Mill was built in 1518 by the prior and in 1558 fell into secular hands, then burgh ownership; in the late 1890s it was sold to the gas company. The Windmill is mentioned by 1598 by the Cow Wynd (cf. modern Windmill Road), and it was probably erected as a tower mill in the 1580s on the site of an earlier mill, and might have been one of those 'ready made' mills that were imported from Ghent at this time.

To the west of the town lie the lands of Strathtyrum and here stood, before 1400, the Strathtyrum Cross. Once the Culdees drew tithes from this land conferred by Bishop Roger de Beaumont in the twelfth century. After the Reformation, Strathtyrum estate was resumed by the Crown and conferred on the family of the Duke of Lennox. By 1596 the estate passed to James Wood of Lambieletham and was later assumed by the Inglises who sold it to Archbishop James Sharp in 1669; Sharp's dwelling has long vanished. Soon after this the estate was subdivided and in 1782 Strathtyrum was acquired by James Cheape. Strathtyrum house dates from 1720–40 and is a three-storey building with a south-east section of 1805–15, stables of 1817 and a mausoleum of 1781. Strathtyrum Lodge dates from 1821 and the gates are early eighteenth century. In the early part of the nineteenth century the sea still washed up to Strathtyrum gates in a mass of sea marshes and rivulets. The property was leased in Victorian times by John Blackwood (1818–79), the Tory publisher who issued the works of George Eliot; to Blackwood's house parties at Strathtyrum came a great gathering of eminent writers including Anthony Trollope.

CHAPTER 9

Fisherfolk All

On New Year's day, I heard them say, Just at St Andrews pier, man,
The *Packet* then was quite mista'en-Out of her course did steer, man.
It was nae joke, she struck the rock,
Right on the Burn Stool, man;
Being dark, I fear she missed the pier—
Their compass was nae rule, man.

George Bruce, *Reminiscences of St Andrews Bay* (1884)

Fishermen have said for centuries that there are no more changeable waters than those in St Andrews Bay; a morning calm can soon give way to an afternoon of endless chains of breakers lashing the beaches and headland by the harbour. On New Years Day 1817, the cargo vessel *Packet*, having just discharged coal at Haig's distillery at Guardbridge, came to grief on the Burn Stools rocks at the entrance to St Andrews harbour. It joined many such wrecks in the harbourmaster's disaster log from the Macduff sloop *Janet* (1800) to the Dundee steam tug *Osprey* (1871). It was the *Janet*'s fate that caused St Andrews to acquire its first lifeboat around 1801. For around 138 years the burgh retained its own lifeboat; the era ended in 1938 when, because of the decline of the fishing industry, it was difficult to recruit skilled volunteers. The last lifeboat was the 25-foot self-righting Rubie-type *John and Sarah Hadfield* which had been put into commission in 1910. The vessel was sold to Valvona of Portobello to be used as a pleasure cruiser.[1]

For generations St Andrews folk pursued the cod, codling and herring-rich waters of the bay until one fateful day . . . Soon after daybreak on 4 November 1765, St Andrews fleet of five small fishing yawls set off for the cod waters of Carr Rock. The fishermen had hardly cast their hook-studded three-string lines when the sky darkened rapidly and a storm battered the fleet. Running for harbour the yawls were denied shelter of the quays by the contrary running tide and the yawls were dashed to pieces on the rocks. Twelve men drowned and the entire St Andrews fleet was destroyed.[2] Fishing on any commercial scale was abandoned in St Andrews until the early 1800s, when two Shetland yawls began to ply from St Andrews. By 1882 the St Andrews fishing fleet had grown to twenty-four vessels.[3] The first local motor-powered fishing vessel to be used at St Andrews was the deep-sea herring boat *Theodosia* owned by Will and John Cross of 1911.

The nearest fishing havens to St Andrews harbour were at Boarhills and Kinkell and here boats tied up when rough weather kept them out of the harbour. St Andrews harbour walls were rebuilt in 1654 with stones from the castle and the quay was rebuilt and the harbour was widened and deepened during 1845–46. Despite rapid silting St Andrews harbour was bustling during 1770–1925 with fishing boats and ships for exporting potatoes and grain, and the importation of coal, iron, paving stones and timber. A passenger packetboat plied to Leith from 1830 to 1914. The development of the present harbour was largely due to the efforts of the philanthropist, poet and musician George Bruce (1825–1904) who lived in Market Street. The son of a surgeon, Bruce became an apprentice joiner and set up his own builders business; his projects included the 'Royal George' and 'Great Eastern' tenements. A town councillor for forty years, Bruce played a key, if dissenting role, in St Andrews society and promoted many improvement schemes while castigating the ideas of others.

He was immortalised in his sponsorship of the Bruce Embankment. In 2005 a £1.5m partnership project to improve access to the West Sands included an upgrading of the Bruce Embankment locations. The pier at St Andrews was originally of wood, but this was destroyed by the storm of December 1655; thereafter a half-length pier was built with stone from the castle and regularly repaired. There was a lighthouse at the end of the 290-yard-long pier until 1849, and a new beacon was placed beyond the pier to replace a decayed oak one on Lady Craig's Rock. The cross pier was built in 1722 and was damaged by the storm of 1727 and rebuilt; it was repaired in 1938. The East Bents (with its putting green of 1925) was regularly breached by the Kinness Burn, and a protective wall was erected here in 1877. The inner harbour dates from 1785–89 and was crossed by the Shore Bridge (just beyond Balfour House) of around 1789; in the thirteenth century this bridge was known as Stermolind ('Mill Bar') and Bow Bridge by 1655; the footbridge linking The Shorehead and the East Bents dated from 1927 and was replaced in 2004.

St Andrews harbour was not the burgh's most ancient seaport. Large schooners and sloops from as far as the Baltic sailed up the Eden well into the Victorian era to the anchorage at Guardbridge; this was the quays for the sawmill and Haig's Seggie distillery and for agricultural products. The port had been granted a charter as far back as 1140 by David I to the 'Layde Burn' or 'Water of Eden'.[4] The port had its own Regality and Admiralty and granted cockets (custom house certificates) to make it an important 'international port' for Continental shipping.[5] Thus this was the main harbour of the

46. Crew of the British Channel fleet parade at St Andrews harbour, c.1910, on what was once known as Battery Pier. The Shorehead tenements are clearly seen with the now-vanished gasworks at the rear.

Metropolitan See of St Andrews but declined after the Reformation. The Shorehead of St Andrews was formerly the site of two taverns and a malthouse, and fishermen's stores; it developed as a tenement, with the name of 'The Royal George' and was condemned as a slum in 1935. The site was redeveloped with flats and houses during 1965–6. At the east end of the new block is Bell Rock House of around 1750, restored in the early 1950s. Behind the Royal George site at East Kirkhill, lies the old signal station and the remains of a fifteenth century doorway of the old Provost's Manse. Most of the burgh's working people lived in overcrowded tenements which were given names of ships of the line, like *Great Eastern*, *Great Western* and *The Pembroke*. Although fisher families did live at the harbour edge, the main fishing *quartier* was in the shadow of the cathedral's north-west aspect,

A large number of St Andrews families gained a livelihood from the open sea-fishing, netting locally for ten months, then off the Caithness coast for the other two. St Andrews old fishing quarter was set within that area of land contained by North Castle Street, South Castle Street, Gregory Lane (once Dickieman's Wynd, or Foundry Lane), Gregory Place and the East Scores. The fisher folk had their own school in Gregory Place by 1847 (on the site of the old Salvation Army citadel) which moved further east in 1856 to become the East Infants' School. Gregory Lane was the site of a fishermen's reading room and social club set up in 1907, of which the main donor was the Scottish Coast Mission; a former reading room for fishermen was sponsored by Captain Cox of the coastguard and Dr A.K. Lindesay, and the new one was opened by Major W. Anstruther-Gray MP. Marine Place was built by the old charity of 1643 known as the Sea Box Society (ended 1921), abutting the Ladyhead, which street led to Gregory's Green (sited in front of the war memorial of 1922) named after Professor David Gregory (1712–66).

The focal point of the fisher community was their own Cross, known as the 'Little Cross'; it was sited opposite to 52 North Street and was removed around 1800. This cross was repaired around 1616 and there was probably a fish market in the

47. The Fisher Quarter, North Street, near to the site of the medieval fisherfolks' 'Little Cross', c.1910 [Alexander Brown Patterson]

vicinity although the bulk of St Andrews fish was sold at the Buttermarket. At one time fish could only be sold at these markets; transgressors were fined (from £1 to £10 in 1800) and were incarcerated in the Tolbooth until such fines and court expenses were paid. Regularly townsfolk of St Andrews complained that the fisherfolk used North Street for the deposit of stinking fish guts and as a depot for their gear. Several of the fisherfolk and seafarers worshipped in Holy Trinity Church where a 'Sailor's Loft' was sited until 1789.

Many of the old established fisher families, like the Gourlays, the Wilsons and the Chisholms, still have descendants in the town. As the fishing industry declined in the burgh, some of the fishermen became golf caddies and retained their blue jerseys and peak caps. Several of the old fish-sellers walked as far as ten to fifteen miles radius of the town each day to sell their fish. One great personality in the town was the fish-seller Mrs Henry Clark, known locally as 'Joan'. She wore the distinctive costume of the traditional Scottish fishwife of white stockings, elastic-sided boots, a striped skirt over a multitude of brightly cloured petticoats, a red knitted jacket, a red shawl and fisher apron. Joan's spotless house, from which she issued to sell flounders, white fish and cod from her wheelbarrow, was at 11 South Castle Street. She was working hard up to ten months before her death on 4 September 1927, aged 75.

Like most fisherfolk, those in St Andrews were a very superstitious group. They did not like seeing a clergyman before they set sail, for instance, and they evolved a taboo language in which such words as pig, orange and storm were never used in conversation lest bad luck ensue. Because many of them had the same surname nicknames were very common among the fisherfolk.

For years the fisherfolk claimed the right to collect the mussel-scalps on the Eden estuary which they used for bait. The scalps formed one of the burgh's oldest and most remarkable industries. The fishermen had long claimed them as a free perk, but ultimately they were charged so much per basket by the Town Council who had been granted a monopoly in early charters. This led to a continual argy-bargy between the fishermen and the authorities. The fish trade had so declined by the 1940s that the scalp foraging died out because of labour and transport costs.

Press Gangs

During the Seven Years War, 1756–63, the press gangs were active in St Andrews. Originally the pressmen were employed to force paupers, vagabonds and criminals into the army and navy; but in time of war they were unscrupulous recruiters of those who had seamanship skills. During the years 1759–60, three naval press gang lieutenants were active in the burgh; these lieutenants, Fowler, Betson and Bruce, got friendly with the fishing population with a view to recruitment. Alcohol was a common bribe and when the recruits were well oiled they were shanghaied by the twelve-man press gang. Although the Provost of the time, James Lumisdaine of Rennyhill, and the magistrates complained, it had no effect, although there are no records of the numbers of recruits 'taken' by the press gangs in the burgh.

CHAPTER 10

The Haunts of Academe

'St Andry', Love's for thee not dead, Whate'er thou
taught's of knowledge, In days when we, not deeply read,
Were yet red-gown'd at College!

John Donald Sutherland Campbell,
9th Duke of Argyll (1845–1914)

When Queen Victoria's son-in-law (as Marquess of Lorne he
married Princess Louise, fourth daughter of Queen Victoria, in
1871) penned these words in 1902, the University of St Andrews was heir to a thousand years of learning. Tutelage
ostensibly in the Gospels and the metrical set of canonical rules
of such as St Maelruain had begun in the days of the Culdees at
Kilrymont.[1] In their settlement a *ferleiggin*, or 'man of letters'
had charge of records and the teaching of a school. Apart from
offering instruction to pilgrims the *ferleiggin* taught *scologs* ('a
band of scholars') whose number were destined for church
service.[2] We know too, that the life of St Regulus was written at
royal command by Thomas the Ferleiggin at Kilrymont making the place an early seat of knowledge.[3] A fundamental part
of the early teaching, albeit in the vernacular (i.e., Gaelic),
would be the study of Latin, the language of society, and the
ancient Celtic twenty-character alphabet of script known as
Ogham.[4]

The running conflict between the Culdees and the Augus-
tinians about who had the superior right to do what at
Kilrymont and the early diocese included the education of
novices, the early students. It was not until around 1211 that
Archdeacon Laurence the Ferleiggin was allocated funds by
Bishop William Malvoisine for teaching within the priory of St
Andrews. It is likely that the Culdees continued a teaching role
under the Augustinians until the former's total absorption.

The University Established

The motivation for Scotland to have her own university came about through politics and war. Although Scots scholars continued to study at Oxford and Cambridge, after the Wars of Independence, the increasing troubles with England and the Great Schism in the Papacy from 1378, wherein England and other nations supported a Rome-based Pope who was not acceptable to the Scots, allies of France, drove Scottish students to seek their advanced education elsewhere, notably at Paris and Orleans.

The origins of the University of St Andrews came in three well-defined steps. The need for establishing advanced education was brought into focus by the diocese of St Andrews' senior clergy under the leadership of Bishop Henry Wardlaw, with the support of King James I (still a prisoner in England), Prior James Bisset and Archdeacon Thomas Stewart. Abbot Walter Bower tells us that after the Feast of Pentecost, 11 May 1410, a *Studium Generale Universitatis* was founded.[5] This meant that teaching began on this date with the main objectives of advancing learning and maintaining the Catholic faith. At this point the 'university' was a voluntary society of teaching clergy who were chartered on 28 February 1412 in the chapter house of the priory, by Bishop Wardlaw. This was an important step as the intent of the charter was to bring about a working and amicable understanding between the burgh and the new university teachers. Wardlaw made it easy for the two to flourish together and the teachers were under the protection of the bishop in terms of their liberty and privileges and now the teachers were able to buy their needs in the burgh without tax.

A number of university personalities began to show themselves.[6] Within the faculty of Canon Law were: Laurence of Lindores, who expounded the fourth book of *Sentences* (opinions) of the scholastic theologian and philosopher Peter Lombard; Richard de Cornell, Archdeacon of Lothian; John Litster, Canon of the Priory of St Andrews; John de Schevez, Official of St Andrews; and William Stephen, later Bishop of Dunblane. In the faculty of Philosophy and Logic were: John

Gill, sometime clerk of the diocese; William de Fowlis, priest of
the diocese of Dunblane; and William Croser, priest of the
diocese of St Andrews.

Bishop Wardlaw's charter gave the school and its staff
protection but it could not confer degrees, neither was it
recognised in Christendom as having any 'university status'.
These important things could only be granted by one of two
heads of Christendom, the Pope or the Holy Roman Emperor.[7]
So far as Scotland was concerned the only lawful pope was
Peter de Luna, Cardinal of St Mary in Cosmedia, who ruled as
Antipope Benedict XIII, from his stronghold of Pensicola in the
diocese of Tortosa, Aragon, Spain. So an approach was made to
Benedict in the name of the infant school, its promoters the
Church of St Andrews, the King of Scots and the Estates, all of
whom formed the sovereign authorities of Scotland. As a
consequence six papal *bulla* were issued on 28 August 1413,
the Feast of St Augustine of Hippo, which formulated the small
school as an equal with the great schools of Europe. Thus it
became a *studium generale* in Canon and Civil Law, Theology,
Arts, Medicine and 'other lawful faculties'. It now had the
power to examine candidates for doctorates and masterships
and to present such candidates to the diocesan bishops for
ubique docendi, the licence which meant that they could teach
anywhere in Christendom.[8] The papal bulls were brought
to St Andrews by Henry de Ogilvy, priest of the diocese of
St Andrews, and they arrived in St Andrews on the Morrow of
the Purification of Our Lady, Candlemas, February 1414 after
a long and arduous journey by land and sea from Spain.

Amid pealing bells the bulls were welcomed by the townsfolk,
and next day, they were formally presented to Bishop Henry
Wardlaw in the refectory of the priory. Once the bulls had been
promulgated, the diocesan clergy and the canons processed into
the cathedral church, singing the *Te Deum*. At the High Altar,
Alexander Waghorn, Bishop of Ross intoned the versicle and
the collect *De Spiritu Sancto* (Of the Holy Ghost): *Deus, qui corda
fidelium Sanct Spiritus illustratione docuisti: da nobis in eodem Spiritu
recta sapere; et de ejus semper consolatione gaudere.* (God, who didst
teach the faithful by sending the light of the Holy Spirit into

their hearts, grant that, by the gift of that Spirit, right judge-
ment may be ours, and that we may ever find joy in his
comfort.) Waghorn also preached the sermon.[9] The day was
spent in feasting with bonfires in the streets at night.

On 6 February, the celebration of the Coming of St Andrew's
Relics, the rejoicing continued; this day Prior James Bisset
celebrated mass with prayers for the infant university.

Rectors and Chancellors

There was little distinction between professors and students in
the new university; all were scholars in the pursuit of learning
within an academic society. The head of this society was the
Rector, elected by the *Comita*, all the people who had been
legally 'incorporated' or matriculated in the university, and
who formed the general congregation.[10] The first Rector of the
university (cf. College of St John) was the theologian philosopher Laurence of Lindores (c.1372–1437), Inquisitor of Here-
tical Pravity in Scotland, who introduced the system that all the
members of the academic community were divided into four
'Nations': *Albania* – Fife; *Angusia* – Angus; *Laudonia* – Lothian;
and *Britannia* – the diocese of Glasgow and Galloway, replaced
by *Fifa* by the sixteenth century. Thus each member was placed
in a 'Nation' according to place of birth. Each of the 'Nations'
had its Procurator, and a proxy (Intrant) for voting. In
medieval times the Rector was elected the first Monday of
March after which a meal of wine and fruit was supplied at the
Rector's expense.[11]

The early role of the Rector was to preside over the university's general congregations, supervise its order and discipline and embody in his person the 'corporate authority' of the
university. He also instituted proceedings over debtors to the
university, aided the students with their commitments to the
university and was the main link between the university and the
townsfolk. In his work the Rector was assisted by a number of
assessors, generally nominated by the 'Nations'. After 1475 the
students were excluded from the election of Rector, and while
the vote was restored in 1625, the actual choice of Rector was

limited to the heads of the colleges, and after 1642 to the Professors of Divinity. No significant alterations took place until 1858, when the system was changed and from that date the Rector no longer represented the 'corporate identity' of the university, and instead of being elected annually he was elected for three years.

After 1862 a certain party political flavour entered the election of Rector with the nomination of the Liberal Fox Maule, 2nd Baron Panmure (and eventually 11th Earl of Dalhousie), Viscount Palmerston's erstwhile Secretary at War, and Perthshire MP, Sir William Stirling-Maxwell who won the election; this strong political flavour continued until 1892. Over the years some Rectors have been outstanding in their work for students and for the university. Others, like Frederick Temple Blackwood, 1st Marquess of Dufferin and Ava whose rectorship 1890–92 showed his little interest in the post, while others like the 3rd Marquess of Bute, dubbed the 'First Working Rector' have been generous benefactors and popular with the students; some have been a thorn in the flesh of Principals; for instance, Bute did not see eye to eye with Principal Sir James Donaldson.

Today the role of Rector, as defined by the Act of 1858, is as 'ordinary President' of the University Court, and general spokesman of the students both inside and outside the university, and he or she is chosen by the students themselves. The Rector consults the Students' Representative Council – instituted 1885 and one of the two component organisations of the students' association – as to students' needs and problems. The Rector appoints an Assessor who sits on the University Court.

The superior of the Rector in medieval times was the Chancellor, and from 1413 to 1689 the office was held (with three brief intervals) by the bishops and archbishops of the (arch)diocese. When the system of episcopacy was abolished the Chancellor was thereafter appointed by the *Senatus Academicus*, who combined the role until 1858 when the prerogative was invested in the General Council.[12] The actual duties of the Chancellor have always been vague, but can be summed up thus:

The office of the Chancellor has existed ever since the foundation of the University and no comprehensive definition of its powers has been made in any modern statute. The most authoritative definition is contained in the return made by the University to the Commissioners of 1826 which states: 'The Chancellor is the head of the University. He is consulted on all public matters relative to its welfare, and he is also Conservator of its privileges. The power of conferring degrees is vested in him.' The Act of 1858 provides that the Chancellor is to be elected by the General Council and to hold office for life. He is the ordinary President of the General Council and must give his sanction to all 'improvements in the internal arrangements of the University' proposed by the University Court. He appoints an Assessor on the Court.[13]

Since the late seventeenth century the office of Chancellor has been held mostly by aristocrats, or say a career soldier (Field Marshal Earl Haig of Bemersyde, 1922–28), a Prime Minister (Stanley Baldwin, 1929 47), or an academic like Sir Kenneth James Dover (retired from the post on 30 December 2005).

The role of the Vice-Chancellor has been defined thus:

From an early date in the history of the University it was customary for the Chancellor to appoint a Vice-Chancellor to confer degrees in his absence. The Act of 1858 explicitly empowers the Chancellor to appoint a Vice-Chancellor who may in his absence discharge his office 'in so far as regards conferring degrees but in no other respect'. By a convention uniformly observed since 1859 the Principal of the University is appointed Vice-Chancellor.[14]

From the birth of the university its teaching and ceremonial were conducted where the lecturers lived, but for important 'congregations' and faculty meetings they met in the refectory of the Augustinian Priory. Tradition has it that from an early date the university used premises in a group of buildings in South Street known to the authorities as the Chapel and College of St John the Evangelist. Here we find the Faculty

of Arts meeting in 1416, and three years later the university
seems to have fully possessed the property. In January 1419
Canon Robert of Montrose, Rector of the Church of Cults and
Chaplain of Honour to the Apostolic See gave a tenement of
land on the south side of South Street 'to found a College of
Theologians and Artists' all confirmed in honour of 'Almighty
God, to the Blessed Virgin Mary, and especially to the Blessed
John the Evangelist and All Saints'. This property was vested in
Laurence of Lindores, first 'Master, Rector and Governor of the
said college'.[15]

The site of the first building of the university today is the
western end of the Parliament Hall, South Street, and we know
that in medieval times the 'College of St John' was a long
double tenement incorporating a chapel and a small chantry
college. The Feast of St John the Divine, Apostle and Evangelist, author of the fourth Gospel, was the main official festival of
the college, and was held on 27 December when the Master
would say the Collect *Ecclesiam tuam, Domine, benignus illustra*
(Lord, cast thy gracious beams of light upon thy Church) while
the most senior clergymen present would intone the mass of St
John. The next building developed for the university came with
the granting of a tenement by Bishop Wardlaw in 1430 for a
Pedagogium on a site just west of the College of St John.[16] This
was replaced by the founding of St Mary's College in 1537.

The Colleges

Before the end of the Middle Ages the society of scholars at St
Andrews had formed themselves into three endowed colleges,
St Salvator's (1450), St Leonard's (1512) and St Mary's
(1537). In 1747 the colleges of St Salvator and St Leonard
were united into a single United College and have so remained
in modern times, although St Leonard's College was revived as
a non-statutory college to encourage and support research
students and care for postgraduate students.

The College of St Salvator was founded as a consequence of
the university going through a bad patch in the mid-fifteenth
century. With the expulsion of the English scholars from Paris

in 1436, Scottish students renewed their traditional gravitation to France and denuded the university's potential intake. This, combined with inter-college squabbling at St John's and the Pedagogy, led to a decline in the university's funds and influence, and the whole needed a new focus. To this end the asthmatic Bishop James Kennedy (c.1408–65) founded a new college dedicated to the Holy Saviour on 27 August 1450 in North Street. The college remains on the same site today and its dedication to St Salvator comes from the English rendering of the Scots *Sanct Salvatour*. Kennedy's foundation was confirmed by the bull of Pope Nicholas V in February 1451, and reconfirmed in an updated charter by Pius II in 1458.[17]

Today the college founded to teach Theology and Arts with a faculty of thirteen persons to symbolise Our Lord and His Apostles, and funded by teinds from the parishes of Cults, Kemback, Dunino and Kilmany, remains one of the most noteworthy assemblages of architecture in Scotland.[18] It was the first real academic college in Scotland and its charter says that its members were 'to live together in a collegiate manner, and to eat and sleep within the bounds of the college'. The original buildings of the college were arranged round a cloister court, with the upper stories being used as living quarters and the ground floor as lecture rooms. Only the frontage of the medieval buildings remains, but the college formerly had a hall against the wall of the south end of Butt's Wynd, a walled garden to the back leading to the riggs of Stanycroft next to the Swallowgait; in front of the chapel, and now under the roadway of North Street was the collegiate church cemetery. The cloister court was demolished in 1763. What can be seen today is Lower College Hall of 1846, the East Wing of 1831 (with extension of 1906) and the Cloister building of 1846 set around the Quad. The gateway now set outside the college chapel in North Street probably came from the cloister buildings of Kennedy's time.

The tower of Bishop Kennedy's college remains as a landmark in the town and dates from the 1450s; the original spire of timber and lead was erected by Archbishop James Beaton

48. The Quad and Chapel of St Salvator's College, founded by Bishop James Kennedy in 1450

around 1530, and it was destroyed during the great siege of the castle of 1546–47, whereupon the tower was used as a gun emplacement to attack the castle – the present spire was added by Archbishop Hamilton around 1550 and its parapet was added in 1846. The tower archway, which gives access to the old college court and the modern quad, is surmounted by a panel showing Kennedy's arms, flanked by niches for now vanished statues; these would probably be of religious figures hacked down at the Reformation. The coat of arms of Bishop Kennedy, surmounded by its mitre, is to be found on various parts of the college and the college arms themselves were only officially matriculated in 1949 and depict an orb surmounted by a Latin cross. The tower was restored 1999–2000. In the belfry hangs the great bell of the college traditionally called 'Katherine' and the tower would probably have a clock from medieval times. The faces of the modern clock were refurbished during the recent tower restoration. The bell called 'Katherine' measures two feet seven inches in diameter across the mouth and bears the inscripion:

SANCTUS IAC[OBUS] KENNEDUS EPISCOPUS S[ANC]TI ANDREA AC FUNDATOR COLLEGII S[ANC]TS SALVATORIS ME FECIT FIERI ANNO 1460 KATHARINAM NOMINANDO D[OCTOR] JAC[OBUS] MARTINUS EIUSDEM COLLEGII PRAE-POSITUS ME REFECIT A.D.1609 ET D[OCTOR] ALEX[ANDE]R SKENE EIUSDEM COLLEGII PRAEPOTIUS [sic] ME TERTIO FIERI FECIT: JOHN MEIKLE ME FECIT EDINBWRCH ANNO 1686 ET DOCTOR JACOBUS COLQUHOUN IRVINE EQ[UES] EJUSDEM COLLEGII PRAEPOSITUS ME QUARTO FIERI FECIT ANNO 1940.

[That holy man, James Kennedy, Bishop of St Andrews and founder of the College of the Holy Saviour, had me cast in the year 1460, giving me the name of Katherine. Dr James Martine, Provost of the same college, re-cast me in the year of our Lord 1609; and Dr Alexander Skene, Provost of the same college had me cast a third time: John Meikle cast me at Edinburgh in the year 1686; and Dr James Colquhoun Irvine, Knight, Principal of the same college, had me cast a fourth time in the year 1940.]

'Katherine' is accompanied by the old bell of St Leonard's College called 'Elizabeth' cast at Ghent around 1512 to be recast in 1724 and 1940; 'Elizabeth', a somewhat unusual name for a bell, was brought to St Salvator's when the steeple of St Leonard's College was demolished in 1764. 'Elizabeth' stands one foot six inches in diameter across the mouth and has this inscription:

ME ELIZABETHAM LEONARDINAM ANTE BIS CENTVM ANNOS GANDAVI FACTAM ET TEM-PORIS INIVRIA DILAPSAM COLLEGE [sic] LEO-NARDINI IMPENSIS REFECIT ROBERTVS MAXWELL ANNO 1724 ED[INBURGI] ET ME BIS CENTVM ANNIS ITERUM ELAPSIS IAM FRACTA VOCE SENESCENTEM REFICIENDAM CURAVIT

JACOBUS COLQUHOUN IRVINE HUJUS COLLEGII
PRAEPOSITUS 1940.

[I am Elizabeth of St Leonard's cast at Ghent two hundred
years before and impaired by the ravages of time, Robert
Maxwell re-cast me at Edinburgh in the year 1724 at the
charges of St Leonard's College; and after the passage of
another two hundred years, when my voice cracked and
when I was growing old, James Colquhoun Irvine, Principal
of this college, took care to have me re-cast in 1940.]

In medieval times St Salvator's was a sumptuous place with
side chapels and altars rich in gifts from private benefactors.
The focus was the high altar with its cover of blue velvet and
cloth of gold. At its centre was a huge gilt crucifix in honour of
the Blessed Virgin, St John and the twelve Apostles. For
services a 'richly bound and enamelled gospel book' was placed
on the altar.[19] Here too, was a solid silver image of Christ with
diadem of precious stones, flanked by silver gilt chalices and a
jewelled reliquary cross thought to contain what purported to
be a sliver of the True Cross of the Crucifixion.[20] The church
contained a number of tombstones like that of Hugh Spens,
Provost of the College (1534); but the main burial was of the
founder set to the left of the eastern apse and the sacrament
house. It is probable that Kennedy's tomb was designed for the
cathedral, where one would expect the diocesan bishop to be
buried, but some time between the consecration of the church
in 1460 and Kennedy's death in 1465, a change of plan was
carried out. The tomb is formed of a Gothic niche with a tomb-
chest covered with a black marble slab; on this may have rested
a now-vanished effigy of the bishop destroyed by the Reformers. The stone is grey micaceous freestone, but the carving is
of the Tournai school to Kennedy's own design with the theme
of the Bringing of Good (Christianity) to a world of sin and
death. The stone chapel roof was renovated in 1773, and this
work destroyed much of the early decoration and maybe the
tomb too; and considerable restoration took place in 1930, a
stone screen being erected at the west end of the nave and the

49. Chapel of St Salvator's College. The tomb of the founder
Bishop Kennedy is on the far left.

famous 'John Knox' pulpit replacing an earlier one. At the time Kennedy's tomb was opened, and not for the first time; in 1842 an excavation took place wherein Kennedy's bones were examined and in 1862 the bishop's bones were gathered and placed in an oak casket made by Charles Conacher, the St Andrews cabinet maker, for £3 2s 7d (£3.13½p). By 1930 this casket was disintegrating and a new silver/bronze casket, supplied by Sir Henry Shanks Keith, replaced it to contain the bishop's remains. James Kennedy also had his own barge, the *Salvator*, 'the biggest that had been seen to sail upon the Ocean',[21] which it is thought transported the stone for his tomb; the barge with the tomb cost Kennedy a great deal of money and the vessel was wrecked off Bamburgh, Northumberland, in 1473.

Something of the beauty of the medieval embellishments of the church can be seen in the celebrated mace of St Salvator's College. The mace was ordered for the college by Bishop Kennedy in 1461, and has a hexagonal open shrine as its head with the Holy Saviour as a main emblem. Angels show the symbols of the Passion (a cross, a scourging-pillar, a spear) and the shields of St Andrews, Bishop Kennedy and St Salvator's College are displayed along with the figures of a king, a bishop and a Franciscan friar (or, perhaps a merchant). An inscription on the base reads:

Johne Maiel (*Jean Mayelle*) Gouldsmithe and Verlette off Chamer til the Lord the Delfyne has made this Masse in the Toun of Paris the year of our Lorde mcccclvi.

A silver-gilt medal (attached to the rod of the mace by a chain) says:

AVISEES A LA FIN JACOBVS KANEDI ILLVSTRIS SAN[C]TI ANDREE ANTISTES AC FV[N]DATOR COLLEGII S[ANCT]I SALVATORIS CVI ME DONA-VIT ME FECIT FIERE PARI[S]IIS AN[NO] D[OMI]NI MCCCCLX.

[*Avise la fin* . . . the French equivalent of the Latin *Respice finem*, 'Consider the End' . . . James Kennedy the illustrious bishop of St Andrews and founder of the College of St

Salvator, to which he gifted me, had me made at Paris in the year of the Lord 1460.]

The mace shows that it was repaired several times particularly in 1685. The university owns other maces, the Mace of the Faculty of Arts, commissioned 1414–15 and completed 1418–19, and the Mace of Canon Law made pre-1457. There are also two modern maces, that of the School of Medicine of 1949 and the University Mace of 1958.

At the Reformation the church's medieval religious services came to an end, although the educational functions of the college continued in part and it was reduced to a Protestant Arts college. The church was stripped of its 'papist' furnishing and it stood empty and desolate, and was ultimately used, along with its vestry, as a meeting place for the new Commissary Court, which replaced the pre-Reformation Church Court. The church was 'occasionally used for preaching' in the late sixteenth century. In 1747 United College was formed of the colleges of St Salvator and St Leonard and from 1759 to 1904 the parishioners of St Leonard's worshipped in the church. The University entered a full occupancy of the chapel as a 'university chapel' on 16 October 1904.

Many prominent figures in Scottish history have passed through the quad of St Salvator's as students and graduands. Perhaps the most famous was James Graham, 1st Marquess of Montrose (1612–50) the signatory Covenanter of 1638 turned royalist, who was hanged, drawn and quartered at Edinburgh. Montrose was at St Salvator's during 1627–29; a student dilatory in learning, Montrose spent more time on the links, riding or at the archery butts situated behind what is now Lower College Hall, where he won the Silver Arrow in 1628. In raising the flag of monarchy in Scotland, Montrose displayed his own philosophy learned at the butts:

> He either fears his fate too much,
> Or his deserts are small.
> Who dares not put it to the touch
> To give or lose it all.[22]

Hardly a major Scots burgh did not have a prominent citizen who had not attended St Salvator's in the sixteenth and seventeenth centuries. Neighbouring Dundee sported several like Alexander Guthrie (burgess 1559) and Latinist James Gleig, Regent of St Salvator's (burgess 1606).[23]

Despite all these famous names, one other stands out in the history of the college. Patrick Hamilton (b.1504) was made Commendator of the Premonstratensian Abbey of Fearn, Ross, as a boy and went to France to graduate at Paris in 1520. Thereafter he studied at Louvain and while on the Continent he absorbed Lutheran doctrines. On his return to Scotland in 1523 he advocated reforming theology at St Andrews and had to flee because of his opinions in 1527. In Germany he met Luther and others which honed his reforming beliefs; he returned to Scotland and continued preaching his beliefs but was arrested by the signature of Archbishop James Beaton, tried for heresy in an indictment led by the Blackfriar Alexander Campbell, convicted by the assembled senior clergy, and sentenced to burning at the stake at the gates of St Salvator's on 29 February 1528. The initials 'P.H.' set in the causeway in front of the gate act as a permanent memorial backed up by a plaque on the wall nearby commissioned and donated by the late Professor Emeritus Jack Allen in 1988. A student tradition has it that should an undergraduate step on the initials he or she will fail their final exams. Should the visitor look above the arms of Bishop Kennedy on the forefront of the tower they will see the weathered stone in the form of a 'face', which the pious declared was the image of Hamilton etched in stone by the psychic power of his martyrdom.[24]

With the decline of the pedagogy, the sixteenth century opened for the university with financial and recruiting problems, and these were confronted by the young Archbishop Alexander Stewart; in the event he was to die with his father the king at Flodden in 1513. Alexander had studied under Erasmus's tutelage and was a scholar of note. Events developed so that an ancient hospital adjoining the church dedicated to the sixth century Gaulish abbot St Leonard became available – this had been an institution that had belonged to the Culdees and

50. Weathered stone set within the south face of the tower of St Salvator's College. It is said by the faithful to depict the face of the reformer Patrick Hamilton who was burned at the stake in front of the tower in February 1528.

had been given to the Augustinians in 1144 by Bishop Robert, and which had subsequently been turned into an almshouse for old women; the old women were expelled for being neither spiritual nor worthy. On 20 August 1512 a charter proclaimed the conversion of the hospital, once a haven for pilgrims to the Shrine of St Andrew, and Church of St Leonard into 'the College of the Poor Clerks of the Church of St Andrews'; confirmed by James IV in 1513, the college became known as the 'College of St Leonard's' and was largely founded by the work of Prior John Hepburn, and initial accommodation was found for the library and tutorial rooms at the priory. At first a master, who was a canon of the priory, four chaplains and twenty poor scholars, who were effectively Augustinian novices, made up the college which was run on monastic lines with football (and such 'dishonest games') being forbidden and no woman was allowed within the college precincts, except a laundress who had to be at least fifty years of age and inordinately plain. The college was to last through the vicissitudes of the Reformation and Episcopacy until in 1747 it was united with St Salvator's and its buildings were sold as private residences. For instance, Samuel Johnson's host, Dr Robert Watson, was one of the residents.[25]

The site of St Leonard's College is incorporated in St Leonards private school, but there is public access to the college chapel from The Pends. St Leonard's College was revived in the 1980s as a non-statutory college to care for post-graduate students, and encourage and support research activities. The oldest part of the chapel extant is the nave and west portion of the choir which dates from around 1144; the rest of the chapel is Romanesque; the buildings were extended eastwards around 1544–50 to include a now vanished western tower and south porch. It functioned as a parish kirk after 1578 and remained so until abandonment in 1761, whereafter the church became ruined. In 1853 the interior of the church was cleaned out and the windows unblocked; and in 1910 the University Court renovated the building, re-roofed it and re-glazed the windows, but nothing further was done on the church until the extensive renovation in 1948–52.

The chapel contains an early piscina, probably taken from the cathedral, and several interesting monuments including a much worn example thought to be that of the college founder John Hepburn. Prior Hepburn's body was exhumed in the 1840s, under the supervision of professor of humanity, Thomas Gillespie, and the cadaver was found to be in a shroud and enclosed in lead, but with no coffin. Also exhumed were Robert Stewart, Earl of Lennox, and Bishop-elect of Caithness; he fled to England on a charge of treason in 1544. He joined the Reformers and used the style of bishop until his death in 1586.

51. Chapel of St Leonard's College; originally built around 1144, the chapel was extended in the sixteenth-century and extensively renovated 1948–52.

His Romanesque-type mural monument is set against the east
end of the north wall with the inscription:

IN[P[ORTV FLVCTVSQVE OMNES CLASSEMQVE
RELINQVO ME SPECTANS MVNDVMQVE OMNEM
PASCESQVE R[ELI]NQVE.

[Safe in harbour I put behind me the ocean and my fleet.
Behold me, put behind you the whole world and your
burdens.]

Exhumed at the same time was James Wynram, sub-prior and
after 1560, Superintendent of Fife, who died at the age of
ninety. His epitaph reads:

1582 MVLTA/CVM DE/AMBVLAVERIS DEMVM RE/
DEVNDVM/EST HAC CONDITIONE [IN]/TRAVI
V[T]/EXIREM.

[Long as your pilgrimage has been you must return at last. I
came on condition that I should depart.]

St Mary's College was founded on 12 February 1537 by
Archbishop James Beaton, and was designed on the advice
of French masons working at Falkland Palace. The college was
completed 1543–44 and was based on the existing 1430 Pedagogy to teach Theology, Law, Physic and other 'Liberal disciplines', all 'under the invocation of the Assumption of the
Blessed Virgin Mary'. Archbishop Beaton's probable intention
in his foundation was to promote the teaching and recruitment
of well-educated secular clergy for his archdiocese. When the
archbishop died in 1539 the continuation of the college scheme
was carried out by his nephew Cardinal David Beaton, but the
buildings were completed by Archbishop John Hamilton
around 1553–54. The original buildings were set around a
four-sided court of which only the much-altered north and west
blocks remain; the Common Hall of the college stood to the
south and the college chapel to the east.[26]

Divinity is taught in St Mary's whose entrance is in South Street leading through an archway into the quad. The distinctive iron gateway bears the motto 'IN PRINCIPIO ERAT VERBUM' ('In the beginning was the Word': John 1.1) and the coat of arms incorporates devices of Archbishop James Beaton and archbishop James Hamilton with the *fleur de lis* representing the orginial dedication to the Blessed Mary of the Assumption. To the west the quad is bounded by the Principal's House (1544), the Frater Hall (1544) and the Stair Tower (1552), outside of which is the thorn tree whose predecessor is deemed to have been planted by Mary, Queen of Scots in 1565. The belfry was the home of fan-tailed pigeons from around the late 1880s. On the South Street exterior wall of the Principal's House is the Royal Coat of Arms with *In defens anno domini 1613*. The north range of St Mary's incorporates Parliament Hall and Library, bearing on the South Street side the arms of former Chancellors of the university while the south side displays a fourteenth-century emblem of the passion from the earlier church on the site dedicated to St John the Evangelist.

Parliament Hall gains its name from events of a time of anxiety during the Civil War, when following defeat at the battle of Naseby Charles I surrendered to the Scots. After St Andrews graduate the Marquis of Montrose's triumphant victory at Kilsyth, Royalist troops were welcomed into St Andrews by the provost.[27] Yet, by 13 September 1645 Montrose was defeated at Philiphaugh and St Andrews was again Presbyterian orientated and Montrose and his supporters (including the provost) were condemned before the Parliament of Scotland which met at St Mary's College 'Public School' from 26 November 1645 to 4 February 1646 under the Chancellor, John Campbell, 1st Earl of Loudoun. The parliament met here to escape the plague which raged at Edinburgh at the time; and, for which St Andrews landlords were paid 6s (30p) for lodgings per night for gentry and 4s 6d (22½p) per servant.

The south range of St Mary's incorporates the Reading Room of 1890 and the Carnegie Library of 1908. In the middle of the quad is the evergreen holm oak (*quercus ilex*) of around

52. St Mary's College showing the Frater Hall (1544) and Stair Tower (1522) and the famous 'Queen Mary's Thorn'

1750. Nearby is the offshoot of the Glastonbury Thorn (from the Benedictine Abbey of Glastonbury, Somerset, itself mooted to have been planted by St Joseph of Arimathea) planted to commemorate the Moderatorship of the Church of Scotland of Principal George Simpson Duncan. The old University Carnegie Library has been converted for use by the Department of Psychology. South of the quad now lie the Bell Pettigrew and Bute buildings for the study of Biology and Medicine. The Bell Pettigrew Museum of Natural History (1838), at the Bute medical building, was transformed in 2005 to promote interest in Natural History to school pupils and the general public. A memorial to James Bell Pettigrew (d.1908), Professor of Medicine and Anatomy 1875–1905, and founder of the Gatty Marine Laboratory, the museum was developed by the mildly eccentric Professor Sir D'Arcy Wentworth Thomson (1860–1948), himself a character in the Kate Kennedy Procession.

The Place of the University

The constitution of the university developed steadily from 1410. Its substance is not set out in any one document. Its traditions and customs have been prescribed by the enfolding Universities (Scotland) Acts 1858–1966. The University Court is the supreme governing body of the university, in which all of the university's revenue and property are vested. The Court is made up, and prescribed by statute, of around twenty people drawn from the university and outside bodies. Its ultimate responsibility is for the maintenance of properties, management of residences, appointment of staff, finance and business management. The *Senatus Academicus* holds autonomous authority in matters academic, which elects six members of the Court. It is made up of the principal, the professors and certain other members of the university *ex officio*, and elected non-professorial staff and four students. The office of Principal of the University dates from 1858, although it was only created as such in 1953. The academic structure of the university is made up of three Faculties – Arts, Divinity and Science (with Medical Sciences).

The Students Association (Union), a social centre of student life, is situated in St Mary's Place on the site of the old West Park Hotel; here too are the Student Support Services and the Travel Office. The Union developed from the provision of a Common Room or Reading Room for students in the chapel cloister, around 1864, but a scheme for a more substantial Union was set afoot in 1885. As funds grew, temporary quarters were found in the now-defunct Imperial Hotel, North Street, but a move to Butt's Wynd was made in 1892.

The site was the much-altered fifteenth- and sixteenth-century residence of a former alumnus, 'the Admirable' James Crichton of Eliock; his descendant, the 3rd Marquess of Bute, bought the house for the Union and paid for its restoration. An eastern reconstruction was carried out in 1923. A Women's Students' Union was established in the early 1900s and a permanent home for them was subscribed by Mrs Andrew Carnegie of Skibo in the western half of the North Street Union. The two unions were amalgamated in 1963–64 and the coat of arms (incorporating the arms of Low of Blebo and Crichton-Stuart of Falkland, principal benefactors) granted to the Men's Union in 1949 was adopted by the new amalgamated union under the motto *Stat Scotia, Stat Aula* ('Stands Scotland, Stands this House').

Today students either live in one of the halls of residence or in private accommodation. To date there are twelve main residences, the oldest being the University Hall of Residence for Women Students opened in 1896, four years after women first appeared at the university. University Hall was expanded to include the neighbouring mansion of Westerlee of 1865–67 and is incorporated in the annex of Wardlaw Hall Residence. When it was opened in 1930, St Salvator's Residence ('Sally's) was the most up-to-date in Europe; nearby in North Street is Gannochy House of 1971. John Burnet Hall (1965), formerly the Atholl Hotel (built around 1890–1900) was donated by Captain H.K. Salvesen of the Salvasen Shipping Co and was named after Professor John Burnet the noted Greek scholar; Andrew Melville Hall (1968), North Haugh, takes its name from the founder of Scottish Presbyterianism. Dean's Court (1951) was opened as an annexe to St Salvator's Hall in 1931, and is set apart as a residence for postgraduate students. Dean's Court with its incorporated twelfth-century vaulted core was part of the first archdeacon's house in St Andrews and the residence includes a frontage at the end of South Street with the sixteenth century Roundel at No. 1. McIntosh Hall (1930) was the gift of Emeritus Professor William C. McIntosh (1838–1931) and was formed around his basic bequest of his house 'Chattan House', 2 Abbotsford Crescent. The whole has extended to include the entire sweep of Abbotsford Crescent from the basic reconstruction of 1939. Two other residences have interesting histories: Hamilton Hall (1949), with Eden Court, was once the Grand Hotel (1895) and is named after Archbishop Hamilton and the House of Hamilton. During the 1930s this hotel was the venue of 'royal' visits by blue-bloods and celebrated golfers and was used by the Air Ministry during World War II.

53. Dean's Court was part of the first archdeacon's house in St Andrews. It was opened as an annexe to St Salvator's Hall in 1931, and is now a postgraduate residence.

In 1948 a proposal was mooted to sell the hotel to the Roman
Catholic Bishops of Scotland as a teachers' training college; but
this caused a furore amongst the local Presbyterians and the
bishops' offer was rejected and the university bought the
building in 1949. In 2005 the university sold the property
for private development. St Regulus Hall (1944) adjoins the
gardens of St Mary's College and is set at the foot of Queens
Gardens. Formerly the building was the first home of the St
Andrews School for Girls Co. (later St Leonards School), then
it became the St Regulus Hotel and the building was bought
from the Younger Estate in the 1920s. The hotel was favoured
by Their Royal Highnesses Princess Helena Victoria (1870–
1948) and Marie Louise (1872–1957) – the daughters of HRH
Princess Helena, daughter of Queen Victoria – who took a suite
here in 1886; they caused much local stir and attended services
at Holy Trinity Church. More recently St Regulus Hall has
been supplemented by an annexe in nearby Queen's Terrace.
New Hall on the North Haugh is also a more modern development. Staff houses are also located at Albany Park, Fife Park,
Angus House (off St Mary's Place) with Stanley Smith House.

Over the years some residences have vanished. David Russell
Hall (1971) at Wester Langlands, Buchanan Gardens, for
instance was named after Sir David Russell, a former Chancellor's Assessor and university benefactor. The site was demolished in 2004, but David Russell Apartments abut the site by
Fife Park. Hepburn Hall, opened in 1947, was named after
Prior Hepburn, founder of St Leonard's College and was sited
in Hepburn Gardens opposite the university sports pavilion; it
was sold by the University for private development.

From its early beginnings, St Andrews University educated
most of the leading figures in Church and State in Scotland.
After 1659 it became the focus of the new national scheme of
education grounded in the parish schools which rose out of the
Reformation. Although its life was continually interrupted by
the political troubles of the sixteenth and seventeenth centuries,
the university retained its academic influence in the education
system in Scotland. Following the Act of Union of 1707,
though, and the earlier abolition of Episcopacy, the political

and economic shift to Edinburgh and Glasgow greatly affected the university and the town and during the eighteenth century the university went through a period of acute depression. During 1826–30 the university was subject to a searching investigation by a Royal Commission and this gave the impetus for the supplying of new buildings and changes in constitution, and under such principals as Sir David Brewster and Sir James Donaldson the university was given a new lease of life, and, thus refreshed, it entered the twentieth century with a new strength and reputation which was further enhanced by principals Sir James Irvine and Sir Thomas Knox who between them spanned the years 1921–66.

The affiliation of the University College of Dundee in 1881 to 'make it form part of the University of St Andrews' was effected in 1897 and in 1898 the Conjoint School of Medicine was established at Dundee. The foundation of the University of Dundee in 1967 brought all of these arrangements to an end and the university is now wholly in the town of its birth.

CHAPTER II

Rectors, Pageants and Traditions

> I look upon the history of St Andrews as especially
> precious here as a continual expression of and witness
> to, the spirit of the Scottish nationality in the higher
> spheres of thought and activity.
>
> <div align="right">John Patrick Crichton-Stuart,
3rd Marquess of the County of Bute,
<i>Rectorial Address</i> (1893)</div>

Poets, politicians, priests, philosophers and poltroons have all
had a chance to be Rector of the University of St Andrews. The
office began in the very foundation decade of the university in
1411 and was a position second only to the Chancellor of the
university in range of powers and authority.[1] The first Rector
was the lecturer priest Laurence of Lindores.[2] He took up the
position in 1422 and held a strong administrative influence at
the university until his death in 1437.

Today the unpaid position of Rector is an honour for which
conferment the student body hold an election. The mode of
election changed over the years and the students did not always
get their way. For instance in 1825 their nomination of Sir
Walter Scott was ruled null and void.[3] Exactly one hundred
years later, when the Student Representative Council, became
more closely involved with the election, there were no less than
eight nominations put forward for the post from Edward,
Prince of Wales to composer Sir Edward Elgar. In the event
the election of 1925 saw success for Norwegian explorer Fridtjof
Nansen (1861–1930).[4]

In 1982 the students elected the first female Rector in
journalist Katherine Whitehorn, and each decade's whims
and fashions have elected an eclectic band of personalities from
future and past Prime Ministers in Arthur James Balfour

54. Sir Wilfred Thomason Grenfell (1865–1940), medical missionary and author, arrives at St Andrews railway station on the occasion of his installation as Rector, 1928.

(1886) and Arthur Philip Primrose, 5th Earl of Rosebery (1910) to soldiers like World War I Commander-in-Chief Sir Douglas Haig (later 1st Earl of Bemersyde: Rector 1916) to non-British citizens like South African statesman and Prime Minister Jan Christian Smuts (1931) and Italian physicist and inventor Guglielmo Marconi (1934).

The rectorial addresses of several Rectors became important news items to be re-published for public consumption. One such was the address entitled *Courage* by Sir James Matthew Barrie (1860–1937: Rector 1919–22). He delivered it three years into his rectorship on 3 May 1922 at the Volunteer Hall, St Mary's Place, as the Younger Graduation Hall was not opened until 1929. Chancellor Earl Haig presided and Principal Sir James Irvine gave moral support to a nervous Barrie who had tinkered with his text up to the last minute.[5] After Haig introduced Barrie there was a long silence. He began to speak, but his voice was hardly audible. He fiddled with a paper-knife on the desk before him. Then out of the sea of students a voice rang: 'Put it down Jamie! You'll cut your throat!' Laughter engulfed Barrie; it was just what he needed

and launched confidently into his address. It remains as perhaps the most bizarre piece of public oratory ever declaimed to
St Andrews students. So much of it sets out ideas that Barrie
himself did not subscribe to, and holds coded clues as to his own
complex character. Yet out of it came a spark that would revive
an old tradition at the university.

In his rectorial address Barrie speculated what it would be
like to walk with some of the famous folk who had touched the
university's history.[6] He would have liked to have walked with
Dr Samuel Johnson. 'I should like to have the time of day
passed to me in twelve languages by the Admirable Crichton. A
wave of the hand to Andrew Lang; and then for the archery
butts with the gay Montrose, all a-ruffled and ringed.'[7] These
words were mused upon by two students Donald Kennedy and
James Doak, who founded the Kate Kennedy Club in 1926.
The consequence being the revival of the famous Kate Kennedy Pageant. This colourful event appears to have originated
in 1849 as an end-of-term frolic by final-year arts students. It
takes its name, tradition has it, from the supposed christian

55. Sir James Matthew Barrie (1860–1937), Rector of the University 1919–22

name of Bishop James Kennedy's niece, one Kate Kennedy, who the speculators of history further added, also gave her name to the tower bell at St Salvator's.[8] Whatever the truth at the 1849 frolic one student dressed up as 'Kate' and capered at the centre of the noisy masquerade which, in time, spilled out into the streets of St Andrews. When the frolic became more boisterous in succeeding years the professors tried to ban it and this suppression made it a symbol of undergraduate freedom. In the 1860s Kate Kennedy Pageant had become a procession through the streets and in time the students' high spirits on this day brought them into conflict with the local authorities and the whole thing was banned in 1874; this ban remained almost total until 1926.

So in 1926 Kennedy and Doak saw the revival of the procession as the nearest thing to Barrie's idea. Today over one hundred characters take part from St Andrew himself to Field-Marshal Earl Haig, and new characters are added from time to time to the pageant of late spring. Traditionally Kate Kennedy is played by a male student, and 'she' rides in a carriage with her uncle the bishop who is dressed in full canonicals. The procession comes out of the university Quad and proceeds down North Street to the castle, via The Scores. Then, by way of Market Street, the West Port and the cathedral it returns to the Quad. Traditionally too, the Kate Kennedy Club is an all male society; in 2002 there was a protest from female students that the pageant was 'sexist and elitist'. There were calls by such as the female students of the 1892 Society (women students were admitted to the university in this year) to have it banned; in this the protesters were supported by the Principal Dr Brian Lang and leaders of Fife Council. Town and gown opinion was split, supporters of the Club saying that the tradition should not be undermined by 'political correct-ness, nor by 'political posturing' by Fife Council councillors. By 2002 female students were taking part in the pageant which still survives. The stated aims of the Kate Kennedy Club are to 'preserve traditions, to raise money for charity and to foster town–gown relationships'.

Sir James Barrie dedicated his rectorial address 'To the Red

Gowns of St Andrews'. The scarlet gown is still worn by students at St Andrews and is considered a post-Reformation tradition.

Rector Andrew Carnegie (1835–1919) has been hailed as 'The Last of the Great Benefactors' to the university.[9] The

56. Andrew Carnegie (1835–1919), Rector of the University 1901–07, often dubbed 'The Last of the Great Benefactors'.

record of his rectorship reveals a number of interesting facets of university life. Carnegie was Rector during 1901–07. He was installed in October 1902 at the Volunteer Hall, St Mary's Place, the Younger Graduation Hall, North Street, not being opened until 1929. Representing the university on the platform sat Principal (later Sir) James Donaldson, the Chancellor Field-Marshal Douglas Haig, while the town was represented by Provost James Welch. Carnegie had been elected unopposed by the students who collected him and Mrs Louise Carnegie and themselves (unharnessing the horses) dragged his carriage from St Andrews railway station to the principal's house on The Scores; in the evening the 'ex-ironmaster from Pittsburgh' was entertained with student songs and a torchlight procession.

At the graduation ceremony Carnegie was to learn that the students would be boisterous having researched the 'weaknesses' of their chosen representative. One of which was 'Carnegie's hostility to dead languages'.[10] Principal Donaldson rose to administer the rectorial oath in Latin. From the body of the hall came a strident voice: 'Oh! Jamie, why don't ye tell Andra what ye're saying?' Met with gales of laughter, hearty cheers filled the hall when Carnegie replied to the principal with the Latin response *Juro* ('I swear'). As Carnegie gave his address there were constant interruptions. Carnegie took it all in good spirit; indeed it was his second draft. His first sent to Principal Donaldson had dwelt on his 'religion and philosophy' honed in his childhood Dunfermline days, his mother's Unitarian beliefs, his aunts' Swedenborgian teachings and lessons derived from Herbert Spencer, Charles Darwin and Matthew Arnold. Donaldson declared it out of step with then current thinking and vetoed the content.[11] Carnegie changed tack and talked about American influence in the world.

Carnegie was elected Rector for a second time in 1904. On this occasion a group of students, ostensibly 'bored with two successively uncontested elections', moved for Carnegie to be challenged. Classicist, alumnus Andrew Lang was asked to stand; he initially agreed but withdrew his name just before the ballot, realising that he only had the support of a rump of disaffected students.[12]

For his second rectorial address on 17 October 1905, Carnegie used the theme of peace and his address was published as peace propaganda in a Europe where war clouds were emerging. He quoted French political philosopher Jean Jacques Rousseau's (1712–78) words 'War is the foulest fiend ever vomited forth from the mouth of Hell', and exhorted the students to support a 'League of Peace'.[13] He also encouraged the 'women students of St Andrews' to raise their voices 'in stern opposition to war before it was declared'.[14] Carnegie lived to see World War I decimate student populations in Europe and saw his dreams of peace shattered.

Carnegie was a generous benefactor to the university and still today there are stories that some of his gifts were obtained by sleight of hand. The most persistent was made much of by Professor Douglas Cuthbert Colquhoun Young (1913–73) who taught classics from 1947 to 1968 at St Andrews. Young noted 'the tongue of scandal' that 'Principal Donaldson pulled a fast one' to relieve Carnegie of funding. It appears that St Leonard's College had held title to lands in the Buchanan Gardens area of the town and these lands had passed to United College in 1747 and were thus owned by the university. A new university sports park was now mooted for the land, but funding was tight. Also the property was held in trust. To get round this, money had to be found to reimburse the trust in lieu for the land if sold. A price was quoted for the land; Carnegie averred that the price was high. Donaldson explained that wealthy jute barons from Dundee were eyeing the land for private housing which put the land at a premium. Carnegie did produce the money and the university bought 'a tract of land that it already owned'.[15] Carnegie's most agreeable function while Rector happened in Philadelphia, not St Andrews. It was April 1906 and the American Philosophic Society was commemorating the second centenary of the birth of statesman and scientist Benjamin Franklin (1706–90); in 1759 Franklin had received the degree of LL.D from St Andrews. In honour of the event the *Senatus Academicus* agreed to confer an honorary degree on Franklin's great-granddaughter Agnes Irwin, Dean of Radcliff College, Harvard. Dressed in his rectorial robes Carnegie conferred the degree in Philadelphia and considered it 'one of those colourful triumphs' at which he shone.[16] Incidentally although Franklin had had his degree conferred in absentia, he visited the town late in 1759.

Education was set at the core of Carnegie's endowments from the $480 million US banker J. Pierpont Morgan had paid him for his share of the Carnegie Co. in 1901. Out of this fund, and in the same year, Carnegie founded the Carnegie Trust for the Universities of Scotland. His original endowment was $10m (equivalent to £2m in 1901) ensuring that the four Scottish universities shared approximately £100,000 per annum.[17] Out of the trust meetings came the 'established custom' of the principals of the four universities making annual visits to Carnegie's home at Skibo Castle; this he called 'Principal's Week'.[18]

Carnegie was introduced to certain student traditions during his service as Rector. In medieval times the age of entry to the university was thirteen and each student conformed to a seniority system, with the *bejaunus* being the youngest, rising to *bachelor* after third year (with *semi-bachelor* as an intermediate stage) and *magistrand* in final year. Eventually the term *bejant* applied to first years students, *semi* for second year, *tertian* (bachelor in the nineteenth century) for third year and *magistrand* for fourth.

The custom of 'Raisin Monday' probably goes back to the earliest days of the university. By tradition each *bejant* (female *bejantine*) acquires a 'Senior Man' or 'Senior Woman' from the third or fourth year to whom they can turn for assistance in their first year; these 'academic parents' introduce them to friends and into the university social circles.

During the first term (Martinmas) the honoured custom of 'Raisin Monday' is held in which *bejants* and *bejantines* present their academic parents with a pound of raisins (now usually in the form of a bottle of wine) in exchange for a ribald receipt in Latin. The whole carnival atmosphere, which expects the *bejants/bejantines* to dress up in outrageous costumes, is a unique feature of St Andrews student life. On the prescribed day students involved congregate in the Quad of St Salvator's

College and plaster each other with shaving cream. The academic year is now focused on two semesters, Martinmas (September to January) and Candlemas (February to June).

At the end of morning service at St Salvator's Chapel, on any Sunday during term, the Pier Walk takes place. It is thought that its inspiration goes back to the time when students escorted a visiting preacher to his boat in the harbour. Some historians aver that the walk by red-gowned students honours the bravery of one John Honey, a Divinity student who rescued five men from the shipwreck of the sloop *Janet* off the East Sands, on 5 January 1800.[19]

CHAPTER 12

Priests, Prelates and Presbyterians

Of priests we can offer a charmin' variety,
Far renowned for larnin' and piety.

Andrew Percival Graves (1846–1931),
Father O'Flynn

For centuries until the Reformation, St Andrews was the ecclesiastical capital of Scotland. So the most prominent group of persons in the medieval streets of the burgh was the clergy. After this time the clergy were rather fewer, and sometimes an ecclesiastical 'sight' was witnessed. In August 1773 when Dr Samuel Johnson and James Boswell were in St Andrews, Boswell observed:

It was somewhat dispiriting to see this ancient archiepiscopal city now sadly deserted. We saw in one of its streets a remarkable proof of liberal toleration: a nonjuring clergyman [i.e. Episcopalian] strutting about in his canonicals with a jolly countenance and a round belly, like a well-fed monk.[1]

As well as the cathedral, the Church of St Mary of the Rock and the hospital and college chapels, there were other medieval churches and two further important religious houses in St Andrews, namely the foundations of the Dominicans (Blackfriars) and the Franciscans (Greyfriars).

Friars

The Order of St Dominic of Friars Preachers was founded at Toulouse in 1215 by St Dominic (1170–1221) of Caleryega who was anxious to promote the skilful defence of the Catholic faith against heresy and the better instruction of the people in the

Greyfriar (Franciscan)   *Blackfriar (Dominican)*

57. The Greyfriars (Franciscans) and the Blackfriars (Dominicans) had important houses in medieval St Andrews [Sankey, Hudson & Co.]

principles of the Catholic faith and piety. The background of the Dominicans was an order founded on traditional monastic lines living a contemplative life linked with an emphasis on the study of theology, but free from priestly or pastoral work and with a mobility to become itinerant preachers. As teachers, the Dominicans first introduced a systematic course of education in Scotland. They took a vow of poverty and were therefore a mendicant order. They received their name of Blackfriars from their distinctive garb of white robe, scapular and cowl, and black open mantle with a cowl. The Blackfriars are recorded in the *Chronica de Mailros* as having come to Scotland in 1230, a fact confirmed by the *Scotichronicon* which says that they were encouraged to do so by Alexander II. It is Archbishop Spottiswoode who says that they were brought to Scotland by Bishop William de Malvoisine of St Andrews, led by Friar Clement, and a house was founded for them in what was to become South Street, in 1274, by Bishop William Wishart. The actual date of the foundation is confused and is a matter of historical controversy, but the house did survive and was restored in 1516 by a legacy from Bishop Elphinstone's estate and in 1519 the Dominican priories of St Katherine at Cupar and St Monan at St Monans, and the Hospital of St Nicholas were all united with the St Andrews house. It is known too, that over the period 1464–1516, Blackfriars was not only restored in fabric but as a place for study of sacred literature; and Dominican scholars were funded within the university. Up to 1481 when their own province was founded, the St Andrews Blackfriars were ruled by the English province chapter of the visitation of York, whose local representative called every four years. In 1547 Blackfriars was burned by Norman Lesley and destroyed by the Reformers in 1559 when John Knox preached in the burgh; and in 1567 Mary Stuart granted the properties of the Blackfriars to the provost, magistrates and council and community of St Andrews.[2]

Today all that remains of the house of the Blackfriars, dedicated to the Assumption and Coronation of the Blessed Virgin Mary, is the c.1525 three-sided north transept of their chapel; the boss in the vaulted roof bears the Emblems of the Passion of Christ and the fragment of building remains the only example of its type in Scotland. The conventual buildings lay under the present site of Madras School, and it is known that some of the medieval buildings were incorporated in Dr Young's school of 1622, demolished in 1833. The western part of the friary known as the 'Old Palace' was used as a dwelling until the early nineteenth century, and the remaining medieval religious site was handed over to the Board of Works in 1911. The house of the St Andrews Blackfriars was some 25 feet wide (with length unknown) and probably had a square, spireless tower with cloister to the south with a central well; a garden

58. Relic north transept of the House of the Blackfriars, South Street. The
architecture dates from around 1525.

probably ran down in tofts to the Lade Braes. Possibly there was a prior's house with outbuildings as well as a chapter house, sacristy and frater abutting the cloisters. Of the tombs within the chapel it is probable that all of the priors were buried in the aisle, and Sir James Balfour averred that Cardinal David Beaton was buried in Blackfriars in 1547. The Blackfriars cemetery was to the north side of the remaining transept and is now under South Street.

When the mendicant Order of Friars (Franciscans), founded by St Francis of Assisi (around 1181–1226), came to Scotland is a matter of dispute, but King James IV declared that his grandmother, Mary of Guelders, had introduced the Observant Friars of St Francis in the mid-fifteenth century. Whatever the truth we know that the Franciscans were founded in their house at the corner of modern Greyfriars Gardens and Market Street by Bishop James Kennedy in 1458, with a grant for a large house being gifted later by St Andrews' first Archbishop, Patrick Graham, in 1478. These grants were confirmed by the charter of James IV in 1479. The St Andrews house of the Observant Franciscans was colonised by Greyfriars from Edinburgh.[3]

The extent of the property of the Greyfriars, the name by which the Franciscans were best known in St Andrews, may be set out by a line drawn from Woolworths, Market Street, to the site of the Northgait (opposite numbers 144–6 North Street), with a parallel line from the site of the Marketgait to Murray Place car park. A fragment of the eastern wall of the friary runs behind modern Greyfriars Garden, and a fine arched gateway was removed from the North Street entry to the friary in the eighteenth century. The 48-foot-deep friary well is in the garden of 4 Greyfriars Garden, the site being where the friary cloister was located; the well was rediscovered in 1839 and cleaned out in 1886 when the parapet and iron guard was fitted. The chapel of the friars was on the garden site of Greyfriars Garden with the high altar location under the foundations of the modern Woolworths building.

Greyfriars cemetery was discovered when work was being done on the nearby houses in 1904, and it was found to contain

St Andrews burghers and their families buried in the chapel. The simple and unpretentious house of the Greyfriars was burned by Norman Leslie in 1547 and made over by its last Warden (Prior), Symon Maltman, to the St Andrews magistrates in May 1559, to be destroyed by the Reformers in June of the same year, but remained the property of the magistrates until the grounds were confirmed as being the property of the burgh by Mary Stuart in 1567.[4] The two dozen or so Greyfriars at St Andrews acted as confessors to the students of St Salvator's College and influenced the spiritual life of the university within their role as evangelists rather than academics. Bound by vows of poverty, obedience and charity, the St Andrews Greyfriars went forth from the burgh to 'promote and fortify the Catholic faith, to strengthen the Christian religion and to sow the word of God more abundantly in the hearts of the faithful' in the major towns of Scotland. One of the most prominent of the St Andrews Greyfriars was Friar Robert Keith, a distinguished theologian who was the house's first warden.

Other Churches

Two other now-vanished medieval churches were to be found in St Andrews. One 'St Peter's Overlooking the Sea', was situated at the junction of Gregory Lane and the East Scores; stones from the church were found in 1887 and 1927. Another church, the Chapel of the Holy Trinity, the Virgin and St Duthac, sited opposite St Leonard's Lane, was possibly founded by James III in 1487; but the building had gone by 1538. St Duthac of Tain (d.1065) was the Bishop of Ross, venerated for his miracles and prophesies and had quite a following in the East Coast villages of Fife.

Two venerable parishes are associated with modern St Andrews and its environs, the seaboard parish of St Andrews itself, taking in the old town, and the parish of St Leonards which was once made of four detached parts mostly surrounded by the parish of St Andrews. By an Order of the Boundary Commissioners of 1890 the two parishes were reconstituted in part, but the old St Leonards parish had its origins with the

Hospital of St Leonard and the College of poor Clerks of the Church of St Andrews (St Leonard's College). Within these parishes certain town churches were established.

The Scottish Episcopal Church has a strong showing in St Andrews within a sea of Presbyterianism. A province of the Anglican Communion, the Scottish Episcopal Church had survived the vicissitudes of the alternating religious climates from the Reformation to the seventeenth century, and was disestablished after the unfortunate audience between William Ross, Bishop of Edinburgh, and William III in 1688, when the bishop was considered to have snubbed the monarch. An Act of Parliament of 1689 established a Presbyterian Church of Scotland. There followed a period in which Episcopalians were harried, persecuted, impoverished and held in scorn. Although they were evicted from the establishment, many of the Episcopalian clergy and congregation took courage from the Act of Toleration of 1712. If they were prepared to accept the House of Hanover they were given freedom to worship, but many Episcopalians were Jacobites and brought their church into bad odour because of their support of James Francis Edward Stuart (the only son of James VII and II and Mary of Modena, considered King James VIII and III by the Jacobites) in 1715 and 1745. The St Andrews Episcopalians had a perfectly legitimate 'meeting place' in a house on the south side of South Street.[5] yet, after the Jacobite army's defeat at Culloden in 1746, local tradition has it that their altar table and furnishings were dragged out into South Street and burned. Nevertheless the St Andrean Episcopalians survived in secret and records of their activities are extant; some of these were found at the beginning of the nineteenth century in a tobacconist's shop, where portions of the document pages had been used to wrap snuff. The documents showed that the Episcopalians were active in St Andrews during 1722–87.

The first modern Episcopal Church in St Andrews was sited in North Street; its foundation stone was laid on 27 August 1824 and its site abutted the modern university College Gate of 1953. Consecrated in 1825, and dedicated to St Andrew, the church survived until 1870 when it was shipped stone by stone aboard the *Sea King* to Buckhaven having been bought by the Free Church of Scotland for £130.

The Episcopal congregation was soon to have a new church, St Andrews, Queen's Terrace. Its foundation stone was laid on 31 July 1867, with full masonic honours and the church was built to the plans of Sir Robert Rowland Anderson; dedicated in 1869, the church was consecrated in 1877. The tower of the church was erected in 1892, but demolished as unsafe in 1938. A church hall was added to the west end in 1938.

By 1895 this 600-seat church was proving too small for the burgeoning congregation which included many 'poor fisher-folk' who could not afford the 'pew rents'. So, in 1903 a temporary iron mission church was established for the fisherfolk in North Castle Street; soon the seventeenth-century neighbouring Castle Wynd House was purchased for the Priest-in-Charge. It came with its resident ghost, the 'Brown Lady', and is now rented as student accommodation. In 1907 the dedication stone was laid for a stone chancel and by 1909 a bell tower was added to the church now dedicated to All Saints'. Locally it was known as the 'bundle kirk' because of the parcels handed out to the needy. After World War I moves were set in motion by Mrs Annie Younger, the wife of Dr James Younger of Mount Melville, to complete the church in stone and additional land was acquired around the site; the fisherfolk who lived in houses on this land were rehoused in Saint Gregory's building, Gregory Lane, set on the site of an old foundry. The church now acquired a nave, chapel and baptistry with subsidiary buildings, and a rectory was completed in 1939. Mrs Younger's provisions for the church were lavish from vestments to font, and all buildings and endowments were in memory of her daughter and son-in-law. The old Guide Hall and its gymnasium above were converted into a bookshop and tearoom taking the title of the old fisher quarter of Ladyhead. The courtyard of the church is particularly fine, dominated by the crucifix of the war memorial constructed of Forest of Dean stone; this memorial was unveiled by Field-Marshal Earl Haig of Bemersyde in 1924. Inside the church is a fine carving of the Madonna and Child by Hew Lorimer which was set to the south of the nave as a memorial to Mrs Younger who died in 1942. Another memorial also catches the visitor's eye; the ship model hanging in the north-west part of the nave was presented in memory of the novelist Hugh Walpole (1884–1941) by his sister Dr Dorothea Walpole in 1954. The Chapel of the Blessed Sacrament, with its dark green panelling of marble and alabaster altar, is moving and memorable.[6]

The congregation of Hope Park Church, City Road, had its roots in 1733 as a consequence of the Great Secession, itself the forerunner of the Disruption of 1843 which splintered the Presbyterian Church. These events were concerned with the preservation of freedom to worshop God without dictation or financial support of an 'establishment', and spoke of the fierce independence of the Presbyterians who in 1559 split from the Church of Rome. The forefathers of Hope Park Church began worship at a prayer meeting at Balone Den, near St Andrews, in 1738 and this emergent congregation first made up the Associate Congregation 1738–47 to become the 'Burgher Kirk' in St Andrews. One of their early meeting places during 1749–74 was the pantiled house, a former barn, at Imrie's Close, 136 South Street; next they moved to Burgher's Close, 141 South Street, where they worshipped until 1827 when they moved to a chapel on the site of what is now 52 North Street as the United Presbyterian Church. By now the Associate Congregation had passed through the phase of being the general association of 1747–1820 when the 'Burghers' and 'Anti-Burghers' united to form the United Secession Congregation. These were the days when to be seen inebriated in public drew a personal denunciation from the pulpit and perceived moral turpitude a public reprimand. The United Presbyterian Congregation was formed in 1847 when the United Secession and the Relief Churches united. By 1865 the United Presbyterian congregation had moved to Hope Park Church and by 1929 the United Free Church congregation was formed out of the United Presbyterian and Free Church congregations. Thereafter Hope Park reverted to the Church of Scotland. The present church was built in 1864 and the church hall was opened in 1900.[7]

Martyrs' Church was born out of the Disruption of 1843. It

was formed out of an Association in connection with the Free Church, and one of the founding members was Sir David Brewster, Principal of the United Colleges of the university 1838–59 himself a staunch supporter of the Free Church movement. At first regular services began in the Secession Church (now Hope Park), but the first church for the congregation was opened in November 1843 on the site of the present church in North Street. A spire and new frontage were added in 1851 and the first manse was built in Kennedy Gardens during 1856–57 (a new manse was built in Irvine Crescent in 1967). In 1883 it was decided to introduce hymns as well as the psalms for the services and this engendered much protest particularly from the local historian Dr David Hay Fleming. He 'denounced the innovation' from his pew on the day of their introduction. Hay Fleming carried his protest 'by standing at the prayers and sitting at the singing of the psalms'; his protests were intensified at the introduction of instrumental music (which preceded the purchase of an organ in the early 1900s). The church was renovated in 1887.

At the union of the Free and United Presbyterian Churches in 1900, the church took its name from Martyrs' United Free Church and by 1914 there was a movement to build a new church. The plans were thwarted by World War I, but in 1925 the scheme was revived. The church of 1843–44 was demolished in 1925 and the present church was opened in 1928, funded largely by the bequest of Henry Maitland of Balmungo. With the reunion of the United Free and the Church of Scotland in 1929, Martyrs' became the latter's charge.[8] A church hall was added in 1933–34 and today the church contains a set of fine stained glass memorial windows dating from the Forgan Window of 1929.[9]

From time to time town and gown have been at loggerheads and one celebrated occasion was when the *Fife News Almanac* of 1905 highlighted the 'St Leonard's Church Case'. This, according to the press, 'became notorious over the land'. The case arose from these historical circumstances; during 1903–04 the university authorities reclaimed the chapel of St Salvator's College for their own use. Now since 1759 the congregation of the dilapidated chapel of St Leonard's had been worshipping at St Salvator's alongside the students; they were now thus dispossessed. Until the ousted congregation acquired their new church at Rathelpie (in modern Donaldson Gardens) 'there was protracted litigation', said the papers of the day.

The new St Leonard's Parish Church was dedicated and ready for worship on 28 July 1904. The church of Nydie quarry stone cost £5000 and was designed by architect Peter Macgregor Chalmers in mock-Norman style. The university as land heritors continued to be obstructive and a new manse was not ready for occupation until 1907; a church hall was completed in 1938; reconstruction of the site took place in 1966 and 2002. Symbolism that would have been recognisable to medieval St Andreans is seen in St Leonard's Church stained glass, from ' St Margaret of Scotland' (1949) to the 'Transfiguration' (1954), and from 'St Leonard Liberating the Prisoners' (1943) to the 'Crucifixion and Emmaus Story' (1926).[10]

At the Reformation a goodly part of the clergy of the medieval Church in St Andrews espoused the new faith, and the Church of Rome disappeared from Scotland. During the ensuing centuries the only Roman Catholic clergy to appear in Fife would be a few travellers and scholars and hardly any Roman worship took place in St Andrews until after Pope Leo XIII (1810–1903) restored the Scottish Roman Catholic Hierarchy in 1878, although there were Roman Catholics identified in St Andrews by 1849 when the burgh was placed in the Cupar Mission. There seems to have been regular monthly masses in St Andrews from around 1881, but there was no resident priest.

A scheme to build a Roman Catholic Church in St Andrews was backed by the Tory lawyer James Robert Hope-Scott before his death in 1873 and it was on his land on The Scores that a Catholic Mission was planned and a temporary iron church was erected funded by the Marquess of Bute. The first priest, who was to become a St Andrews ecclesiastical personality, was Father George Angus (1842–1909), an Anglican turned Roman Catholic who first came to St Andrews during September 1884 and was housed at 22 Queen Street (now Queens Gardens – his house was on the site of a portion of

St Regulus Hall); until the iron church was ready Father Angus conducted services in his home.

The iron church, known in the community as the 'Tin Tabernacle', was opened in 1885 and was dedicated to St James, Apostle and Martyr and cousin of Our Lord. A stone presbytery for the priest was ready by 1886, next to the iron church. Curiously enough the excellence of Father Angus' extempore sermons brought a large non-Catholic congregation to his Sunday evening services, but all of his early Roman Catholic congregation were Irish.

Despite his popularity in certain quarters Father Angus had to endure hostility from some local Presbyterians nervous of anything Popish taking root in their burgh. Presbyterian rowdies demonstrated under his windows and the postmaster of the day objected to the use of 'Presbytery' in the address, proclaiming to all who would listen to his bigotry that the title belonged to the local Presbyterian clergy alone. One occurrence is noted: that the Roman Catholic Church was broken into and altar vessels thrown into the sea. Even so, Father Angus was received as a friend at the tables of such local clergy as Dr A.K.H. Boyd of Holy Trinity and the Baptist Minister and in due time the priest was made a member of the Royal & Ancient Golf Club.

In 1908 the St Andrews Roman Catholic Mission became a properly constituted parish taking in the area from the River Eden to Earlsferry and during 1909–10 the iron church was replaced by a stone edifice designed by the architect Reginald Fairlie funded by Mrs Annette Harmer of Canmore, The Scores. Her house was purchased in 1947 by the White Fathers as a study centre for their order; today it is the Roman Catholic chaplaincy of the university.

The present building of the Baptist Church, South Street, adjoining Rose Lane, was refronted 1901–02, but the original foundation of the congregation goes back to 1841–43. In those days the people who were to form the Baptist congregation worshipped at the Independent Church, which became the Congregational Church, itself established in Bell Street in 1856. The original Baptists formed a congregation in 1841 with their first meetings in the Old Town Hall; a Baptist Sunday School was established in 1844. A Christian Institute was functioning 1907–53 on the site of the old Post Office of 1892 in South Street, the present location of the Citizen Bookshop annexe. The Religious Society of Friends (Quakers) began regular worship in St Andrews in 1964 meeting at various sites. The Salvation Army began its work in the town in 1893, but closed down in 1904 to carry on once more in 1910–17. The work of the Army did not commence again until 1934. The Army had premises in Gregory Place, at the original fisher school of 1847, but moved to North Street; these premises were sold in the early 2000s.

The 'Town Kirk'

The most historical and ecclesiastically important parish church in St Andrews is Holy Trinity, South Street, colloquially dubbed 'the Town Kirk'. Dedicated to the Holy Trinity, a parish church of around 1144 stood at Kilrymont just to the south of the east gable of the cathedral, probably founded by Bishop Robert who had granted it to the Priory as a vicarage in 1165. The church received its formal dedication in 1234 by Bishop David de Bernham and was frequently utilised as a meeting place for the bishop's judiciary court and for some early university meetings. Probably stone from this old parish church was used by Prior Hepburn in the building of his precinct walls. The twelfth-century church was removed to the present site of Holy Trinity in 1410–12. Drastically altered in 1798–1800, the church we see today dates from the last reconstruction of 1907–09.

Those who wished the burgh to have its own parish church, within the town and away from the everyday influence of the cathedral chapter, were encouraged in their efforts by Bishop Henry Wardlaw; the folk were greatly assisted too, by Prior James Bissett, who had built the parish church of Cupar in 1415. The first vicar of the new parish church was William Bower, a canon of the Priory, who probably established the first manse for Holy Trinity in east North Street around 1434; the manse was demolished in 1882. The site of the new parish

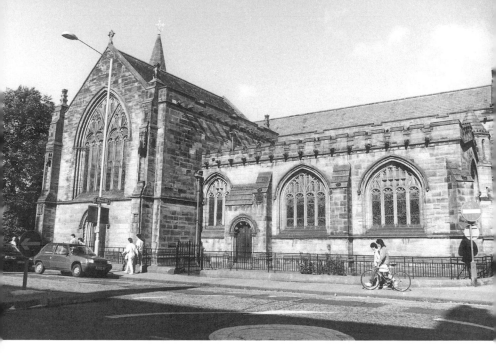

59. Holy Trinity Church, South Street, the 'Town Kirk'. Set on its present site 1410–12, the church was altered 1798–1800 and reconstructed 1907–09.

church was on the lands of Sir William Lindsay, Lord of Byres, and Bishop Wardlaw gifted a neighbouring rig in 1430 to enlarge the cemetery which then took in most of the modern roadway in South Street beside the church and today's Church Square; in this graveyard was interred in 1574, John Douglas, the first Protestant Archbishop of St Andrews and erstwhile Principal of St Mary's College. The only surviving portions of the medieval building are parts of the west wall, some of the internal nave pillars and tower; the latter was often used as the town jail. The tower contains a change of seventeen bells, a memorial to Dr Patrick Macdonald Playfair (d.1924), minister of the First Charge of St Andrews and chief promoter of the restoration of Holy Trinity. The city curfew is still rung from the tower every week evening at 8 p.m.

The bishop of the diocese was the superior of medieval Holy Trinity, and the rector of the church was the Prior of St Andrews who dealt with the church's financial and legal affairs; the vicar saw to the everyday running of the church assisted by a curate, both overseeing the duties of the master of works, who tended the fabric, while the parish clerk was the link man between the burgh and the clergy. In medieval times the parish clerk would be in holy orders and he sang the mass, and cared for the church security and bells, and directed the secular clergy (sacristan, beadle) who rang the bells, attended to the church's more domestic arrangements and acted as doorkeeper.

Some 30 priests served the church, with its 33 altars, and 12 of their number acted as choristers, all under a procurator or hebdomador (second only to the vicar) for their order and discipline and to maintain the canonical services basically which, with some grouping, followed those of the cathedral. It was usual for the civic bodies of the town to maintain the altars within the parish church, while some were founded by individuals for the good of their immortal souls. When the church was built, the Holy Trinity Altar, for instance, was erected by the burghers in honour of Sir William Lindsay who endowed the South Street site, and the city magistrates and council were the patrons of the altar of St Andrew. The devotion to the Holy Trinity, from the prayer *Gloria Patri, et Filio, et Spiritu Sancto* (Glory be to the Father, and to the Son, and to the Holy Ghost), was strong in medieval St Andrews and the First Day of the Holy Trinity (the Sunday after Whitsunday), which had been established as a feast by St Thomas Becket the Martyr of Canterbury in 1162, was one of pious devotion in the burgh calendar. The Altar of St Aubert, Bishop of Cambrai, was founded and maintained by the town's Bakers' Craft, or Guild, while the Altar of St Eloy of Limoges was maintained by the town's Hammermen.[11]

The church sports many interesting windows and artefacts from the West Window (a gift of the Women of the Congregation, 1914), the memorial font to Dr A.K.H. Boyd, minister of the First Charge 1865–99, the Playfair (family) Aisle, the onyx, alabaster and Iona marble pulpit and the John Knox Porch commemorating the Reformer. It was in Holy Trinity that Knox preached his inflammatory sermon on 11 June 1559 (on Our Lord's ejection of the buyer and sellers from the Temple) which incited the mob to follow the stage-managing of the rapacious Protestant lords to unspeakable vandalism against the treasures and culture of the Medieval Church.

The Sharp Aisle contains the white and black marble tomb and monument remembering another famous murder with which St Andrews is connected. James Sharp (1618–79), Archbishop of St Andrews, was a Royalist who went to England when the Covenanters abolished episcopal government in 1638. He came back in 1643, taught for a while at St Andrews University and became the minister of Crail in 1649. In due time his skill as a negotiator won him high praise and he was appointed Professor of Theology at St Andrews; as leader of the 'moderate party' he was chosen as Archbishop of St Andrews and consecrated in 1661. To those of the fanatical Covenanting persuasion Sharp was now a turncoat and a 'government man' willing to agree to anything to secure his position; anathema to the Covenanters was Sharp's apparent willingness to accept the Act of Supremacy of 1669 which gave the monarch complete authority in the church. An attempt was made on Sharp's life in 1668, but his enemies finally succeeded in his murder at Magus Muir, where he was dragged from his coach and stabbed to death on 3 May 1679.[12] The monument to Sharp in Holy Trinity is of Dutch work and was erected in 1681 by Sir William Sharp of Scotscraig, the son of the slain archbishop. At Sharp's funeral on 16 May 1679, the sermon was preached by John Paterson, Bishop of Edinburgh, and Andrew Bruce, Bishop of Dunkeld, composed a Latin epitaph. The inscription details Sharp's qualities and recounts how:

> nine sworn assassins, inspired by fanatical rage, did with pistols, swords and daggers most foully massacre [Sharp] with his beloved daughter and his personal attendants bleeding, weeping and protesting . . . when he had fallen on his knees to pray even for his murderers.[13]

When Sharp's tomb was opened in 1848 it was found to be empty of bones or relics. On the sarcophagus is a marble figure of the kneeling archbishop, and from a white marble cloud an angel holds out a martyr's crown. Behind the archbishop's head are the gold-painted words PRO MITRA, PRO MITRA CORONAM. A plaque below depicts the archbishop's martyrdom.

60. Popular Victorian etching of the murder of Archbishop
James Sharp on Magus Muir on 3 May 1679

61. Tomb of Archbishop Sharp in
Holy Trinity Church

CHAPTER 13

Tinderest Teachers: Local Education

Good Dick, a teacher much respected,
Boys from all quarters had collected,
And by the powerful aid of tawse *leather strap*
Enforced his pedagogic laws.

Doggerel by Professor Andrew Duncan (1744–1828)
on Richard Dick Master of St Andrews Grammar School

For almost a thousand years St Andrews has promoted schools of various kinds, from groups in cloistered college walls to dame schools where teachers knew little more than their oldest pupils. Some, too, added a certain fashionable eccentricity. In the late eighteenth century a popular dancing school was founded in St Andrews. Here two future Lord Chancellors, John, Baron Campbell (1779–1861), and Thomas, Baron Erskine (1750–1823) as students were 'initiated into the rhythmic gyrations of the Shantrews, the single and the double hornpipe'. All to the great disapproval of the university authorities.[1]

Early Schools

Education, albeit with the sole intent of sifting out likely recruits for the church, was first developed in the town by the priors of St Andrews, within their cloistered setting. All this came to an end at the Reformation and a Latin grammar school developed in the town out of the turmoils of the religious upheavals. The Latin Grammar School, which was probably developed from around 1570, was set on ground between the then ruined site of Blackfriars, South Street, and Lade Braes Lane. The grammar school served the town until another public school was founded around 1755 on the site of the public library; this was the English School where no Latin was taught, but pupils were grounded in reading, writing and arithmetic. The English school was built largely at the expense of George Dempster of Dunichen, Provost 1760–76. These two schools were to form the basis of a new educational foundation.

Opened in 1833, 'The Madras College' was founded on the 'Madras', or 'Monitorial', system of education invented by the Rev. Dr Andrew Bell (1753–1832), Prebendary of Westminster Abbey, and Master of Sherburn Hospital. A native of St Andrews – he was born in a house which stood on the site of 107 South Street where the modern Citizen Bookshop is located. The son of a St Andrews barber-wigmaker, Bell was educated at the Latin Grammar School and entered United College in 1769. After graduating he was employed as a tutor in Virginia, USA, and was ordained as a clerk in holy orders in the Church of England. In due course he embarked for India and became superintendent of the Madras Military Orphanage Asylum, India, a foundation for the care and education of the orphans and Eurasian offspring of deceased British soldiers. Gradually Dr Bell evolved his Madras monitorial system of education in which youthful members taught younger children. He returned to Britain in 1796 to become more involved in parish duties as a clergyman and as Master of Sherburn Hospital.

Long before the Madras College was opened, Andrew Bell had started to work on the idea of opening a school in St Andrews where both poor and privileged children could be educated in one place. Eventually plans were agreed upon and the Jacobean-frontaged school was begun with the foundation stone being laid on 9 April 1832. Bell was not to live to see the opening of his school of Strathkinness stone built to William Burn's design as it rose to blend with Blackfriars ruins, but the incomplete school was opened 1 October 1833 to teach pupils at a full fee of 3s (15p) a quarter, with other pupils receiving free education. The first intake formed the pupils of the English School and probably others from the private schools in the town. Children were to come from all over the UK to be taught at Madras, and they lodged with the masters or with people in the town. By 1834 the pupils of the old Latin Grammar School

62. Madras College opened in 1833 as the inspiration of the Rev. Dr Andrew Bell (1753–1832). The foundation stone of the Jacobean-frontaged school was laid on 9 April 1832.

moved into Madras, and although it was a co-educational school from the first in spirit, few girls attended in the early years; a Lady Superintendent was not appointed until 1864, then girls appeared in greater numbers. New buildings for Madras College, Kilrymont Road, were occupied by Madras pupils in 1967, and were officially opened in 1968.

The school's early records throw up interesting facts. The appeerence of the school, for instance, the largest public building to be erected in St Andrews since 1559, did not please everyone. After his visit to St Andrews in 1844, the lawyer diarist and Lord of Session Henry Thomas Cockburn (1779–1854), wrote: 'The thing called Madras College is at present a great blot. There should have been no commonplace, vulgar, bare-legged school there.'[2] Early facilities at the school were spartan; privies were not added to the school until two years after it opened and it seems that Madras College always had a reputation of being cold despite ducted-air heating; one Rector 'Put on two sets of woollen underwear in October and kept them on till April'. Classes could begin as early as 6 a.m., and pupils were forbidden to bring firearms to school in 1836, and in the early days parents paid separate fees for each class, selecting the classes that their children should attend. The school was a prominent landowner in the town, purchasing the farms of Priorletham, Waterless and Pipelands in 1846 and Cairns in 1856; in this spirit Dr Edward Woodford, the classics master, kept a pig in the tiny yard behind his lodgings at Madras House East; eventually the school Trustees brought his pig-keeping to an end.[3]

Madras College former pupils included Professor William McIntosh, who endowed the university's McIntosh Hall and historian Dr David Hay Fleming. Two men were to carry on Dr Woodford's eccentricity. One was the colourful soldier-cum-writer Robert Marshall, who wrote the golf classic *The Haunted Major*, and the other was Martin Anderson (d.1932); Anderson was the artist who under the pseudonym of 'Cynicus' was celebrated for his satirical cartoons – he built his red-sandstone folly castle (demolished in 1939) at Balmullo in 1903.

Writing in 1838, Dr James Grierson reported on the desirability of the then extant infants' school:

So soon as the child can speak or walk, he may be subjected to a course of kind and interesting training under the management of an experienced lady in an infant school. Here exercise, music and elementary learning are beautifully mixed and alternated, that the infant of four or five years of age is far happier than if set free from all instruction and management whatever. All this may be obtained by every parent for a mere trifle. The infant school forms a proper nursery school for Madras College. There English reading and spelling are admirably taught so low as one shilling [5p] a quarter, whilst writing may be added for only three pence [1½p] per quarter more.

Grierson was writing of the infants' school, called Dr Bell's Infants' School, sited behind the town church 1832–44. In 1844, at the cost of £800 the West Infants School was built in

St Mary's Place and was hailed as 'a masterpiece of modern education'. Today the building is no longer used as a school but houses the town's registrar's office and other local government departments. After the 1890 Education Act a board school was established in Abbey Walk and continued as a part of 'comprehensive' education with Madras as a junior high school until 1967.

The Education Acts

Education in St Andrews was greatly reorganised by the passing of the Education (Scotland) Act, 1872, by which every parish and burgh had its elected school board for the direction of education for children 'who might otherwise have grown up in ignorance and been nurtured in vice'. One of the immediate tasks of the school boards was to 'regularise' the school system, build extra schools and enforce attendance as far as was possible. To pay for all this parish education there was a charge of around three pence [1½p] a week, but after the Education Act of 1890 elementary education was virtually 'free' in that it came out of a local rate levied for education.

Up to the 1872 Act the schools in St Andrews were a mixture of private schools of various kinds including 'adventure' schools, so called because they were a financial 'adventure'; the schools were run by many who had only a smattering of education themselves. It was not unusual for tradesmen, from cobblers to public-house keepers, to run a school from their establishments. For young ladies and gentlemen of the middle class and the gentry there were private schools run by many an untrained 'Dame' or 'Gentleman of Letters'. A glance at a national directory of 1873 shows the list of schools in St Andrews to include that of the Misses Moir for young ladies at 4 Alexandra Park, Thomas Hodges at West View, Annie Morton, 42 North Street and the Rev. Jack George of Seaton House. Miss Murray ran a school on the site of the Tudor Inn and several of the children of the poor received instruction at the hospital at South Lodge.

Some of the private schools were of the highest probity. Such included Dr Fogo's Boys' School, Edgecliff, The Scores, which flourished from 1889 to 1906; and Kilrule Private School for Girls at 140 Market Street, which was in existence until 1900; Dr Cleghorn's Academy was sited at 5 Alexandra Place and Dr John Browning's boarding school was at St Leonard's House. All the town's private schools prepared boys for the university, the armed forces and the Indian Civil Service as well as boarding boys and girls whose families worked abroad.

The first small private school of any note was started in St Andrews by Dr J. Smeaton (d.1871), who had come to the burgh in the 1840s and was a teacher at Madras. He commenced his school in Market Street and purchased Abbey Park around 1869. In 1889 the Abbey Park Institution for Young Gentlemen was transferred to Leask, and the site was taken over by St Leonards School.

Clifton Bank School was founded around 1860 by John Paterson, another master from Madras, and this was taken over by Messrs Macmillan and Lawson in 1892, and then by Walter G. Mair, also a former teacher at Madras in 1904. Clifton Bank, set on The Scores, survived until 1917 when its building was taken over by St Katherine's junior school. Perhaps the school's most famous former pupil was Field-Marshal the Earl Haig of Bemersyde, the commander-in-chief of World War I.

St Salvator's School at 2 The Scores, on the site of the present Scores Hotel, was founded in 1881 by one Gerald Blunt, who remained its headmaster until 1903. Two supporters of Blunt's enterprise were Professor William Knight, Professor of Moral Philosophy and Political Economy, and Emeritus Professor Lewis Campbell, Professor of Greek, through whose influence the school's name was allowed by the university authorities. In 1903 the school was purchased by Alfred George Le Maitre (1866–1943), who developed it into a prominent preparatory school for boarders and day boys. The school was classics orientated with no science being taught at all, and the maximum number of boys at any one time was fifty, who were prepared for such public schools as Fettes, Edinburgh, and Sedbergh, Cumbria, and for the Royal Navy; in those days entry for the latter was at 12½ years old. The school did not have its own playing fields but rented ground, then known as Mount Pleasant, from the Strathtyrum Estates, which was located where the Madras playing fields are today. The school hospice was at 9 Golf Place (once Kirk's Place). Alfred Le Maitre sold the school in 1931 to Mrs King who developed it into a hotel. The school trophies and cups were purchased by Lathallan School who absorbed the pupils then being educated at the time of the sale.

The Fisher School, known also as the 'East Infants' (1856), was supported by the burgh's community of mariners, fish-curers, pilots and fishermen for the education of their own children. The school took pupils in the age range 4–14, but not all of them were of fisher stock; in the 1850s there were complaints in the burgh that town children were filling places that should have gone to fisherfolk children. The school opened in the evenings for sewing, reading, writing and arithmetic as many of the children worked during the day baiting the fishing boat lines.

St Andrews was long in the forefront of the development of education for women. Here in 1862 Elizabeth Garret Anderson (1836–1917) obtained the support which was to lead her to become the first English woman to enter the medical profession, and in the 1860s there evolved the idea to found a public school for girls in the burgh. Who had the idea first is hard to say, but certainly it was mooted in the social circle in which the widow and daughters of Dr Cook, Professor of Hebrew, were wont to circulate. In 1868 Miss Harriet Cook was present at an occasion in Miss Elizabeth Garrett's house in London when the possibility of forming a women's college at Cambridge was discussed; this was eventually to develop into Girton College (1869), Cambridge, and two of its students, Rachel Cook and Louisa Innes Lumsden, were to be involved in the school for girls that was to be founded in St Andrews. The fact that these women passed the Classical Tripos at Cambridge, as the first women to do so, caused a stir in St Andrews, and this and the fact that Miss Cowan's school for girls in Queen Street (today's Queen's Gardens) was to close, gave the promotion of a new school for girls in St Andrews a great boost.

Practical plans for a girls' school at St Andrews were formulated at Kirnan, the home of Lewis Campbell, Professor of Greek. Leading lights were Mrs Lewis Campbell and Mrs Matthew Rodger, the wife of the minister of St Leonards parish, and the members of the Ladies Education Association. Approaches were made to Miss Lumsden and her friend Miss Constance Maynard, also of Girton and later Principal of Westfield College, to assist in the setting up of the school and on 5 January 1877 a Council was formed for the St Andrews School for Girls Company. So on 2 October 1877, in the building which now houses St Regulus university residence in Queen's Gardens, the school was established with Miss Louisa Lumsden as the first headmistress. The school was funded by shares taken up by individuals and income from school fees and a total of fifty girls enrolled in 1877 of whom ten were boarders. The school offered a high standard of academic subjects and provided a gymnasium and playground which was unheard of in Victorian Scotland, and it was regarded askance by the residence of Queen Street. Gymnastic lessons, known in Scotland as 'physical drill', did not appear in the Scottish Day School Code until 1895. In 1927 now Dame Louisa Lumsden summed up the spirit of the emergent school:

Truth was its inspiration, truth in thought and deed and word. Intellectual work was to be thorough, not slight or shallow, but honest, which of course means hard. Play was to have its fitting place, it was not to be frivolous but in its way as honest as work. The girls were to learn to govern themselves, to be worthy of trust and to be trusted, and the older and leading girls were to be responsible for a share in government.[4]

Louisa Lumsden resigned as headmistress in 1878 but remains the most prominent 'personality' in the school's history. She was to continue to be a leading figure in St Andrews too; from 1895 to 1900 she was warden of University Hall and in 1925 she was created DBE; one commentator writing in the press about her state honour described her as 'of the race of those great adventurers and pioneers who have made the British Empire what it is'. Dame Louisa died in 1935, aged 95, but remains significant as a 'character' in the annual Kate Kennedy procession.

The school remained in Queen Street until 1882 when it moved into the house and grounds of the old Playfair residence of St Leonards, Pends Road, from which it drew its new name. Today the school, known as St Leonards School and Sixth Form College, has properties covering some thirty acres of parkland roughly bounded by Pends Road and Kinnessburn, although some of its southern acres were sold in the late 1980s for development as Greenside Court. The school's main buildings, apart from the swimming pool, science and main school blocks include the former residence of Principal James Forbes, Bishophall (1862); this was once called College Hall (1868), then Bishophall the residence of Charles Wordsworth (1806–92), Bishop of St Andrews, Dunkeld and Dunblane, until the school bought it in 1887, the property was extended in 1936. St Rules dates from 1895–1896 as school property and fronts

63. St Leonards School, founded in 1877

the remains of the Priory guest house of around 1350, it has now reverted to the old name of East and West. The Hospice (1894), on the site of the *Hospitium Novum* is now called Ollernshaw. St Katherine's, the Sanatorium in 1899 on the Abbey Mill site was extended in 1974 and is now called Hepburn House. St Nicholas (1930), Abbey Park House (1815, extended 1853; taken over by the school in 1899) and St Leonards [in the] Fields were all sold in the early 2000s for private development.[5]

In 1894 a preparatory school was opened in the Georgian house at 91 North Street under the name of St Katherine's to replace the junior department at Priorsgate. The house had been built around 1815 with extensions of 1830 and retains its portico with four columns. When St Katherine's was sold the building was developed in 1978 as a Centre for the Arts. St Leonards School badge and motto remember the old Priory associations in that they incorporate the motto *Ad Vitam*, the crosier and shield of Prior James Hepburn.

A private school for boys was established at New Park, Hepburn Gardens in 1933 by Cuthbert Dixon (d.1949), formerly of Merchiston Preparatory School, Edinburgh. It was to remain an all male staff until World War II when a 'petticoat brigade' of women joined; among these teachers was Willa Muir, the wife of the poet Edwin Muir (1887–1959). The school was extended in 1936, and originally incorporated the old Plash Mill Cottage later known as New Park Cottage, parts of which date from 1658. In 2005 St Leonards junior and middle schools merged with New Park to become one unit. New Park properties were thereafter sold and the new unit is called St Leonards–New Park and is housed in Hepburn House (the old St Katherine's).

More Recent Times

Apart from Madras and St Leonards–New Park, the burgh is served by Canongate Primary School (1971), Maynard Road, Langlands School (1957), Kilrymont Road and Lawhead Primary School (1974), Strathkinness Low Road. The teaching of Roman Catholic children in terms of their own denominational instruction was done largely outside school hours in

64. Visit to St Leonards on Saturday, 1 October 1927, by HRH The Duchess
of York (later Queen Elizabeth the Queen Mother). The duchess was opening
the new library at Queen Mary's House. Here she is seen walking with Miss
Katherine McCutcheon, headmistress 1922–38, and behind them walks the
Rev. C.E. Plumb, Bishop of St Andrews, Dunkeld and Dunblane, Chairman
of the School Council 1924–30 [St Leonards School].

various school buildings in the town. A Catholic Primary School was opened in 1959 staffed by nuns of the Poor Clares of Newry order, under the title of Greyfriars School, with teaching rooms at the church hall of St James's Church on The Scores; teaching was subsequently moved to a house in Queens Terrace. In 1968 the school was taken over by Fife Education Authority and was moved into the old Board School (1889) in Abbey Street in 1969; this time it was staffed by lay teachers. The school was relocated to the Langlands site in 2007. Langlands merged with Canongate School in 2006.

CHAPTER 14

The Party-Coloured Burgh: Parliamentary Representation

The origin of the Scottish Parliament and its early history
are alike involved in mystery.

A.H. Millar, *Fife: Pictorial and Historical* (1895)

It was a March day like no other in St Andrews in 1304. The
calendar showed the thirty-second year of the reign of Edward
of the House of Anjou, bynamed Longshanks, who ruled
England as Edward I. Edward now claimed overlordship of
Scotland, for at the fall of Berwick-upon-Tweed and the defeat
of the Scots under John Baliol in 1296, Edward had added to
his proclaimed titles that of King of Scotland. Crowds thronged
to St Andrews to see Edward, *Malleus Scottorum* (hammer of the
Scots), and his entourage enter the city and make their way to
the cathedral to be received by Bishop William de Lamberton,
newly restored to his temporality, and the Augustinian and
senior diocesan clergy. The parliament was to be a prelude to
the one held at Westminster in September 1305 which drew up
the Ordinance for Edward's governance of Scotland. Edward's
presence in St Andrews was a political move to show dominance in Scotland's ecclesiastical capital. While Edward was in
St Andrews his siege of Stirling Castle was being advanced and
Edward's sappers stripped lead from the cathedral roof for
armaments. Did he pay for the lead? We don't know, but he
assuaged his soul when he and his queen, his second wife
Margaret of France, gave gold and jewelled offerings at the
shrine of St Andrew.

This was the first parliament to be held in St Andrews and
130 landowners from Sir John of Cambo to Sir William Murray
of St Fort queued to pay homage to Edward as overlord.[1]
Ordinary folk in St Andrews had no say in what was happen-

ing; even their chosen burgesses had no role in the important events at the cathedral. But things were moving towards greater, if limited, public representation. Five years on, on 24 February 1309, at the Great National Council at the Church of the Minorite Friars at Dundee, Robert I, the Bruce, was accepted as King of Scotland, yet it was still the senior clergy who represented the people. Only after Robert I's parliament at Cambuskenneth Abbey on 15 July 1326 was there any appearance of a 'Commons' (i.e., the burgesses and middle class) in the Scottish Parliament.[2] Representation for the Commons was patchy for Fife and only freeholders of property could seek representation, and only if business discussed was relevant to them were they summoned to parliament. After the

65. The National Government Fete at Earlshall, 1 July 1939. Margaret Walker presents a buttonhole to National Liberal MP, Leslie Burgin, Minister of Supply. Coalition National Governments served the UK from August 1931 to 1945. In the photograph are young Margaret's grandparents Sir Michael and Lady Nairn and (later Sir) John Henderson Stewart, National Liberal and Conservative MP for East Fife (1933–61). [St Andrews Research and Lecture Projects]

Revolutionary Settlement of 1689 ecclesiastical representation was removed.

After the Treaty of Union (1707), parliamentary representation for St Andrews in particular became more positive, with the establishment of the first Parliament for Great Britain. In these days St Andrews was united with Cupar and lumped with Perth, Dundee and Forfar to send one member to parliament. The first elected parliament of 12 November 1713 saw a new electorate defined as St Andrews Burghs, while the 1832 Reform Bill placed St Andrews in with Anstruther Burghs. The redistribution of Seats Act 1885 saw one MP sitting for St Andrews Burghs: (including Anstruther–Easter, Anstruther–Wester, Crail, Cupar, Kilrenny and Pittenweem).

From the earliest records the roll-call of St Andrews parliamentary representatives these names stand out:

Anstruther, Henry Torrens. Advocate. 1886, 1892.

Anstruther, Sir John. Master of Works in Scotland. 1708–11, 1713–41.

Anstruther, Sir John. Son of the above. 1766–82, 1790–93. Accepted the Chiltern Hundreds twice.

Anstruther, Lt-Gen. Philip. 1715–54.

Arnot, John. 1612. Commissary clerk.

Arthur, Henry. 1621.

Austin, Joseph. 1798–10. [Constituency included Perth etc.]

Balfour, Duncan. 1583, 1588. Conventions of Estates, 1594, 1612.

Bell, Laurence. 1357.

Bonar, William. 1456, 1468. Auditor of complaints, 1417.

Carstairs, Andrew. 1650, 1661–63. Dean of Guild.

Dempster, George, of Dunnichen. 1761–90. Advocate. Provost. Director of the East India Company. [Constituency included Perth etc.]

Eassone, John. 1681–82, 1685–86. Provost. Merchant.

Ellice, Edward of Invergarry. 1837–80.

Forret, David. 1599. Conventions of Estates.

Geddie, John, of St Nicholas. 1667, 1669–74, 1678. Conventions of Estates. Provost.

Geddie, Martin. 1569. Conventions of Estates.

Haldane, Patrick. 1715–22. Advocate. King's solicitor. Commissioner on Forfeited Estates. [Constituency included Perth etc.]

Johnston, Andrew of Rennyhill. 1833–37.

Kirkyntolach, Adam of. 1357.

Leirmonth, David. 1524.

Leirmonth, James. 1524, 1535, 1540, 1543, 1544. Provost.

Leirmonth, James of Dairsie. 1587, 1593, 1600.

Leirmonth, Sir Patrick, of Dairsie. 1567–69. Conventions of Estates. Provost.

Lentron, James. 1646–47.

Lentron, Robert. 1665. Conventions of Estates. Provost. Merchant.

Lepar, John. 1639–40, 1644–46.

Leslie, Charles. 1722. [Constituency included Perth etc.]

Leslie, Thomas of Stenton. 1743–61. Equerry to the Prince of Wales, 1742. Barrack Master of Scotland, 1748–69. [Constituency included Perth etc.]

Murray, Captain George, of Pitkaithly. 1790. Vice-Admiral of the White, 1796. [Constituency included Perth etc.]

Robertson, James. 1645, 1648.

Robertson, Thomas. 1617. Conventions of Estates and Parliament.

Russell, David. 1579, 1590 Conventions of Estates

Russell, William. 1586, 1596, 1602. Conventions of Estates,1604–05,1607–08.

Sibbald, Alexander. 1571. Conventions of Estates.

Smith, James. 1689. Conventions of Estates, 1689–1702.

Stuart-Wortley, John, younger of Belmont. 1830 till his election was declared void. [Constituency included Perth etc.].

Sword, James. 1641, 1649–51.

Tailyour, Robert. 1617, 1625. Conventions of Estates, 1628–33, 1643–44.

Wallch, Thomas. 1572. Conventions of Estates.

Watson, Alexander of Aithernie, 1702–07,

Watson, David. 1593, 1597. Conventions of Estates, 1598.

Watson, James, 1630. Conventions of Estates.
Wedderburne, Sir David of Ballindean, 1805–18. Postmaster-
General for Scotland. [Constituency included Perth etc.]
Welwood, Thomas. 1578. Conventions of Estates.
Williamson, Leonard. 1568.
Williamson, Stephen, 1880–85. Tied with Sir Robert An-
struther at the polls and retired in the latter's favour.
Yeaman, George. 1710–15. [Constituency included Perth
etc.][3]

In Scotland two new university seats were created by the 1867
Reform Act and St Andrews was grouped with Edinburgh. The
first MP elected by the Chancellors, the members of the
University Courts, professors and members of the General
Councils was (Sir) Hugh Lyon Playfair, who served 1868–85
as a Liberal. The first Conservative to win was the Rt Hon.
J.H.A. MacDonald who served from 1885 to 1888; thereafter
the Conservatives (as Unionists, Liberal Unionists and Conservative Unionists) predominated. Later the two university
seats were combined to represent four universities (St Andrews,
Aberdeen, Glasgow and Edinburgh) with three MPs and
described as the Scottish Universities constituencies, balloted
for by proportional representation. The university seats were
abolished by the Representation of the People Act 1948 and no
longer appeared after the February 1950 election. Sir James
Matthew Barrie was asked to stand for the Liberals for the
university seat in 1900, but declined, yet perhaps the most
celebrated MP who sat for St Andrews was the writer John
Buchan, who served as a Conservative from 1927 to 1935 in
which year his appointment as Governor-General of Canada
made him ineligible to sit.

During the nine years of the reign of Edward VII, four Prime
Ministers held sway two Conservatives in the Marquess of
Salisbury and A.J. Balfour, and two Liberals, Sir Henry Camp-
bell-Bannerman and H.H. Asquith. In these years St Andrews
district constituency was firmly Liberal. At the new parliament
of 1901, Henry Torrens Anstruther (1860–1926) was re-elected
(he had served since 1886) as a Liberal Unionist and continued

until 1903 when he was appointed Director of the Suez Canal. His place was taken by Captain Edward Charles Ellice (1858–1934), Liberal, who was subsequently defeated in 1906 by Major William Anstruther-Gray of Kilmany (1859–1938), the Unionist Candidate. In the election of 1910 Anstruther-Gray was defeated by (Sir) James Duncan Millar (1871–1932), Liberal, who sat from January to December 1910, when he was defeated by Anstruther-Gray, who represented the constituency until he retired in 1918.

After World War I there were to be some political changes affecting St Andrews. The Reform Act of 1918 brought St Andrews Burghs into the East Fife Constituency and there was to be some political controversy when Col. Alexander Sprot, the Unionist candidate, defeated the ex-Liberal Prime Minister H.H. Asquith (1852–1928) in December 1918; Sprot represented the seat until 1922. (Sir) James D. Millar, the Liberal Nationalist held the constituency during 1922–24 and 1929–32, having been ousted from 1924 to 1929 by the Conservative, Commander the Hon. A.D. Cochrane. Sir James Henderson-Stewart, the National Liberal and Conservative, sat for East Fife from 1933–61, and thereafter it was held by Sir John Gilmour until his retirement in 1979.

The seat was held for the Conservatives again by Barry Henderson until 1983, whereupon the constituency became Fife North East and Henderson served 1983–87 until he was defeated by Liberal lawyer (Sir) Walter Menzies Campbell who became leader of the Liberal Democratic party in 2006. Campbell was elected Chancellor of the University of St Andrews on 10 January 2006 by the University's General Council; under the terms of the Universities (Scotland) Act 1888 he can hold his office for life.

CHAPTER 15

Victorian Peepshow: Edwardian Spectacle

> The streets he paved – the wrath he braved
> Of the fishwife progenie:
> The 'Mussel Scalp' re-bel-lion
> He quelled with stern decree –
> This Provost of St Andrew's town,
> St Andrews by the sea.
>
> Nineteenth-century squib on
> Sir Hugh Lyon Playfair

Victorian Peepshow

Queen Victoria, the last member of the House of Hanover, was born at Kensington Palace on 24 May 1819, the only child of HRH Prince Edward, Duke of Kent and Strathearn (1767– 1820), and his wife Her Serene Highness Mary Louisa Victoria of Saxe-Coburg-Saalfeld (1786—1861). Victoria ascended the throne on 20 June 1837 on the death of her uncle William, Duke of Clarence (b.1765), who ruled as William IV.

Victoria was crowned at Westminster Abbey on 28 June 1838 and in St Andrews there were great rejoicings with representative processions made up of municipal dignitaries, freemasons and schoolchildren. Arches of flowers hung across Union Street and bunting festooned St Rule's Tower and the castle, adding to the colour of the day, and bonfires lit up the evening sky; throughout the day junketing took place in both public house and middle-class parlour alike and food was distributed to the poor. On 10 February 1840 Victoria married her cousin HRH Prince Albert of Saxe-Coburg and Gotha (1819–61) and by then the town settled down to a new era.

In Victorian St Andrews, one man stands out above all others to be dubbed 'The Man who made Modern St Andrews'. Hugh Lyon Playfair was a son of the manse, born at Meigle,

Angus, on 17 November 1786. Educated at Meigle, Newtyle and Dundee Grammar School, Playfair finished his academic training at St Andrews where his father Dr James Playfair was Principal of United College. He entered military service at Woolwich completing his training in 1805 as an artillery officer serving until 1817. A private tour in Europe lasted three years; he was made a freeman of St Andrews in 1820, married Jane Dalgleish of Scotscraig (d.1872) the same year and returned to India to continue service in artillery. A furlough from the Indian Army in 1833 saw him back in St Andrews where he devoted some time to the regeneration of the Golf Links. He retired from active service in 1834 and returned to St Andrews to take up residence at St Leonards which he had bought in 1827. Playfair devoted time to developing a theatre, within a lavish theme garden for 'instruction and recreation' which he opened to the public. From time to time Playfair opened his home to the tourist. The family sometimes found strangers wandering around the rooms 'leisurely inspecting the paintings and furniture' having dispensed with the need of an invitation. In the town Playfair was known as the 'Major'.

Playfair was appointed to St Andrews Town Council in 1842 and set about harmonising the various warring fractions on the council and retrieved the burgh funds that had been dissipated. With military precision he undertook a survey of the burgh to see what needed to be done. St Andrews was in a sorry state: weeds flourished in the streets, public sewers were inadequate for the population, pavements were fractured, buildings were run down, dunghills of animal and fish waste festered in wynds and corners

The first task was to lay footpaving along the whole length of South Street from The Pends to the West Port, and an alignment of the buildings on the street; lime trees were added 1879–80. Street lighting was improved to make St Andrews one of the best-lit places in Britain. Improvements were made to The Scores, Lade Braes, the harbour and the cathedral burial ground, and Playfair Terrace, constructed 1846, was named after the Major. None of these projects was easily accomplished. Many thought Playfair an interfering bully and he encountered much vested-interest opposition and lethargy. Yet with a mixture of diplomacy and hectoring he was able to set the tone for the development of modern St Andrews.

Playfair's work was contentious and one controversy stands out in the burgh's history. For generations the local fishermen had collected mussel scalps from the Eden estuary to bait their lines. Most of the collecting was done by fisher-family women. Playfair believed that this threatened their 'mental and moral' fabric; after all, he said, the mussels were being 'stolen'. There was uproar when Playfair suggested that the Town Council organised the mussel collection and sell them to the fishermen. Playfair got his way and after 1843 fishermen could be fined for illegal removal of the mussels.[1]

Nevertheless Playfair was knighted in 1856 for his services in India and St Andrews. He was Provost of St Andrews for nineteen years and added to his honours in 1854 that of Honorary Custodier of the Property of the Crown in St Andrews. Playfair died on 21 January 1861 and was buried in the cathedral burial ground.[2] In recent years scholars have opined that Playfair's work has been exaggerated and a more significant part was played in the development of modern St Andrews by Dr John Adamson (1819–70), who as Medical Officer of Health completely overhauled the burgh's sanitary arrangements.

Playfair, Dr Adamson and a whole range of local architects from Jesse Hall (1820–1906) and David Henry (1835–1914) to John Milne (1822–1904) and George Rae (1811–69) gave Victorian St Andrews an architectural boost that had not been seen since the Middle Ages. The existing roads were widened, new highways were constructed, and buildings were reconstructed or demolished and new ones put in their place. North and South Bell Street evolved between 1834 and 1858, as did Queens Gardens, Gillespie Terrace, Gibson Place and Playfair Terrace. Wagons carrying sandstone from such quarries as those as Blebo Craigs and Strathkinness regularly trundled into the town and permanent employment was offered to St Andrews craftsmen from carpenters to masons during this period. Of the main public buildings erected, the Gibson

66. Popular postcard view of the West Port and West Port Garage, mid-1930s. The garage is now the site of new private residences. South Street pavements and lime trees date from 1879–80.

Hospital is a worthy example of Victorian enterprise in the town, projected and endowed by Bailie William Gibson of Dunloch, as a home for those 'aged sick, and infirm poor' who were natives of St Andrews or St Leonards parishes; these conditions of admission were altered in 1934 to include those who had lived in St Andrews for ten years. Gibson had proposed such an enterprise in the 1860s but it did not come into operation until 23 June 1884; the foundation stone of architect David Henry's classical themed building was laid in 1882 by J.Whyte-Melville, with full masonic honours.

Regularly St Andrews appeared in the national press for one reason or another. During the autumn of 1876 St Andrews folk were all agog as it was fixed that on Wednesday 27 September, HRH Prince Leopold would visit the burgh to be installed as Captain of the Royal and Ancient Golf Club. Leopold, Duke of Albany (1853–84), the haemophiliac eighth child and fourth son of Queen Victoria, married Princess Helena of Waldeck-Pyrmont (1861–1922) in 1882, and they became the parents of the very popular HRH Princess Alice, Countess of Athlone

67. Typical house with forestair, St Andrews

(1883–1981). Prince Leopold was looked upon as a 'Scottish adoptee' as his title had originated in 1398, in the reign of Robert III; Mary, Queen of Scots had bestowed it on Henry Darnley and it had descended through the Hanoverian line to Leopold. The prince duly arrived and was hosted by John Whyte-Melville of Mount Melville and was installed as Royal and Ancient Captain, and Provost Walter Thomas Milne was

68. This postcard scene of the Martyrs' Monument, the R&A, with the links and the West Sands of the mid-1930s became one of the most famous in the world as St Andrews' tourist trade developed.

presented. The prince lunched with Principal Tulloch and visited St Mary's College with a walk to the cathedral, the castle and an unexpected call at the Ladyhead to meet the fisherfolk. He dined at the Royal and Ancient and the next day he attended a meet at the Fife Fox Hounds at Mount Melville, played golf and appeared at a civic ball at the Town Hall. Leopold was presented with an album of photographs by Thomas Rodger Jr and was much taken by the bonfires, street decorations and warmth of welcome. He was accompanied by his equerry, the Hon. Alexander Grantham Yorke, who wrote letters of thanks to the provosts of St Andrews and Cupar. Leopold left St Andrews station on 29 September, walking through a guard of honour mounted by the St Andrews Artillery Company. This had been the first royal visit since that of Charles II. Leopold returned in 1877 and photographic studio portraits of him were taken by Thomas Rodger which are still to be found in the Royal Archives at Windsor.

St Andrews was in the forefront of the birth of photography in Scotland because of the mutual interests of three men, Sir

David Brewster (1781–1868), Principal of United College, William Henry Fox Talbot (1800–77), the English inventor and practitioner of the calotype photographic process and Dr John Adamson (1809–1870). They joined to promote photography in Scotland and Dr Adamson produced the first calotype taken in Scotland in May 1840. The first commercial studio in Fife was that set up in 1849 by Thomas Rodger in the vicinity of Abbey Street.

Prince Leopold's visit and other events were recorded in great detail by the *St Andrews Citizen*, a newspaper which had its birth in 1870. The *Fife Herald* (1823) had developed from Robert Tullis's *Cupar Herald* in 1822 and in 1870 the managing editor of the *Fife Herald* and *Fife News*, John Innes, instituted a St Andrews edition of the *Fife News* which was to be amalgamated with the *Fife Herald* in 1910. The Fife Herald had absorbed its main rival in the area, the *Fifeshire Journal*, in 1893. In 1879 John Innes purchased the whole business and the properties of the printer Robert Tullis (1775–1831) of St Andrews. Thus 'St Andrews-orientated news' was promulgated from a small house and printing shop at the corner of South Street and Church Street; this included the post office run by Provost George Murray (d.1908) which was moved to new premises next door in 1892. The post office site was the home of the Christian Institute from 1907 to 1953. The print shop was rebuilt as the Citizen Office in 1928 and the shop next door was absorbed in 1965. Here too had been the type foundry (1742–44) and birthplace of Adam Bell in 1753. Bell's erstwhile collaboration with Alexander, dubbed 'the father of Scotland's letter founders', was responsible for the first casting of the dollar sign for use in the United States. The town was also catered for in news reportage by the *St Andrews Gazette* which ran from 1862–63, then as the *St Andrews Gazette & Fifeshire News* until 1883. The *St Andrews Pictorial Magazine* was first published in 1831; its contents were of general and national interest, with short stories, fashion notes, travel, natural history and puzzles; basically there was little local material published apart from births, marriages and deaths. The publisher, in 1859, P. Thomson of 51 South Street, included a plea for 'anything not generally known in the history of any of the old buildings in the town'.

Travel for the Victorian St Andrean was restricted to private carriage and gig, hired coaches, or a weekly public coach between the town and Cupar; and a twice-weekly coach from such inns as the Black Bull (at 27 South Street – the old Co-op buildings – and until 1840 it was the town's chief hostelry; it closed in 1850). This supplemented the much used sea transport from St Andrews harbour and the Eden port.

Fife's first passenger railway was opened on 29 June 1847 from Burntisland to Cupar and Lindores by the Edinburgh and Northern Railway Co. This company developed as the Edinburgh, Perth and Dundee Railway in 1849, to be taken over by the North British Railway in 1862 (LNER, 1923; British Railways, 1948) and it was the E., P. & D.R. company which operated the St Andrews railway. When this railway opened St Andrews passengers were picked up by local coaches for the link to and from Leuchars. In 1850 the St Andrews Railway Co. was formed to link Leuchars with St Andrews, via Guardbridge, and the line was opened by the directors, said the *Fifeshire Journal*, on 29 May 1852. The town's first station was located on the site of the modern Old Course Hotel and Country Club and was known as the Links Station. Under the date 3 July 1852 *The Scotsman* recorded the opening of the St Andrews line:

This event, highly important not only for the town of St Andrews, but for the whole of Fife, took place on Tuesday at midday. Strangers, especially those belonging to the chief towns in the county, had been invited by the directors to be present. A number of additional first class carriages had been provided to conduct them along the main line to Leuchars. When the Leuchars station was reached, a little after twelve o'clock, the directors, Mr Ellice [Edward Ellice MP] and a large number of the inhabitants were there to receive strangers, and accompany them along the new line to St Andrews. After a short delay, incident on the exhange of courtesies, all took their seats. They filled some eight or ten first class carriages. On starting, the Leuchars folks, crowds of them had gathered at the station, cheered loudly and lustily. The progress was both swift and smooth. The time occupied in travelling from Leuchars to St Andrews station was between thirteen and fourteen minutes. At the station a number of ladies and gentlemen of St Andrews were waiting. A dinner took place in the Town Hall at which seventy-three gentlemen were present. Mr Ellice MP was in the chair and the talent and affability of the honourable gentleman carried the company guickly and smoothly along. He was supported on the right by Major Playfair of St Andrews, and Provost Sang of Kirkcaldy, and on the left by the Rev. Dr Buist and Prof. Alexander. Mr W.F. Ireland and Mr Alex Meldrum, Easter Kincaple, officiated as croupiers. The line was opened on Thursday for regular traffic. The fares are extremely moderate. The railway has been made cheaply, and is to be travelled very cheaply.

The cost of the building of the railway was £5,625 by the notorious Sir Thomas Bouch whose Tay Bridge collapsed in 1879. By 1857 the journey from St Andrews to Leuchars was twenty minutes, and in 1877 the line was absorbed into the North British Railway.

On 16 July 1883 there was an authorisation for a link between Anstruther and St Andrews Railway, and the North British Railway at St Andrews, but only by 1 June 1887 was the link completed via Kingsbarns and Boarhills. The link between St Andrews and Boarhills which opened in 1883 was made by coach operated by the Rusack family, then proprietors of the Star Hotel. St Andrews now had a new station situated nearer the town centre than the Links, off City Road. When the Forth Bridge was opened 4 March 1890, St Andrews had convenient links with Edinburgh and the south. All of which led to the further opening up of the East Neuk to tourists and increasingly speedy deliveries of agricultural and fishery products. The Links Station of 1852–87 became the goods station, with its engine shed, coal yard and offices. The Station Master's house is still retained as the Jigger Inn.

The railway system at St Andrews began to decline in the 1920s when, first, the through services from St Andrews to Perth were closed. The decline was gradual, though; in 1930 the stations at Kingsbarns, Boarhills, Stravithie and Mount Melville were closed to passengers and in 1954 Dairsie station closed. By 1964 the St Andrews to Crail line closed to freight and by 1965 the St Andrews to Leven link was closed to passengers. Freight was also closed in 1966 from Guardbridge to St Andrews and on 6 January 1969 the Leuchars to St Andrews line was finally closed to passengers.

Since 1969 the old railway track has been part developed to the south as car parks and walkways; the short tunnel under Doubledykes Road is sealed, as has been the aperture under the humped-back Lade Braes bridge, and the Canongate bridge was demolished. Householders in Drumcarrow Road and Spottiswoode Gardens long purchased the railway embankment for garden extensions. The station site is now a car park and the embankment to the west still abuts Windmill Road, and Petheram Bridge over the line of the modern A91 was demolished. In this area the Victorians had a curling pond where the line from the biblically named Jacob's Ladder path meets the A91 and they played on natural ice but were disturbed by railway workings; a new artificial pond was constructed at Law Mill in 1905. St Andrews Curling Club formed in 1846.

A prominent transportation group in Victorian St Andrews was the Carters, also known as the Whiplickers, whose society had been re-established in 1872. St Andrews' carters had been extant as a group from the Middle Ages, when they struck their bargains before the altar to their patron St Michael, set in Holy Trinity Church. The rendezvous of the carters, on the day they held their annual races, was the 'Blue Stane', which used to be in the middle of the road across from Hope Park Church; today the old whinstone nestles by the railings in the garden of The Raisin [what was The Alexandra, then The Station Hotel] at the north-west of Alexandra Place. The Blue Stane's origins are unknown, but tradition dates it from Pictish St Andrews where it may have been a boundary stone for the ecclesiastical enclave. One local myth tells how a giant, angry at the influence of St Rule, picked up the stone at Blebo Craigs and threw it at the saint's cell on the Kirkhill. The stone fell short and landed at the end of Market Street. The stone has had various locations from Magus Muir to the West Port and tradition invested it with sanctity down the years of such potency that hoary farmers doffed their hats to it, the pikemen off to Bannockburn in 1314 patted it for luck, and women curtseyed to it – or so the old folk said. For a number of years, after its foundation in 1880, a Coachman's Ball was held in St Andrews for the coachmen in the area.

Writing in 1793 the Rev. Dr John Adamson, Minister of the First Charge at St Andrews defined a Town Council in the burgh as follows:

> The government of the city is vested in a Provost, Dean of Guild, and 4 Bailies, who with the town-treasurer, are called the office-bearers in the council, and are elected annually at Michaelmas [29 September, the medieval feast of St Michael]. The Dean of Guild here has the precedence of the Bailies, and is president of the council in absence of the Provost . . . No-one is eligible into the council who is not a burgess and guild brother.[3]

Adamson also noted that in his time the Town Council was made up of 29 elected members representing the guilds and crafts; by 1793 the following crafts still had influence in the town the smiths, bakers, tailors, shoemakers, weavers and fleshers (i.e., butchers). During the Victorian period St Andrews was served by a Town Council of 23 councillors, a provost, 3 bailies, a Dean of Guild and a treasurer, and most of them were elected by the old town guilds. After 1901 the council was reduced to 12, to include the provost, two magistrates and a Dean of Guild. The longest-serving provost was W.T. Milton (1869–81) and many prominent businessmen and academics served in the office in Victorian and Edwardian times, including John McGregor the furnisher, Professor John Herkless and Andrew Aikman of grocers Aikman and Terras.

69. Provost Walter Thomas Milton served the burgh from 1869 to 1881, to be the longest-serving provost. During his time the burgh developed its modern aspects. [St Andrews Community Council]

The provost who served the shortest period was Major C.H.M. Cheape during 1915, and the town had to wait until 1952 to elect its first woman provost in Jessie L. Moir. The town's first woman councillor, elected in 1919, was Frances Jane Warrack (1865–1950). Although David I had given the city and royal burgh of St Andrews the right to use certain ensigns, it was not until 1912 that the town petitioned the Lord Lyon King of Arms to matriculate the city ensigns. The town's provost's chain of office was presented to St Andrews by the Marquis of Bute in 1897.

In terms of public entertainment the Victorians had open-air dancing and swimming at the Step Rock. Young men and boys usually swam naked in the sea and a future Archbishop – Cosmo Gordon Lang (1864–1945, he became Archbishop in 1928) – remembered bathing naked in the sea at St Andrews during a holiday in the 1870s.[4] There was a skating rink in operation on The Scores (opposite the Craigmount Nursing Home) from 1875 to 1890. 'Ice-Day' holidays in which large numbers of young and old went to Kilconquhar, Strathtyrum and Leuchars to skate were popular too. Musically there was a Choral Society started by Mr Salter, the organist of the Episcopal Church in North Street, in the 1860s, and the City Band was founded in 1879. There were various clubs and associations established too, like the St Andrews Burns Club which was instituted on 25 January 1869 at the Royal Hotel on the 110th anniversary of the birth of the poet. When the new Town Hall was completed in 1861 the hall above the council chamber was fitted out as a lodge for the local Freemasons; their rooms were completed in 1897. There was a lodge of Freemasons in St Andrews as early as 1600 but the current lodge dates from the 1720s and is one within the Province of Fife and Kinross.

The town also had a burgeoning number of hotels stimulated by the expansion of Victorian tourism of which Rusack's Marine Hotel has an interesting town and family history. By the time that Johann Wilhelm Christof Rusack died in 1916 he had made 'The Marine' hotel into an internationally respected golfing hotel. During his forty-year stay in St Andrews, Rusack

70. Rusack's Marine Hotel overlooking the 1st and 18th greens of the Old Course. The hotel was constructed and developed 1887–92, the work of Johann Wilhelm Christof Rusack (d.1916). [Forte PLC]

saw the ancient burgh develop from a little-known holiday resort into a place of great tourist potential. Born in 1848, Rusack came from the fashionable summer resort of Bad Harzburg, Lower Saxony, and was of Huguenot extraction. His forebears had been of the old French family of De Rousac, Huguenots who had emigrated to Germany from Normandy in the seventeenth century. He came to Britain in 1871 after serving in the Franco-Prussian war, and became a naturalised citizen in 1885. Soon after he arrived in St Andrews, he started up the 'Rusacks Private Hotel', Abbotsford Crescent, and by 1877 he had taken over the former Star Hotel, Market Street.[5] He also ran Kinloch House and the Temperance Hotel. Convinced that St Andrews was to become an important watering place, Rusack acquired a piece of land on the Links in 1887. Enlargements were made in 1892 and by 1896 the family were also owners of Bogward Farm which became Rusacks Home Farm. The hotel was to become the most famous in Scotland for golfing holidays patronised by royalty, particularly HRH

Edward, Prince of Wales, the famous Rothschild financiers and by such golfing celebrities as Bobby Jones, Bobby Locke, Peter Thomson and Ken Nagle, the latter two of whom stayed with their families during the 1984 Open. Even 'James Bond' otherwise known as the actor Sean Connery stayed most years during the autumn. William Rusack served on the St Andrews Town Council and was Dean of Guild; he took an active part in the masonic movement. On his death the hotel was carried on by the Rusack family but was ultimately acquired by the St Andrews Links Trust in 1980 and was bought from them in 1985 by Trusthouse Forte Hotels who sold to Macdonald Hotels in the early 2000s.

St Andrews became one of the most 'modern towns' in Britain; the telegraph came to the town in 1870 and the first telephone was obtained by R. Niven, flesher, in 1885. Street lighting in the burgh was boasted of as 'the best in Scotland', with its distinctive Victorian livery of white and Venetian red.[6] Oil lamps were replaced by gas. Manufacture of gas began in St Andrews in 1835 under the active enterprise of Provost Kirkby Dalrymple and a new gas tank was erected in 1878. The St Andrews Gas Co. ceased to exist after October 1949 when it was taken over by the Gas Board, and gas was produced in the town until 23 February 1962 when the works were closed. Electric current was switched on in 1905.

As befitted a town which had won a living from and on the sea, St Andrews was in the forefront of Victorian marine innovation. The first marine laboratory in Britain was established in St Andrews in 1884 at the East Bents and set in the old isolation fever hospital which stood on the site of the present putting green. The research here was directed by Professor William Carmichael McIntosh (1838–1931) and contributed much to marine knowledge internationally. In time the old wooden fever hospital became inconvenient to use and a new laboratory was built in 1896 through the generosity of Dr Charles Henry Gatty (1835–1903). Today the 'Gatty' is an important international Research Institute which incorporates the Sea Mammal Research Unit and the rock pools of St Andrew Bay offer important field studies of marine biology.

71. From the 1850s St Andrews developed westwards with Victorian and Edwardian architects and designers bringing the best features into the houses of the prosperous middle class. [Mr & Mrs Robert Thomson]

The old fever hospital survived until it was destroyed by fire in 1905.

Within Westburn Lane, and later to be a private wash-house, was the site of St Andrews' first bank opened in 1792 as a branch of the Bank of Scotland and run by the agents Charles Dempster & Co. This bank was relocated several times but in 1870 it was moved to the corner site of South Street and Queens Gardens. By 1845 St Andrews was served by the Eastern Bank (W.F. Ireland, agent), the Clydesdale (Walter Walker) and the Edinburgh & Leith (Ireland & Murray). A savings bank was established in St Andrews in the Town Hall in 1846, which was to become the Dundee Savings Bank at 12 Church Street where it was moved in 1921. The 1930 Dundee Savings Bank was reconstructed in 1937 and was taken over in modern times by the Trustee Savings Bank. In 1930 too, the National & Union Bank, South Street (the site of the current John Menzies shop) was opened under the agency of A. Gilchrist of Queens Gardens; the bank's coat of arms remains on the frontage. [Queen Victoria died at Osborne House, Isle of Wight, in the arms of her grandson Kaiser Wilhelm II of Germany, and her physician Dr Sir James Reid, at 6.30 p.m., 22 January 1901. The new king, born Albert Edward, Prince of Wales, on 9 November 1841, was sixty-one years old when he was proclaimed at the Cross of St Andrews, Market Street, on Saturday, 27 January 1901, by Provost James Ritchie Welch (d.1903). A royal salute was fired by the Voluntary Artillery at Kirkhill, and by this year the folk of St Andrews had gone a long way towards becoming 'Anglicised' in their private and public life. Most of the town's upper strata were educated at English public schools and the town commerce was run along the lines of Anglo-Saxon capitalism interlarded with Calvinist thrift.

72. William Wilson, motor trader, St Andrews. By 1903 the Motor Car Act had licensed vehicle and drivers. Wilson was one of the early promoters of motor vehicles in St Andrews. [STARALP]

73. Wilson's garage and motor works was at 193 South Street; they also had premises at Alexandra Place [STARALP]

St Andrews' Edwardian society reflected the affluence and ostentation of the period, and the age of strict social discipline, peace and plenty for those who could afford it. Edward's reign was a time of transition between the leisurely self-confidence of the Victorian Age and the bursting forth of the revolutionary years which were to be heralded by the advent of World War I. Yet, no-one who took part in the coronation festivities in St Andrews on Saturday 9 August 1902, had an inkling of the coming horrors of Flanders Fields. Instead they craned their necks at the official proclamation procession as it wended its way round the town to Divine Service at Holy Trinity and oohed and aahed at the fireworks which burst across the burgh, and strolled under the Chinese lanterns and padella lights in South Street and Market Street. St Andrews' administrators had had plenty of time to make their arrangements for the displays, as the coronation had been postponed from 26 June

1902, because the king had to have an emergency operation for perityphlitis.

The Edwardian Age began in the wake of tremendous change. Britain had lost her supremacy in foreign commerce and on 13 July 1902 the Victorian Conservative Prime Minister, Lord Salisbury, resigned in favour of A.J. Balfour and in 1905 after a decade out of office the Liberals were given a mandate to try to satisfy the needs of the people. In 1902 too, there had been a signing of a treaty of alliance between Britain and Japan which underlined the end of that 'splendid isolation' which had been Victorian Britain's international role since the Crimean War. Rich and poor St Andreans, Tory or Liberal, all looked to King Edward's reign with great optimism. Many believed that it had been Britain's misfortune that Edward had not come to the throne at least ten years earlier.

Edwardian Spectacle

Edwardian St Andrews was a place of bustle and the burgh streets reflected the clutter of the average home. People were out and about from the early hours, the first on the pavements being the milk vendors, the bakers with their baskets of steaming baps, and the home produce sellers. It was a scene of noise with the wheels and horses of drays, carriages and carts being the noisiest. By eight o'clock the itinerants were out; the knife grinders, the pan menders and the fish-sellers, bynamed the cadgers, all jostling for business. Folks were busy, but wages were low and the distress was only too apparent if you went down such places as Crail's Lane and Abbey Street; the extent of the state of the poor was to be brought into focus by Conservative Prime Minister A.J. Balfour's Royal Commission on the Poor Law and the Relief of Distress by 1905. Half of St Andrews' town houses had one or two rooms with shared extramural sanitation. Many were dark, draughty, cramped, malodorous and vermin infested. A two-roomed house in South Castle Street could cost as much as 3s 6d (17½p) per week, while a one-roomed cottage would fetch 1s (5p). This was a high sum for an unskilled worker on 18s (90p) a week. Wages were by no means equitable for physical work done; a full-time shop assistant at W.M. Greig, outfitters of 65 South Street, might earn £30 per year, while a science master at Madras could command £140. But most people settled in St Andrews to the average 22s 6d (£1.10) a week pay of the farm worker. The standard of living of such families as that of the Very Rev. Principal Alexander Stewart of St Mary's was dependent on a low rate of income tax (1 shilling in the pound above £160 per annum) and on the plentiful supply of domestic servants. A maid in St Andrews might earn £12 a year, with ambition to climb the dizzy heights of being a local lawyer's housekeeper at £80 a year.

The Second Boer War, begun in 1899, the worst war Britain had ever suffered with over 100,000 casualties, and conducted by an army that was half-starved at times, ended on 31 May 1902 by the Peace of Vereeniging and the nation wanted to forget. The *St Andrews Citizen* had published updates of the war's progress and the *Fife News Almanac* had printed regular galleries of the prominent local war dead. A memorial fountain of polished Peterhead granite, made in Aberdeen, was set up at the junction of Logie's Lane and South Street (the memorial is now sited in Kinburn Park, by the bowling green) and reads:

DEDICATED TO MAJOR GENERAL R.S. BADEN-POWELL AND THE OTHER IMMORTAL HEROES AND HEROINES OF MAFEKING.

> We shall tell our sons your story,
> How facing a hostile world:
> Starving, fighting, and dying
> You kept your flag unfurled:
> And the length and breadth of the Empire,
> Today with thanksgiving ring,
> In praise to the God of Battles
>
> CHRISTIAN BURKE
> For the Heroes of Mafeking
> 18th May 1900

Mafeking, capital of the Northwest Province of South Africa was the site of the famous siege at the beginning of the Second Boer War wherein (then Colonel) Baden-Powell (1857–1941), founder in 1908 of the Boy Scouts, made a resourceful defence. One local Boer War casualty was the golfer Freddy Tait (Lt. Frederick Guthrie Tait), born in 1870, killed at Koodoosberg (Battle of Magersfontein) on 7 February 1900. In the year that the war started Tait had won the Autumn Meeting of the Royal & Ancient golf tournament.

The first hospital in St Andrews, since the Middle Ages, was sited in a rented house in Abbey Street, a memorial to Lady Elizabeth Douglas (1798–1864) of Dunino and Grangemuir, Pittenweem, widow of Lord William Keith Douglas, Lord of the Admiralty 1822–27. Thereafter the town hospital was always referred to as the 'Memorial'. The South Lodge, in Abbotsford Place, was acquired using money subscribed for memorials to Dr John Adamson and Dr Oswald Home Bell. The hospital had female wards paid for out of a memorial fund set up by the Douglas family and male wards were financed out of the Adamson-Bell fund. South Lodge was used as a hospital from 1871, but by the turn of the century it proved too inadequate in size and facilities and a proposal was launched for a new hospital in Abbey Street, on ground feued by George Bruce. The Cottage Hospital was opened on Wednesday, 27 August 1902, by the mother of F.G. Tait whose memorial fund was a principal financial plank, and the Freddy Tait memorial ward was named within the hospital in recognition. The original hospital, on the site of a cottage then by the old sea beach which stretched way up the Kinness Burn, was in the form of a T and cost £3000. Because of the stipulations of donations certain groups of patients were given preferential treatment, namely professional golfers, caddies and (Black Watch) soldiers. Extensions were made to the hospital in 1924, 1927, 1931 and 1938 and the hospital was upgraded during 1987–88.

Donations to the hospital flooded in and one benefactor was Major Donald Lindsay Carnegie (1840–1911), who lived in a house he built in 1873 in Playfair Terrace; he furnished the hospital surgery and supplied the X-ray apparatus. Major Carnegie also presented an ambulance wagon to the burgh in 1906, commissioned from Reid the coachbuilders of Perth and he also gifted a Merryweather fire engine to the town in 1901, and one of its first jobs was to put out a fire at the old Links Station. The town had secured its first fire engine at the Crawford Priory sale of 1834 and bought a replacement in 1865; a Leyland fire engine was bought in 1921. Today a modern fire station is sited in Largo Road.

Hospital health care in St Andrews was supplemented with the opening of the Infectious Diseases Hospital at St Michaels (now a hotel and private housing complex), Leuchars, in August 1909, and the town was to be in the forefront of pioneer medical research. In 1919 Sir James Mackenzie (1853–1925) founded the James Mackenzie Institute in The Scores, an establishment way ahead of its time. The site was known as Seaton House, and the actual building today is the annex to the Scores Hotel. Sir James was a prominent heart specialist and pioneered investigative clinical procedures towards a basis of preventative medicine. With the help of local GPs, Sir James held regular meetings at The Scores clinic and established a thorough set of medical records of St Andrews townsfolk. This work was carried on into the 1940s when the research endowment passed to the university Faculty of Medicine (and allied academic disciplines) and the Child Care Centre at Dyersbrae. One of Mackenzie's assistants at the Institute was to become one of St Andrews's most celebrated doctors. James Orr (1876–1937) first came to St Andrews in 1900 to be a partner in the general practice of Dr Norman McLeod. He is professionally remembered as a fine clinician of the Institute and bought New Park (which became New Park School in 1933) from his distinguished colleague.[7]

Edwardian St Andrews mirrored the era of cleanliness and fresh air activities. The new Ladies' Bathing Station was opened opposite the Castle Bathing Station in 1904. The site had been used as a ladies' bathing pond from around 1845; here too on the cliff was the site of the public baths of around 1811, bought by St Leonards School for their private use in 1920, the year they bought Castlecliff, the building erected around 1877 and now university property.

The main areas of building in Edwardian St Andrews were in Bridge Street, Murray Park, Links Crescent with City Road and Pilmour Links, Hepburn Gardens with Kennedy Gardens and Donaldson Gardens, to satisfy a population nudging seven thousand by 1914. At the beginning of the Edwardian era St Andrews was to see a new Caddy Master's Shelter in 1904 at the Links, a pavilion of the St Andrews Bowling Club in 1903, the Parish Church Hall in 1902, Greenside Place, the University Pavilion in 1908, Hepburn Gardens, and the Carnegie Library in 1906 in St Mary's Quad.

For entertainment there were concerts, readings and lectures for the St Andrews Edwardians along with visits from concert parties, famous singers' recitals, Sir Robert Fossett's circus, and cinematograph shows at the Town Hall; the first permanent cinema was the 'Cinema House' of 1913 in North Street, which was followed in 1930 by the 'New Picture House' further along the street. Public lectures were very popular too and large audiences were the norm, particularly for such speakers as Sir Ernest Shackleton (1874–1922), the British explorer who made four Antarctic expeditions and who lectured at St Andrews in 1910.

It was a society of voracious readers and intellectual stimulation for the townsfolk was on every hand. Two citizens were prominent among the town as opposed to gown *literati*, both men of divergent character and capability, in Dr David Hay Fleming and W.T. Linskill. David Hay Fleming was born on 9 May 1849 the son of a South Street china merchant. Educated at Madras College, he followed a business career, but wealth inherited in 1883 allowed him to devote himself to academic study, local and Reformation history in particular. Elected to the Town Council in 1881, Hay Fleming moved from 177 South Street in 1889 to 16 North Bell Street (now Greyfriars Garden) and was made a Doctor of Laws of St Andrews university in 1898. He spent the latter years of his life at 4 Chamberlain Road, Edinburgh, where he had moved in 1905. David Hay Fleming was Secretary of the Scottish History

74. David Hay Fleming (1849–1931) lived at 173 South Street. He devoted much of his life to the study of Scottish and St Andrews history.

Society and made a visit to America in 1907. His *Guidebook* (1881) to St Andrews was the standard guide for some seventy years and his work as Honorary Curator of the cathedral museum greatly promoted local history studies and conservation in the burgh.

Up to the work done by Hay Fleming very little had been written about St Andrews in book form for the interested enquirer. From the seventeenth century to the early nineteenth century only three 'histories' had been written. George Martine of Claremont produced his *Reliquiae Divi Andreae* in 1683, but this was more of a history of the see of St Andrews than the town, for Martine was probably secretary to Archbishop Sharp. His manuscript lay in sheaves until 1797 when it was prepared for print by Professor John Rotheram of the Natural Philosophy Department, and was printed by the university printer. In 1807 the Rev. James Grierson produced the first general history of St Andrews under the title *Delineation of St Andrews*, while in 1838 the Rev. J.C. Lyon, presbyter of the Episcopal Church, St Andrews, produced the first standard history. In 1911 there was produced the useful *Handbook to the City and University of St Andrews* by James Maitland Anderson who became chief university librarian. Anderson was born at Rossie, near Collessie in 1852, the son of James Anderson, gardener to Captain James Maitland RN. He started his life as a cowherd and became a newspaper reporter and teacher of shorthand entering the university library in 1873; Anderson died at his residence at Kinnessburn East in 1927, a true Fife 'lad o'pairts'.

Hay Fleming died on 7 November 1931 and his valuable personal library of over 12,000 volumes was bequeathed to the town as the Hay Fleming Reference Library; for many years the collection was on the open shelves of the St Andrews Public Library but now rests in the collection of the University Library. The recently refurbished town library developed on the eighteenth-century site of the English school, which was used as an infant school 1832–44; it then opened as the City Hall in 1845 and was used as a drill hall and auction hall; the City Hall was reconstructed in 1927 for gas company offices an so on. The library moved in during 1951; next door was the town reservoir in 1819 which subsequently became a fire station and later public conveniences. The County Library moved from Queens Gardens to City Hall in 1962.

William T. Linskill was a different character altogether from David Hay Fleming. The son of Captain W. Linskill, Mayor of Tynemouth, and his wife the daughter of Viscount Valentia, Linskill was born in 1855 and was educated at Jesus College, Cambridge. He was brought to St Andrews for holidays in his teens and made the town his home in 1897. Although he had a good working knowledge of the town's history, Linskill's vivid imagination often got the better of him and he went in search of secret passages and lost treasure in the castle and cathedral precincts. Elected to the Town Council, he became Dean of Guild and played a prominent part in the civic and social scene of the town; he was the driving force behind the St Andrews 'howkers' (Scottish for 'diggers') who excavated indiscriminately in the cathedral and castle ruins. A devout Episcopalian and of uncertain temper, Linskill was tutored in golf by young Tom Morris and never tired of telling listeners how he escaped from the Tay Bridge disaster. Linskill is best remembered today for his fanciful *St Andrews Ghost Stories* which he retold with relish; he borrowed his stories from established legends elsewhere and from his own colourful imagination. Linskill died on 22 November 1929.

At the other end of the social scale were such 'literary characters' as 'Donald Blue'. Born in 1846, Donald Blue's real name was James McDonald and he was delivered of his mother Margaret Scott at the roadside somewhere between Pittenweem and St Andrews, or so he said; McDonald was brought up by Mrs Watters of Baker Lane. She dressed him in a bright blue jacket, from which he received his life-long nickname. Educated at Madras College as a free scholar, McDonald was somewhat mentally retarded and held multifarious jobs from ship's cook on a Baltic steamer to a labourer on the Burntisland harbour works. He married around 1891 and at the end of his career worked at the Links; an inmate of one of the town's lodging houses, McDonald died in 1909 and was accorded a pauper's funeral. For years people remembered 'Donald Blue's philosophy'; his maxims were common gossip and included these:

Gouff's guid enuf if yer no a caddie.
It's a camsteerie [perverse] warl' this, ye dinna
    ken wither it's a saxpence or a broken leg ye' re
    tae get the morn's morning.
A wee drappie's a' richt enuf, but ower mony
    drappies [i.e., of whisky] are no easy managed.
    Hooiver, aye waulk as strecht as ye can.

Ownership of a piano, for family recitals, was the aim of many socially upwardly mobile St Andreans, while the playing of the accordion, the fiddle and the bagpipe were the chosen instruments of the lower classes. Those who chose to learn the latter instrument could join the St Andrews Rifle Volunteer Pipe Band, begun in the early 1900s by Pipe-Major Benzie of the 93rd Sutherland Highlanders. The St Andrews Volunteers, by the by, founded in 1859, were disbanded in 1908 and many joined the new Territorial Force (1908), which was to become the Territorial Army.

Celebrated visitors to St Andrews at this period included General William Booth (1829–1912), founder of the Salvation Army, who held a meeting at the Town Hall in 1908; he was welcomed by the town council and drew a huge street crowd. The suffragettes (members of the Women's Suffrage Movement who agitated to get the parliamentary vote for women) also met in St Andrews Town Hall and at Martyrs Monument and were barracked by the students; the prominent English suffragette, Mrs Emmeline Pankhurst (1858–1928), visited the town in 1910 and 1911, to enjoy addressing a meeting lit by the Town Hall's first electric lights of 1909.

Both in Victorian and Edwardian times popular open-air public meeting places were at the memorial fountain (1880), Market Street, set up to remember the Victorian novelist George John Whyte-Melville on the site of the burgh's tolbooth; the bandstand (c.1890) on the Bruce Embankment and its neighbour the Martyrs' Monument. The latter was erected in 1842 to the design of the Edinburgh architect William Nixon (c.1810–48). It commemorates the Protestants Paul Craw (1433), Patrick Hamilton (1528), Henry Forrest (1533),

75. Martyrs' Monument, the Scores. Erected in 1842 the monument is neighbour to the Bruce Embankment, a popular promenading place from Victorian times.

George Wishart (1546), and Walter Myln (1558), who were martyred for their faith in St Andrews.

The Edwardian Age ended on 6 May 1910 when Edward VII died at a quarter to midnight at Buckingham Palace. His son was proclaimed as George V at St Andrews on Tuesday, 9 May, and Provost John Wilson encouraged the townsfolk to prepare for coronation parties. These were held on 22 June 1911 and the civic junketing went on all day, with bonfires at the Bruce Embankment and the harbour, and bunting festooned every street. Coronation mugs, medals and a newly minted penny were given to St Andrews schoolchildren and a loaf, a cake, tea and sundry grocery parcels were given to the poor along with a new shilling (5p); the choice of a jar of Bovril (hailed in *The Illustrated Sporting and Dramatic News* of 1 March 1890 as one of 'Two Infallible Powers: The Pope and Bovril) or a bottle of port was given to the 'invalid poor'. Soon the seemingly ordered, prosperous and sunny days of Edward's reign were to become only a nostalgic memory. Many of the boys who linked with the girls in merry dance down The Scores on Coronation Day would be slaughtered in the mud on the Franco-Belgian border just three short years away.

CHAPTER 16

The Tyrannising Game: Golf and St Andrews

> I think St Andrews was much pleasanter in the old days
> than now. There were no [golf hole] numbers at the start,
> no big hotels, no Calcutta Cups and Jubilee Vase Com-
> petitions, and much fewer dogs and excursion trains.
>
> William B. Skene of Pitlour (1902)

'The Monstrous Game of Golf will ultimately destroy St
Andrews.' This Victorian sentiment, which still echoes down
the years, was given a literary spin by St Andrews poet Robert
Fuller Murray (1863–93):

> Would you like to see a city given over,
> Soul and body, to a tyrannising game?
> If you would, there's little need to be a rover,
> For St Andrews is the abject city's name.[1]

Murray went on to say that 'Rich and poor alike are smitten
with the fever [of golf]', which a hundred years after his death
developed into a multi-million pound business within the
burgh. By 1691 the town was called 'The Metropolis of Golf;
the game replaced the burgh's magnetic ambience as a place of
pilgrimage to the shrine of St Andrew at the cathedral to offer a
new religious experience on the links. The 6,642-yard long Old
Course has become such sanctified turf, that visitors can be seen
stuffing divots into their golf bags as sacrosanct relics to take
home, much as the medieval pilgrim carried away a base-metal
medal of St Andrew. Today the heart and soul of St Andrews
is that ground by Pilmour Links, a 400-acre patch of sandy
'linksand' left behind by centuries of tides, where golf reputa-
tions are made and marred in front of a media world audience
of millions.

The controversy as to who actually 'invented' the game of golf still rages, with St Andrews firmly in the frame as the birthplace. Some brave souls aver that it was Roman soldiers who brought a form of golf to Fife; others suggest it came from the Orient. In 2006 Professor Ling Hongling of Lanzhou University, People's Republic of China, hit the headlines with the claim that (a form of) golf was popular in China from as long ago as AD 945. He noted that the *Dongxuan Records*, written during the Sung Dynasty (960–1279), tell of a game similar to golf called *chuiwan* ('hit ball'). Professor Ling further averred that *chuiwan* was 'clearly the pioneer of modern-day golf and was exported to Europe by Mongolian travellers during the late Middle Ages'. Thus Emperor Hui Tsung was the first 'royal fan' of golf, who played with jade and gold clubs which included a *pubang* (brassie) to a *shaobang* (3-wood), and thus predated Mary Queen of Scots' St Andrews golf playing by several hundred years. Despite all this, Scotland will always be recognised as the cradle of (modern) golf and St Andrews the 'home of golf'.

Today St Andrews has six public golf courses, five of eighteen holes and one of nine holes. The St Andrew Links are the largest

76. Hell Bunker, the Links, St Andrews. Edwardian golfers try their skills.

public golf venue in the world. A seventh golf course is planned to be completed with its associated facilities and club house by 2007. The course at Kinkell Braes is to cover 220 acres of former potato fields and is designed by David McLay Kidd; its character is a coastal clifftop course with a yawning chasm as a feature.

The Old Course (which extends now to 7,279 yards when the Open Championships are played), which originally had twenty-two holes, dates from medieval times and up to the nineteenth century ran at least as far as Murray Park. The earliest known survey of the Old Course was made in 1821, but the 1836 survey reduced it to eighteen holes; teeing grounds were introduced in 1846, and a green staff was employed by then. There have been few changes to the course since 1913, and there is still no Sunday play.

The Old Course was deemed 'the worst course on earth' by Bobby Jones when he first competed on it in 1921; he would win the Open three times in 1926, 1927 (at St Andrews) and 1930, but on his early encounters he walked off in disgust. Some time later he reflected to the press that the Old Course was 'the very best'.[2] The doughty golfer Jack Nicklaus called St Andrews links 'cattle pasture' in 1964, echoing what Sam Snead, the Open Champion in 1946, had said: 'Back home', remarked Snead, 'we plant beet on land like that.' Jack Nicklaus (b.1940) won two Opens at St Andrews (1970, 1978) and played his final Open at St Andrews in 2005. He said: 'If a golfer is going to be remembered he must win the title at St Andrews.'

Today, the Old Course remains by far the most difficult and deceptive to play. When the visiting golfer gazes down the first fairway from the first hole (the 370-yard 'Burn'), a deceptively easy shot is suggested. But under the eagle eye of the 'knowledgeable old-parties' in the Royal & Ancient Golf Club's 'Big Room', his nerve begins to go. On his first round at the Old Course in 1946 Dwight David Eisenhower (1890–1969), the US general and 34th President of the United States, took a few practice shots at the first tee, chickened out as he felt the gaze of the crowd on him and paced off to the second tee (the 411-yard

'Dyke'). Shamefaced he admitted: 'If I whiffed on the first at St Andrews, I'd never live it down.'

Sculpted largely by gale and tide over a period of 6,000 years, the Old Course has slim fairways, once cropped to the earth by grazing sheep, and among the coverts of gorse there are traps for the unwary golfer in the tall spiky marram and sea lyme grasses. More than one hundred bunkers await the player; some are moonscaped pits, while others are small saucers just large enough to hold an apoplectic player and his niblick. Even the names of the bunkers intimidate: 'The Coffin', 'Hell', 'Grave' and 'Lion's Mouth'. Nevertheless the links are shared by a wide variety of plants, from the blue fleabane to the harefoot clover, and wildlife from shelducks to skylarks.

An intriguing piece of architecture on the Old Course is the Swilcan Bridge near the eighteenth hole, the 'Tom Morris' (354 yards). This medieval bridge, in the spirit of the north-country packhorse bridges, was once the only seaward link between the castle and the cathedral with the Eden estuary, the early burgh harbour and the mussel beds.

To school the finest golfer, the Old Course is prone to perverse and illogically timed changes of weather. Sometimes the gales reach 60 mph here and golfers find their well-struck ball arcing behind them. Many remember that this happened to Eric Brown, and others still recall that sunny day in the 1970 British Open when Neal Coles scored a record 65 (7 under par), while Tony Jacklin was 8 under par at the 13th (398 yards 'Hole O'Cross'). The calm day was drenched by a sudden downpour which inundated the links and the game was called off. Next day, with back bent against the wind and rain, Jacklin struggled through the last few holes in 3 under par: 'The Old Course got the last laugh', he later philosophised to friends.

The New Course (6,516 yards) was constructed by the Royal & Ancient Golf Club in 1895. The Jubilee Course was built by the Town Council in 1897 to celebrate Queen Victoria's Diamond Jubilee. This originally consisted of twelve holes, but was increased to eighteen in 1912; a reconstruction of the course was undertaken in 1936 by Willie Auchterlonie,

Open Champion in 1893 and Hon. Professional of the Royal & Ancient Golf Club, 1935–36.

The course was extended and improved in 1981. The Eden Course (6,150 yards) was set out by the town council in 1912 and the Eden Tournament takes place there each August. The Balgove Course of nine holes was built in 1971, primarily for use by children and beginners. And 1988 saw new plans to upgrade the Jubilee Course, alter the Eden Course and build a new eighteen-hole Strathtyrum Course (1993), all of championship calibre, but remaining public. As well as the Duke's Course, owned by the Old Course Hotel, another hotel owns a course on the fringe of St Andrews. This is within the complex of St Andrews Bay Golf Resort and Spa, and comprises two courses, the 7,039-yard Torrance, created by Sam Torrance (Rider Cup captain 2004) and Gene Sarazan, and the 7,400-yard Devlin, designed by Australian Bruce Devlin and Gene Sarazan.

Opinions on the 'playability' of the links at St Andrews have varied down the years. Writing in 1855, David Salmond, one of the proprietors of the *Arbroath Herald*, noted that St Andrews links were very rough:

> There was but one course, and the same nine holes served for the outward as for the inward play. Each hole was marked by a small iron pin, with a bit of red rag attached. The greens were in the 'rough', and the bunkers were in their natural state. If a player went off the narrow course of good ground he was at once landed in very 'rough country', and the course at the ninth hole was all heathery and difficult, across its whole breadth.

These were the conditions that the first 'Greats' of golf, like Allan Robertson (b. St Andrews 1815), the golfball maker who was the first person to break 80 at St Andrews, had to deal with in refining the game.

David I's charter of 1123 ratified the links where golf is now played to be common ground belonging to the people of St Andrews. Golf historians aver that golf was being played here from the early 1400s, but the earliest historical reference to golf in Scotland is found in the year 1457, when James II, forbade the playing of golf (and football) as it kept men away from their archery practice. The local kirk sessions were much against golf too, particularly in the sixteenth century, as it encouraged players to profane the sabbath, and the very officers of the kirk were neglectful of their duties because of the game. The earliest note of golf in St Andrews is dated 1552, when a grant of rights of warren on the links was agreed by Archbishop John Hamilton, guaranteeing the continuing of the rights of St Andrews to play golf on the links as well as 'futeball, shuting and all games, as well as casting divots, gathering turfs (for roofing)'. Once the burghers of St Andrews rode ceremonially around the boundaries of the links to signify to the world the legality of their rights and the extent of their privileges; the ridings continued well into the nineteenth century. The links remained 'common ground' until they were exchanged by deed of excambion in part in 1763 with James Lumsden of Strathtyrum, and to Thomas Erskine, Earl of Kelly in 1797. All this was to get the town council out of debt, and for a while golfers fought a running battle with locals who were allowed to trap rabbits on the links. In 1848 George Cheape of Strathtyrum aquired the links which were brought back into golfers' favour, and by 1893 they were bought back by the town and became 'public property' by the Parliamentary Act of 1894.

Although golf was generally indulged in most actively by the gentry, the game on the Old Course was free of charge to all comers, inhabitants and visitors alike until 1913, then a fee of 1s (5p) was made for visitors. From 1912 to 1945 St Andrews ratepayers could play free, but in 1946 an annual subscription was imposed and the charging of fees per round became functional. By 1995 the St Andrews Links Clubhouse, the first clubhouse in the town freely for the use of visitors was opened, and in 2000 the Eden Clubhouse was opened as the second public venue.

The tradition of golf in St Andrews gave rise to the Royal & Ancient Golf Club, commonly known as the 'R&A'. The club is set overlooking the first and eighteenth tees of the Old Course. According to the records, on 14 May 1754, twenty-two noble-

77. The Royal & Ancient Club House, set overlooking the 1st and 18th tees of the Old Course. The building was erected in 1854.

men and gentlemen of Fife formed themselves into 'The Society of St Andrews Golfers'. They all subscribed towards the purchase of a Silver Club to be played for annually over the links; and, the winner of the match was to be 'Captain of the Golf' for the ensuing year. The Silver Club continued to be played for until 1824, when it was decided to choose the Captain by personal merit alone. Today the R&A Captain still 'plays himself in' with a symbolic stroke at the first tee of the Old Course; the occasion takes place at 8 a.m. on the day of the Club's Annual Meeting and the Captain rewards the caddie who retrieves the ball with a gold sovereign. The caddies whose skill can judge a Captain's potential, place themselves accordingly to retrieve the ball. When Edward, Prince of Wales played himself in as captain in 1922, the story goes that the caddies 'stood disloyally near the tee'.

In 1834 King William IV accepted the invitation to become the club's patron and thereafter the club was designated 'Royal & Ancient'. Club meetings took place in the early days at a number of places in the burgh, from Glass's Inn to the Black

Bull Tavern, and then in the Union Parlour on the site of the Grand Hotel which became the student residence of Hamilton Hall. The present clubhouse was built in 1854 and the R&A remains a private club whose members are 'invited' to join. In 1897 the club appointed its first Rules of Golf Committee, and from that date the R&A was recognised as 'Governing Authority for the Rules of Golf in all countries except the USA, Canada and Mexico'. The latter countries legislated their own rules, but in consultation with the R&A. The R&A conducts the Open and Amateur Championships, which were inaugurated in 1860 and 1885 respectively, and has done so since 1919. By 1888 the R&A had become the sole ruling body of the game. The first Open Championship to be played at St Andrews was in 1873. The R&A Clubhouse contains a multitude of 'golfing treasures', from portraits ranging from that of the longest surviving captain of the club in John Whyte-Melville of Bennochy and Strathkinness, who was a member for sixty years, to a portrait of Edward, Prince of Wales of 1922. The club also displays the old Dutch master *Ice on the Scheldt*, attributed to Van Ostade, presented to the club in 1949 by Robert Boothby, 1st Baron Boothby (1900–86), who was Rector of the University in 1958. Other treasures include cups, medals, trophies and clubs which belonged to famous golfers.

The earliest golf club to be founded in St Andrews, after the R&A, was the Thistle Golf Club which lasted in its first form from 1817 to 1838; this was a club for tradesmen and artisans and went into desuetude in 1839 but was re-formed in 1865 and still exists. The St Andrews Golf Club was instituted in 1843 as the golf club of the town's merchants and tradesmen too, and this club was one of those which retained the red jacket 'uniform' for many years. One of the Club's early captains was Allan Robertson (d.1859), the world's first professional golfer. The New Golf Club was founded in 1902. The first golf club for women in the town was founded in 1867 (also the first women's golf club in Scotland), and St Rule's Ladies Club was founded in 1898, while St Regulus Ladies Golf Club was founded before World War I.[3]

Although the caddying business declined after the introduction of caddie-carts in 1949 – the first caddying car to be wheeled over the Old Course was by the aviator and politician Baron Brabazon of Tara who died in 1964 – the caddies have remained a colourful lot. The name 'caddie' comes from the French *cadet* (junior), a word once used in Scotland to signify an 'errand boy'. With the decline of the fish trade in St Andrews, many of the old fishermen became caddies and added their pawky wit to caddy lore. Before World War I boy caddies were paid 1s 6d (7½p) and men 2s 6d (12½ p) per round. As many caddies had caddied since they were boys they knew the finer points of the game One such, George Smith McIntyre, nick-named Sodger, caddied for the Unionist Prime Minister 1915–16, A.J. Balfour, and remembered the politician consoling himself when he made a bad shot with the comment: 'If I always got what I wanted, I wouldn't play golf.' Other caddies made more caustic comments. Once when the Bishop of London whacked his ball out of the infamous Hell Bunker he said 'Out of Hell in one'. 'Aye, m'lord', said his caddy, 'and ye'd better tak the club wi' ye when ye dee.' The caddies still retain their own 'shelter' by the eighteenth green, dwarfed by the flagstaff once the mast of the famous windjammer *Cutty Sark*.

In 2005 the Professional Caddies Association, founded 2002, set in motion plans to site its 'Hall of Fame' in St Andrews. The association, which promotes golf scholarships for young people, has a range of photographs of famous golfing caddies including 'Tip' Anderson, Peter Colman and Willie Aitchison.

Golf personalities come and go, but the surname Morris will live on in golfing history. Thomas 'Auld Tom' Mitchell Morris (1821–1908) was born in North Street, son of a linen-weaver and letter-carrier; following elementary education at Madras College, he became apprentice to the golf-club and featherie ball-maker Allan Robertson. Eventually he was appointed greenkeeper of the R&A in 1865 and as 'Keeper of the Greens' earned £50 per annum; he continued in this position until 1903. The burgh is still full of Morris-lore and Auld Tom kept the St Andrews links in the premier position amongst British golf courses using the minimum of greenkeeping equipment; he began with a spade, a shovel and a barrow. Local lore has it

78. Thomas Mitchell Morris (1821–1908), legendary greenkeeper of the R&A. Known as 'Old Tom' he went on to win the Open Championship four times.

that he began to play golf at the age of six and he went on to win the Open Championship four times – he failed to beat the celebrated Willie Park by one stroke in 1860 during his first ever Open. The Home Green, the 354-yard 18th hole, was named in his memory; it was considered by Morris himself to be his finest work. Eventually Auld Tom was surpassed in golfing skill by his son 'Young Tom' Morris, who won the Open Championship three times in a row to 1870. Young Tom died in 1875 at the early age of twenty-four. Memorials to the two famous Morrises are to be found in the cathedral graveyard.

Many a skilled golfer in St Andrews began as a cleek-maker, that nineteenth-century word for a golf-club based on the old Scots 'cleekit' meaning hooked. It is not known exactly when club and ball making was begun in St Andrews, but by 1672 the likes of James Pett was supplying such St Andrews *alumni* as James Graham, 1st Marquis of Montrose. 'Forgan is one of the best known names in the club-making trade, and wherever golf has penetrated, clubs turned out by this firm are to be found'. So one correspondent to the magazine *Golf Illustrated* commented about Messrs R. Forgan & Son in the early 1900s. Robert Forgan (1824–1900), who learned club making from his uncle Hugh Philp (1782–1856), official club maker to the Society of Golfers, took over the latter's business in 1856; by 1890 he was employing fifty workmen. In 1863–64, when the then Prince of Wales was elected Captain of the R&A, Robert Forgan made him a set of clubs which won him the ultimate imprimatur to legend all his wares 'By Appointment to His Majesty King Edward VII'; the Prince of Wales' feathers were impressed below the maker's name.

At their premises in Pilmour Links Forgan made golf-balls famous the world over and boasted that they alone employed a man to hand-hammer golf-balls to give them extra drive and straightness. Robert Forgan also pioneered the use of the hickory shafts for clubs, and he bought his wood, from Quebec, at Dundee docks. For more than two hundred years the only accepted golf-ball was a 'featherie', a sphere packed with down, which dated from around 1618. Then in 1845 a St Andrean called Robert Paterson produced a ball of gutta-percha, only bettered by the rubber-covered ball of 1899, still in use today. Golf cleek-making still carries on in modern St Andrews to carry on the traditions of Forgan, Tom Stewart and Laurie Auchterlonie.

The British Golf Museum (1990) in Golf Place at the foot of the Bruce Embankment contains the largest collection of golf memorabilia in Europe. It presents a history of golf from the Middle Ages to the present, highlighting past Open Championships and players, with very early film of golf play.

And so golf goes on in St Andrews and always will while the ancient burgh exists, as George Fullerton Carnegie of Pitarrow wrote:

> And still St Andrews Links with flags unfurl'd
> Shall peerless reign, and challenge all the world.[4]

CHAPTER 17

World Famous City

One does not tire of life in St Andrews town.

Russell Amos Kirk, *St Andrews* (1954)

Never since that day in 1942 when the aircraft of Hitler's National Socialist Reich dropped bombs just south of the Kinness Burn has St Andrews been bothered much with war. Yet there is a kind of ongoing turf war between two opposing groups alive in modern St Andrews. One represents housing developers and golf course planners, while the other includes such as the St Andrews Preservation Trust and the St Andrews Green Belt Forum. The bone of contention is how far St Andrews should develop both inside and outside the old burgh boundaries. A key area of dispute is the extent to which St Andrews will be protected by the green belt protection area, to include Boarhills and Strathkinness, that the Fife Council has proposed. Only through a public inquiry process will the conundrum be solved, if ever, to everyone's satisfaction. To this end too, heritage groups and others are making an attempt to have St Andrews created a World Heritage Site.

Although the population of St Andrews had swollen to 14,500 by 2005, from the 4,590 of the late eighteenth century, the medieval core plan of St Andrews has changed little since the first attempts to depict the town by such as Captain John Slezer (d.1714) in his *Theatrum Scotiae* (1693).

The southern development of St Andrews evolved mainly between 1930 and 1980 with the local abattoir, opened in 1932 to replace the one in South Bridge Street, being the precursor of the tiny edge of town 'industrial estate'.

The St Andrews Preservation Trust is a leading watchdog on conservation and preservation work in the burgh. The trust was founded in 1937, incorporated in 1938, and has the clearly defined object of securing 'the preservation of the amenities and historical character of St Andrews and its neighbourhood'. Preservation work had begun in earnest in the town in the eighteenth century, when through the prompting of the university, the Exchequer repaired St Rule's Tower in 1789 and through the early nineteenth century a large portion of the castle, West Port, priory walls and cathedral were repaired.

There are those who aver that 'vandalism' was mixed with preservation and cite how the medieval town kirk (Holy Trinity) was ruthlessly destroyed as was the medieval hall of St Salvator's College, and several other ancient architectural features. The Preservation Trust's museum at 12 North Street, within the old Ladyhead, contains exhibitions of a distillation of the town's history in the form of an old grocer's shop, and old chemist's shop, early postcards and photographs of St Andrews, and bygones of the town and ephemera of the fishing community. Incidentally, 12 North Street with its moulded doorway dates from 1619 and has a panelled hall; the house was renovated in 1937 and 1963 and its garden redeveloped.

Golfing and housing schemes go on often promoted by outside events; for instance St Andrews house prices soared, some said, because of the 'Prince William factor'; this due to the presence of the royal heir to the throne during study at the university 2001–05. Yet, not all development schemes meet with success. In 1999 the Gateway Centre was built by private developers on a prestigious site at the eastern entry to St Andrews. It was to be a £9 million upmarket golf and leisure club. It did not come to fruition. It was bought by the university in 2004 and re-opened in 2005 to house the new university school of management with temporary university exhibitions, and tourist facilities. Thus the university added more property to be the town's biggest landlord.

St Andrews has been a burgh since the 1140s and its true focus of life is still the medieval old town. The burgh's heart still shows it to be a distinctly Scottish town of home-grown architectural traditions as befits a place that has always played an important role in the history of Scotland. The burgh has survived time, tide and weather and offers a network of wide streets, wynds, quads and leafy squares of honey-coloured medieval sandstone buildings which merge with the grey of Victorian and Edwardian architecture. There is a harmony here of seascape and landscape offering a cosy co-existence for college man and woman as it did once for burgess and cleric. For the visitor the wynds, that lovely soothing Scottish word for a lane leading off a main thoroughfare, in particular have much to offer in surprise views and a semi-private world of character-ful buildings, flowers and trees. And South Street offers the most wynds: there's Baker Lane with its sculpted crowned head of circa the fourteenth century, set into a gable end; there's Crail's Lane, wherein the burgh of Crail was assigned feus in 1517; there's the pantiled houses of Imrie's Close and Rose Lane; there's Ladebraes Lane with its high walls leading to the quiet cul-de-sac by Westview and leafy Queen's Terrace. And Abbey Court leads to the new theatre set in a re-sculpted lang rigg.

St Andrews has played a key role in the development of modern theatre in Scotland. The idea of a theatre in the Old Byre of the Abbey Street Dairy Farm was first conceived by Alexander Brown Paterson MBE (1907–89). A journalist by profession, Alex Paterson was the theatre's administrator until he retired in 1980; he had been the theatre's resident play-wright, actor and major-domo for over fifty years. In tales against himself he regretted turning down Dame Maggie Smith for a job in her early days. The theatre was founded in 1933 and the guiding lights of the enterprise were members of the St Andrews Play Club which had been formed in embryo amongst members of Hope Park Church Bible Class. Plays were per-formed in very spartan surroundings at the Old Byre from 1933 to 1936, then theatrical regulations had to be complied with, and after refurbishment a new performing licence was granted in 1937. Thereafter during summer the Play Club presented a repertoire of plays for both visitors and residents. Activities were called to a temporary halt when war broke out in 1939, but the Dundee Repertory Company were able to stage per-formances from time to time while their theatre was being reconstructed. The first St Andrews Repertory Company was formed in 1940 and somehow the theatre managed to remain open until the end of the war in 1945. In 1969 there was a final season of 'the Old Byre' and preparations were made for a new theatre opened by the late Scottish actor Andrew Cruickshank in 1970.[1] At the end of the 1990s it was decided to build a new theatre and a competition was held to find a suitable design for the new building. Progress was slow as the demolition site was of enormous archaeological significance being part of the earliest development of the burgh from the 1160s. The new complex was opened in 2001, by actress Elaine C. Smith, with studio theatre, gallery and restaurant.

Worth mentioning too is the £750,000 Sea Life Centre constructed on the site of the Step Rock Pool bathing station

79. Alex Paterson (1907–89) was the first to conceive a theatre in the Old Byre, Abbey Street Dairy Farm. Here he surveys the original site. Founded in 1933 the theatre was redeveloped 1969–70 to be transformed into a new complex, opened in 2001. [Alexander Brown Paterson]

80. St Andrews from its southern boundaries in 1925, showing Nelson Street, Largo Road and Claybraes Farm. The LNER railway line sweeps across the Kinness Burn to the left. [RAF Leuchars]

and adjacent to the British Golf Museum. The Centre was opened on 15 June 1989. Coastal erosion has always been a problem in St Andrews, and for hundreds of years succeeding town councils conducted a make-do-and-mend policy. In recent years though the existing sea wall along the worst stretch of erosion, the walkway by Prior Hepburn's Walls, overlooking the harbour, was buttressed to underpin the existing sea wall of 1856–57. Since medieval times as much as three feet of cliff has been swept away by the sea at any one time. The regular planting of *ammophilia areanaria*, known as marram grass, along the West Sands has helped to slow the erosion by sea and wind.

It was the effects of World War II that drastically focused attention in St Andrews both socially and architecturally. The town received its first Air Raid Warning on Friday, 20 October 1939 and on 25 October 1940 the town received 'direct hits' from bombs in Westburn Lane, Kinnessburn, Greenside Dairy

and Alison Place. Hardly a blitz, but enough to sow the seed of
the recognition of the need for future conservation. The war
gave St Andrews a chance to welcome strangers within her
gates on a scale not seen since medieval times when students
came from Belgium, Poland and France to study and make St
Andrews one of the most cosmopolitan places in Christendom.
For, at this time the town welcomed modern generations of
Poles, but under very different circumstances than the pursuit
of learning.

Polish soldiers arrived in St Andrews in 1940 and caused
something of a stir with their distinctive uniforms and cloaks,
and the enthusiastic manner in which they sang their way to
mass at St James's Church on The Scores. The soldiers were
billeted in the hotels, church halls and private houses in the
town and carried out duties as a part of the coastal defence
garrison. Some of them continued their university education
here. The Polish staff officers had their headquarters at Cupar

81. The LNER railway line in the foreground leads the eye to the western
development of St Andrews at Pilmour Links, Gibson Place and Windmill
Road by 1925. [RAF Leuchars]

and the Commander-in-Chief of the Polish Army in Scotland, General Wladyslaw Sikorski (1881–1943) had his main base at Forfar. Sikorski was killed in an air-crash over Gibraltar in 1943; a memorial to him is to be found in Kinburn Park. Several of the Polish soldiers remained in the town after the war and married local girls and their names are perpetuated in telephone book and electoral register. Today a colourful panel in the wall of the Town Hall speaks of the gratitude of Polish soldiers who had received hospitality in St Andrews during World War II.

Wither St Andrews today? The seagulls will continue to wheel and dive over the town; the red gown will remain as a symbol of learning; and the towers of St Rule, St Salvator and Holy Trinity Church will define the skyline as they have for hundreds of years. Or will they? Perhaps a clue to the future of old St Andrews is seen in the timeless permanence of the ruins of Blackfriars in South Street, a fragment when Scotland's and the town's modern history was being made. Today there are parts of the old town centre that would be recognised by old-time visitors Johnson and Boswell, Scott and Lang, but what of the extremities? Developers circle like wolves keen to expand into the fields around St Andrews. Will they succeed? One certainty is that St Andrews will continue its evolution from university city and holiday resort into a golf mega-city as the ever increasing dominance of the 'tyrannising game' swamps all else. Myriad folk come to play golf at St Andrews who never enter the old town to shop or just enjoy the hidden secrets of wynd and close. Once St Andrews was the centre of civilised Scotland, but now her future is still tied solely to the erratic trajectory of a little white ball.

The Bishops and Archbishops of St Andrews

circa 900   *The seat of the Scoto-Pictish kingdom moved to Kilrymont (St Andrews), and there followed a succession of Chief Bishops of the Scots (Scotorum maximus episcopus).*

908   *Cellach.* First Bishop of Alban.

921   *Fothad.* Expelled 955 by Indulph who reigned 954–62. Lived in exile. Died 963.

955   *Malsius.* Disciple of St Duthac.

963   *Maelbrigdi.*

970   *Cellach*, son of Ferdalaig. John Fordun the Chronicler says that this bishop was the first to go to Rome for his confirmation of office.

995   Two little known bishops are mentioned in the *Scotichronicon* as holding the see, namely *Malmore* and *Malsius.*

1025   *Alwyus.*

1028   *Maledirin.*

1055   *Tuthald.*

1059   *Fothad*, called High Bishop of Alban. 1093: *The see was empty for fourteen years.*

1107   *Turgot.* Prior of Durham. Author of *Vita S. Margarete.* Died at Durham, 31 August 1115.

1115   *The See was void until 29 June 1120.*

1120   *Eadmer.* A monk of Canterbury; returned to Canterbury 1121. Died 13 January 1123–24.

1123/24   *Robert.* Prior of Scone. His seal records him as *Sigillum Roberti epi. Scotorum* – thus as 'Bishop of the Scots'. Died 1158/9.

1158–59   The See was probably empty for over a year and Waltheof, Abbot of Melrose, stepson of David I, was chosen as bishop by popular acclaim, but he declined the see.

1160s   Arnold. Second Abbot of Kelso. Founder of St Andrews Cathedral. Died 13 September 1162 and was buried at St Rule's.

1163   Richard. Chancellor to King Malcolm IV. Died 1178 in the *infirmarium* of the Canons of St Andrews

1178   John the Scot. Archdeacon of St Andrews. Chosen by the St Andrews chapter, but expelled by William the Lion. Became Bishop of Dunkeld. Died in 1203 at Newbattle Abbey.

1183   Hugh. Chaplain of William the Lion, was appointed to the See by the king, but his appointment was quashed by Pope Alexander III. He was excommunicated. Served as bishop from 1183–88. Died at Rome, 4 August 1188.

1189   Roger de Beaumont. Chancellor to the King of Scots. Built St Andrews Castle as a residence. Died 7 July 1202 at Cambuskenneth Abbey. Buried in St Rule's.

1202   William Malvoisine. Lord Chancellor of Scotland. Bishop of Glasgow. Died 9 July 1238 at the episcopal manorial house of Inchmurtach. Buried in the cathedral.

1238   (Geoffrey. Postulated. Bishop of Dunkeld. Disallowed by Pope Gregory and Alexander III).

1239   David de Bernham. Sub-dean attached to the court of Alexander III. Chamberlain to the king. Dedicated and consecrated 140 churches. Died 26 April 1252 at the Kelso Abbey property at Nenthorn, Berwickshire. Buried at Kelso Abbey.

1253   (Robert de Stuteville, or D'Etrtrville, Dean of Dunkeld; election disallowed by the King. Became Bishop of Dunkeld. Died 1283.)

1253–54   Abel de Golynn. Archdeacon of St Andrews and papal chaplain. Died the 'morrow of St Andrew' (1 December) 1254, buried in the cathedral.

1255   *Gameline.* Chancellor of the King and papal chaplain. Died on the 'morrow of St Vitalis, Martyr' (28 April) 1271 at Inchmurtach, buried in the cathedral.

1271   *William Wishart.* Archdeacon of St Andrews and Chancellor to the King. Cathedral nave reconstructed during his episcopate. Died 28 May 1279 at Merbotill, Teviotdale. Buried in the cathedral.

1279   *William Fraser.* Chancellor of the King and Dean of Glasgow. The first to assume the title *Episcopus Sancti Andreae.* Died at Artuyl, France 20 August 1297, buried in the Church of the Preaching Friars, Paris. Heart buried in the cathedral.

1297   *William de Lamberton.* Chancellor of Glasgow. Consecrated the cathedral in 1318. Died in the prior's chamber, St Andrews, 7 June 1328, and buried in the cathedral.

1328   *James Ben.* Archdeacon of St Andrews and papal chaplain. Died Bruges, 22 September 1332 and buried in the chapel of the Canons Regular of Eckhout.

1332   *(William Bell, Dean of Dunkeld, elected to See but election not confirmed. Died an Augustinian canon at St Andrews, 1342/43. The Scotichronicon says the See was vacant for 9 years, 5 months, 8 days.)*

1342   *William de Landells.* Rector of Kinkell, diocese of Aberdeen. Died in the Priory of St Andrews, 23 September 1385, and buried in the cathedral.

1385   *(Stephen de Pa, Prior of St Andrews, nominated. Taken prisoner by English pirates on his way to Rome and died in Alnwick Castle, Northumberland, 2 March 1385.)*

1385   *Walter Trail.* Dean of Dunkeld, canon and academic. Died at St Andrews Castle, 1401, buried in the cathedral.

1388   *(Alexander de Neville, Archbishop of York, translated to the See by the antipope Urban VI, but appointment unrecognised.)*

1398   (*Thomas de Arundel, Archbishop of York, then*
         Canterbury, translated to the See by the antipope Boniface
         IX, but appointment unrecognised.)
1401   (*Thomas Stewart, Archdeacon of St Andrews and bastard*
         of Robert II. Renounced rights.)
1402   (*Walter de Danielston, canon of Aberdeen. Never*
         confirmed in office.)
1402–03 (*Gilbert Greenlaw, Bishop of Aberdeen, postulated to the See.*
         Pope Benedict XIII refused to confirm the election. d.1422.)
1403   *Henry Wardlaw.* Precentor of Glasgow. Chartered
         the University of St Andrews. Died at St Andrews
         castle, 1440
         (*N.B: John Trevor was appointed to the See by antipope*
         Benedict XIII in 1408, but the appointment was
         unrecognised.)
1440:   *James Kennedy.* Bishop of Dunkeld. Founder of St
         Salvator's College. Last Bishop of St Andrews.
         Died May 1465, buried in St Salvator's Chapel.
         [St Andrews erected into an archepiscopal and
         metropolitan see by Pope Sixtus IV, 17 Aug 1472.]
1465   *Patrick Graham.* Bishop of Brechin. Great-grandson
         of Robert III. Died a captive at St Serf's Inch,
         Lochleven, 1478.
1478   *William Schevez.* Coadjutor, 1467. Archdeacon of St
         Andrews. Died 28 January 1496/7.
1497   (*James Stewart, Duke of Ross. Provided, 1497. Second*
         son of James III. Probably never consecrated. Died 1504.)
1504   (*Alexander Stewart, bastard of James IV. Slain Flodden,*
         9 September 15. Died at Edinburgh in 1514 before
         securing possession of the See.)
1513   (*John Hepburn, Prior of St Andrews. Disputed his own*
         election.)
1513   (*Cardinal Innocenzo Cibo, appointed to the See by his*
         uncle Pope Leo X. Resigned.)
1514   *Andrew Forman.* Bishop of Moray. Died 12 March
         1520/1.
1522   *James Beaton.* Archbishop of Glasgow. Died 14
         February 1539.

1539	*Cardinal David Beaton.* Coadjutor 1537. Nephew of James Beaton. Bishop of Mirepoix. Murdered by Protestant fanatics, 29 May 1546.
1546	*John Hamilton.* Promoted 1547. Born 3 February 1512, bastard of James, Earl of Arran. Abbot of Paisley, matriculated at St Leonard's College. Keeper of the Privy Seal 1543–56. Treasurer 1545–46. Bishop of Dunkeld. Hanged at Stirling for his part in the murder of Regent James, Earl of Moray. Possibly buried at Paisley.
1551	*(Gavin Hamilton, Coajutor 1551. Abbot of Kilwinning. Served the See during the severe illness of Archbishop John. Hamilton. Slain 1571.)*
1559	When John Hamilton was driven from his See in 1559 the administrative fabric of the medieval Church collapsed, but the Protestant Reformers did not dissolve the titles and benefices of sitting bishops and archbishops.
1572	*John Douglas.* His status was regularised by the Concordat of Leith. Principal of St Mary's College from 1547.
1575	*Patrick Adamson.* Alumnus of St Andrews. Died 1592.
1578	*Bishoprics abandoned.*
1604	*Primacy restored.*
1604	*George Gledstanes.* Titular Bishop of Caithness. Died 1615.
1615	*John Spottiswoode.* Archbishop of Glasgow. Driven into exile by the Covenanters.
1638–61	*Government of the Church by presbyterianism.*
1661	*James Sharp.* Murdered 1679 (see pp. 174–175).
1679	*Alexander Burnet.* Archbishop of Glasgow. Buried in St Salvator's. Died 1684.
1684	*Alexander Rose* (or *Ross*). Last Protestant Archbishop. Died 1704.
1689	*Episcopacy abolished in the Scottish established Church.* The episcopal title of St Andrews disappeared from 1704 until 1842 when it was restored as one of the

constituents in the Bishopric of St Andrews,
Dunkeld and Dunblane. The episcopalians,
however, had used the title for an archbishopric
from 1704 and in 1837 St Andrews was within the
United Diocese of Edinburgh, Fife and Glasgow;
and after 1838 within the United Diocese of
Dunkeld, Dunblane and Fife.

Since 1842 there has been a succession of episcopalian bishops
using St Andrews in their title of which two had homes in
St Andrews, namely Charles Wordsworth (consecrated 1853,
d.1892) and Charles Edward Plumb (consecrated 1908, d.1931).

When the Roman Catholic hierarchy was restored in 1876,
it was placed under the pastorship of an Archbishop of St
Andrews and Edinburgh (to reflect the ancient archepiscopal
See and the political capital).

The Provosts of St Andrews, c.1144–1975

As the head of a Scottish municipal corporation or burgh, the position has been described as that of *Provost* since the late fourteenth century in various spellings. After founding the burgh of St Andrews around 1144, Bishop Robert appointed Mainard the Fleming to be its *praepositus*, a title taken from the Latin for 'president'. While the position was to develop by the fifteenth century as civic head and chief magistrate, Mainard was nothing more than Bishop Robert's agent, acting on the cleric's orders. Mainard's successors, up to the late fourteenth century – if there were any at all – remain almost invisible on record and the role of civic head may have been invested in a senior priest on the cathedral staff. It was not until 1385 that any succession of provosts for St Andrews began to emerge. Even so there are gaps in service records for varying reasons, during which there may have been periods of interregna wherein candidates jockeyed for position. The position of Provost was abolished in 1975 and remains as a title only of Lord Provost as a courtesy in some authorities. As far as records permit, this listing of Provosts can be made for St Andrews:

Mainard the Fleming. c.1144
Andrew Pay. 1385–86
Robert Buteler of Rumgally 1409–10
Richard Kydd 1416–17
John Bower 1418–19
William de Kynnard 1422–23
Richard Kydd 1427–28

Robert Buteler of Rumgally 1428–29
Thomas Ramsay 1430–31
Thomas Arthur 1431–34
John de Carmychell 1434–36
Thomas Arthur 1436–38
David Brown 1447–50
Andrew Ramsay 1450–51
Alan Stewart 1452–53
Robert Maxwell 1453–54
George Martin 1455–59
William Bonar 1459–61
Jota Waugh 1461–62
John Jackson 1465–66
John Lermonth 1473–74
Henry Sheves of Kilwhiss 1475–76
Alexander Lamby 1477–78
Robert Lermonth 1483–84
William Waugh 1488–89
John Carstairs 1489–90
William Waugh 1490–91
Robert Lermonth 1494–98
William Waugh 1502–03
David Lermonth of Clatto 1505–21
Sir James Lermonth of Dairsie 1525–47
Sir Patrick Lermonth of Dairsie 1548–86
James Lermonth of Dairsie 1588–93
Captain William Murray of Pitcairlie 1593–95
James Lermonth of Dairsie 1595–96
William Lermonth of Clatto 1597–1601
James Lermonth of Dairsie 1602–04
Sir John Lermonth of Balcomie 1607–08
John Knox 1609–11
Alexander Winchester 1611–12
Duncan Balfour 1612–13
Alexander Winchester 1613–15
John Knox 1615–16
Duncan Balfour 1616–19
Thomas Lentron 1619–21

John Carstairs 1621–23
Henry Arthur 1623–25
John Carstairs 1625–26
Robert Tailyeour........................... 1626–29
John Carstairs 1629–30
Robert Tailyeour........................... 1630–34
John Lepar 1634–37
Robert Tailyeour........................... 1637–44
John Lepar 1645–46
James Sword 1646–47
James Watson 1647–49
James Lentron............................. 1650–51
James Watson of Aithernie 1651–53
James Sword 1654–55
James Lentron............................. 1656–57
James Wood 1657–58
William Lentron 1658–59
James Wood 1659–60
William Lentron 1660–61
James Lentron............................. 1661–62
Robert Lentron of Kincaple 1662–72
John Geddie of St Nicholas................... 1672–80
John Easson............................... 1680–83
John Geddie............................... 1683–86
Sir William Sharp of Scotscraig............... 1687
William Lindsay 18th Earl of Crawford 1689–98
John Lindsay 19th Earl of Crawford.......... 1699–1710
Alexander Watson of Aithernie 1710–16
Patrick Haldane............................ 1716–20
Colonel Philip Anstruther of Airdrie 1720–24
William Douglas of Glenbervie 1724–46
Andrew Watson............................. 1746–53
James Lumsdain of Rennyhill 1753–60
George Dempster of Dunnichen............... 1760–76
Alexander Watson 1776–79
Colonel John Nairne 1779–82
Alexander Duncan of St Fort 1783–93
John Campbell 4th Earl of Breadalbane 1793–96

Alexander Duncan of Castlefield 1796–99
Thomas Erskine 6th Earl of Kellie 1799–1809
Robert Meldrum of Bonnyton 1809–22
William Haig of Seggie. 1822–33
Kirkby Dalrymple. 1833–35
George Cruikshank. 1835–36
William Erskine of Blackburn. 1836–37
Patrick Wallace. 1837–42
Hugh Lyon Playfair 1842–61
Walter Thomas Milton. 1861–67
Lieutenant-General George Moncrieffe. 1867–69
Walter Thomas Milton. 1869–81
John Paterson LLD – Clifton Bank 1881–87
John Paterson – Kinburn 1887–93
John MacGregor. 1893–99
James Ritchie Welch. 1899–1903
George Murray. 1903–08
John Wilson 1908–11
The Rev. Professor John Herkless. 1911–15
Major Charles Henry Morris Cheape. 1915
Andrew Aikman 1915–18
The Rev. Andrew Sloan DD 1918–24
William Lamond. 1924–27
William Norman Boase LLD 1927–36
John Reid 1936–42
George Bruce 1942–49
William Procter Alexander Tulloch 1949–52
Jessie Love Moir. 1952–55
David Fraser. 1955–58
Robert Leonard 1956–61
Thomas Thomson Fordyce. 1961–70
David Niven MBE JP. 1970–73
John Buchanan Gilchrist TD MA LLD 1973–75

The Streets of Medieval St Andrews

Abbey Street: East margin abutting the priory precinct. Developed as far as Greenside Place by around 1250; name known since 1843. Also identified as Prior's Wynd.

Abbey Walk: Follows priory precinct wall as far as Balfour Place. Tracks south from 1260. Developed as commercial way across Stormolind, or Bow Brig to Tiends Gate in the sixteenth century. Medieval route to and from St Nicholas Hospital.

Argyll Street: Name dates from 1843, but here was a settlement before 1140; probable derivation from Gaelic *Erra-Ghaidheal*, 'borderland of the Gael'.

Baker Lane: Developed 1160–1260. Once Baxter Wynd or Bakehouse Wynd 1500–1700.

Bell Street: Within the burgh development area that had spread by the mid-sixteenth century. Developed as a street after 1844, named after Madras College founder Rev. Dr Andrew Bell.

Butts Wynd: Led to the archery butts.

(North) Castle Street: Extant from the founding of the burgh. During the 1400s it is found in documents as *Vicus Piscatorum* (Street of the Fishermen). Sometimes known as *Vicus Maris* (Sea Street), or Fishergait, or Castle Wynd. Castle Street by 1843.

(South) Castle Street: Extension road from the castle by 1140. Variously known as Rattonrow, or Fisher's Vennel (1400s) to Huxtar Wynd, or Heuksters' Wynd (1500s). Modern name from 1843.

Church Street: Developed from around 1160, named after Holy Trinity Church. Important merchants' lane by early 1400s.

College Street: Developed from around 1160, and known by the early 1400s as Mercat Wynd, then Bucklar Wynd. After 1450 renamed following the founding of St Salvator's College.

Crail's Lane: Herein properties of the Collegiate Church of Crail whose erection was ratified by Archbishop Andrew Forman in 1517. Up to the 1700s known as New Close.

Gregory Lane/Gregory Place: Within the earliest foundation area of the burgh, but only named after Professor David Gregory (1712–66), who held the university chair of mathematics.

Greyfriars Gardens: Runs down the policies of the now-vanished house of the Observant Friars (Franciscans) whose site was granted to the burgh in 1567. Developed 1834–36 as North Bell Street; Greyfriars Gardens after 1896.

Logie's Lane: Extant from around 1160. Once called Logie's Wynd after Thomas Logie, Canon of St Salvator's College, he died in 1474 having held property in this area. Also known as Coffin Row. Medieval thoroughfare led into the now-vanished graveyard of Holy Trinity Church.

Louden's Close: Property running to the west of Blackfriars Friary, within the development of the town after 1260.

Market Street: Developed east–west during around 1160 to 1560. A market developed at its midway point by around the fourteenth century. *Vicus Fori* in documents as well as Mercatgait. Narrow Mercatgait is its oldest (eastward) section.

Murray Park: Although this is a development of the 1890s onwards, the junction with North Street forms the sixteenth-century limit of the burgh and the site of the town entrance known as Northgait.

Muttoe's Lane: Once known as Bakehouse Close, the lane is named after the Mutto family who once owned property here in the sixteenth century. One Thomas Mutto was Town Clerk of St Andrews.

North Street: *Vicus Borealis/Vicus Aquilonalis*. Once Northgait, developed east–west from the foundation of the burgh.

(The) Pends/Pends Road. From Scots 'Pend', an arch, vault, arch
  of a bridge and so on. In this case describes the fourteenth-
  century gateway into the domestic range of the Augustinian
  Priory. Roadway leads down to The Shore and is significant
  within the medieval development of the cathedral/priory
  site.

Queen's Gardens: Although developed 1862–64, the site of the
  1859–61 Town Hall was within a Southgait development
  from around 1160–1260. (Once Queen Street)

(The) Scores: Developed east–west. At the east end it began as
  Vicus Maris, Sea Street, as frontage to the castle site. Thence
  Castlegait. Where the castle precinct ended was the Swal-
  lowgait (now vanished gateway also known as Swallow
  Port). Name derivation, thought to have been from 'scaur',
  a clifftop.

Shorehead: Developed before around 1160. Links with The
  Shore as the medieval mercantile harbour site.

South Street: Vicus Australis/Vicus Burgensium. Developed east–
  west. Once Southgait. This was the main medieval processional way from the cathedral.

Union Street: So named from around 1830, once known as Foul
  Waste from the probable site of a burgh midden.

Notes

Chapter 1

1. Richard Feachem, *The North Britons: The Prehistory of a Border People*, pp. 22, 28.
2. Bruce Walker and Graham Ritchie, *Exploring Scotland's Heritage: Fife and Tayside*, pp.171–3.
3. *Diodorus Historike. History of the World* in 40 volumes, from the Creation to the Gallic wars of Caesar.
4. Strabo, *Historical Studies*.
5. M.J. Rains, D.W. Hall *et al.*, *Excavations in St Andrews 1980–89*, pp.7ff.
6. There are no surface visible remains at Carpow, Newburgh, and the site is on private land not open to the public. See displays of Carpow artefacts at Dundee Museum. See: Lawrence Keppie, Scotland's *Roman Remains*, pp. 153ff.
7. A worthwhile introduction to the Picts is seen in A. Ritchie, *The Picts*.
8. Bede, *Historia ecclesiastica gentis Anglorum*, 731.
9. A. Jackson, *The Symbol Stones of Scotland*.
10. David Hay Fleming, *St Andrews Cathedral Museum*, pp. 3–10.
11. William Reeves, Bishop of Down, *The Life of Saint Columba*, Dublin, 1857.
12. John Lesley, Bishop of Ross, *De Origine Moribus et Rebus Gestis Scotorum*, Libri Decem, Rome, 1578.

Chapter 2

1. For a discussion of legends concerning the Cult of St Andrew, see: Ursula Hall, *St Andrew and Scotland*, Ch. 4.

2. William Forbes Skene (ed.), *Chronicles of the Picts, Chronicles of the Scots and Other Early Memorials of Scottish History*, 1871–72, pp. 138–40, 183–8, 375–7.
3. Hall, p. 60.
4. See: James Ussher, Archbishop of Armagh, *De . . . Ecclesiarum . . . Successione*, 1613.
5. Documents in the British Museum and Wolfenbüttel, Germany.
6. Hall, pp.14–15. James D. Galbraith, *The Sources of the Aberdeen Breviary*, pp.164–7.
7. *A History of Northumberland*, 1896. W.F. Skene, author of *Celtic Scotland*, 1876–80, also gives credit to Richard of Hexham's story.
8. Bede. See: n. 8, Ch. 1.
9. Douglas Young, *St Andrews: Town & Gown, Royal & Ancient*, p. 17.
10. Andrew of Wyntoun, Orygynale *Cronikil of Scotland*; cited c.1420.
11. James Thomson, *The History of Dundee*, p. 11.
12. Thomson, pp. 13–14.
13. D. Brown and T.O. Clancy (eds), *Spes Scotorum: Hope of the Scots, St Columba, Iona and Scotland*, n. 46, p.107; n. 54, p.109. For early bishops, see also: W.F. Skene, *Celtic Scotland*, vol. ii, pp. 323–55.
14. John Dowden, *The Bishops of Scotland*, pp. 1–3.

Chapter 3

1. John Dowden, *The Bishops of Scotland*, pp. 3–4.
2. *Ibid.*, pp. 5–6.
3. D.E. Easson, *Medieval Religious Houses: Scotland*, p. 83.
4. Easson, p. 191.
5. See such texts as: James Houston Baxter, *Copiale Prioratus Sanctiandree – The Letter-Book of James Haldestone, Prior of St Andrews (1418–1443)*.
6. Easson, pp. 78, 79–81.
7. In 1683 there were still sixteen towers according to George Martine, *Reliquiae Divi Andreae*, 1797.
8. James K. Robertson, *About St Andrews and About*, p. 72.
9. W.T. Linskill, *St Andrews Haunted Tower*.
10. Dowden, p. 7.
11. Richard Fawcett and Richard Oram, *Melrose Abbey*, pp. 90, 135, 136.
12. For a detailed assessment of the internal and external architecture and decoration of St Andrews Cathedral, see: David McRoberts (ed.), *The Medieval Church of St Andrews*.

13. Rev. C.J. Lyon, *History of St Andrews*, vol. II, p.157.
14. Reginald of Durham.
15. For sites mentioned, see: Raymond Lamont-Brown, *Fife in History and Legend* and *Villages of Fife*.
16. McRoberts, pp. 96–104.
17. *Copiale*, p. 120.
18. *Ibid.*, p. 454.
19. *175 Years of St Mary's Cathedral*, p. 22
20. Rosalind K. Marshall, *Mary of Guise*, pp. 13ff.
21. McRoberts, p. 118.
22. The books dealing with the muniments (*chartularium*), title-deeds (*carta*), charters of privilege (*privilegia*) of the priory and the cathedral have long vanished. It is known that the following existed: the thirteenth-century *General Cartulary* was added to in the fourteenth century and later, and an eighteenth-century transcript of it is in the National Library of Scotland – Sir Alexander Gilmour of Craigmillar possessed certain folios in the seventeenth century and they were in the collection of the Maule family, Earls of Panmure, and disappeared after 1841. Then there was the great *Magnum Registrum*. In 1924 the letter-book of Prior James Haldestone was rediscovered in the Ducal Library of Wolfenbüttel and was given wide circulation in 1930 as the *Copiale Prioratus Sanctiandree*.
23. David Hay Fleming, *St Andrews Cathedral Museum*, p. xvii.

Chapter 4

1. Margaret H.B. Sanderson, *Cardinal of Scotland: David Beaton c.1494–1546*, pp. 225–8.
2. Tradition has it that the cadaver of the archbishop was taken to the Beaton vault at the East Neuk village of Kilrenny by the archbishop's nephew John Beaton of Balfour. See: Raymond Lamont-Brown, *The Villages of Fife*, p. 108.
3. John Dowden, *The Bishops of Scotland*, pp. 41–2.
4. Alexander F. Mitchell, *The Scottish Reformation*, 1880, p. 59.
5. Dowden, pp. 10–12.
6. Robert Fawcett, *St Andrews Castle*, p. 2.
7. Dowden, pp. 27–8.
8. George Martine, *Reliquiae Divi Andreae*.
9. Francis Grose, *Antiquities of Scotland*, 1789–91.
10. Veronica Smart, *The Coins of St Andrews*, p. 11.

11. Veronica Smart avers that early minting could have taken place at Mainard the Fleming's loft in the region of Abbey Street, p. 17.

Chapter 5

1. Thomas Mutto, Town Clerk of St Andrews, *The Black Book of St Andrews*. *Toft*: A Homestead and its Land.
2. *The Black Book of St Andrews*.
3. George H. Bushnell (ed.), Andrew Lang, *St Andrews*, n., p. 361.
4. The other gateway is the 'Wishart Arch', or 'Cowgait port', Dundee.
5. J.H. MacAdam (ed.), *The Baxter Book of St Andrews*, pp. iii, 13, 301.
6. *Ibid.*, p. vii.
7. Susan Campbell, *Scottish Provincial Domestic Silver*, p. 7.
8. *St Andrews Gazette*, vol. 1868.
9. *Delineations of St Andrews*, 1838.

Chapter 6

1. The cliffs at the Step Rock were dumping grounds for fragmented bones and rubble from the sites of Blackfriars and Greyfriars monasteries during the nineteenth-century redevelopments of the sites.
2. William Andrews (ed.), *Bygone Church Life in Scotland*, p. 171.
3. *Ibid.*, p. 171.
4. See: *Diurnal of remarkable occurrents*; *Register of the Kirk Session of St Andrews 1559–1650*; *Register of the Privy Council*; *Selection from minutes of the Synod of Fife, 1611–1687*; *Rentale Sancti Andree 1538–1546*.
5. Lord Herries, *Historie of the Life of James the Sext*, p. 40.
6. George F. Black (compiler), *A Calendar of Cases of Witchcraft in Scotland 1510–1727*, p. 21.
7. Andrews, pp. 166–7
8. David Hay Fleming, *Mary Queen of Scots*, pp. 518, 522–3.
9. *Calendar of State Papers (Scotland)*, vol. II, p. 120.
10. Aylwin Clar, *Queen Mary's House*, pp. 1–12
11. Antonia Fraser, *Mary Queen of Scots*, p. 249 and n.

Chapter 7

1. Professor William Knight. *Andreapolis: Being Writings in Praise of St Andrews*, pp. 7–8.
2. Aeneas Mackay. *The Life of John Major*, p. 40.
3. Knight, pp. 11–12.
4. John Loveday, *Diary of a Tour in 1732*.
5. Thomas Pennant, *Tour of Scotland*, 1772.
6. A.J.G. Mackay, *A History of Fife and Kinross*, p. 179.
7. Daniel Defoe, *A Tour Through the Whole Island of Great Britain*, pp. 640–1.
8. Knight, p. 19.
9. Defoe, p. 641.
10. Frederick A. Pottle and Charles H. Bennett (eds), *Boswell's Journal of a Tour of the Hebrides with Samuel Johnson LLD*, p. 37. Purists note that Johnson took repast at the Black Bull Inn, on the site of 31–3 South Street. The inn was owned by several generations of the Glass family. Boswell describes the location simply by the family name.
11. Samuel Johnson, *Journey to the Western Islands*, 1774.
12. Pottle and Bennett, p. 44.
13. *Ibid.*, p. 40.
14. Robert Forsyth, *The Beauties of Scotland*, vol. IV, pp. 87–8.
15. J.G. Lockhart, *Life of Sir Walter Scott*, vol. IX.
16. Sir Herbert J.C. Grierson, *The Letters of Sir Walter Scott*, vol. 8, fn., pp. 42–3.
17. Sir Walter Scott, *Journal*, Monday, 25 September 1826.
18. R.G. Cant, *The University of St Andrews*, p. 105, fn. 1.
19. Sir John Skelton, *Macmillan's Magazine*, 1863.

Chapter 8

1. *St Andrews Register*.
2. Raymond Lamont-Brown, *Villages of Fife*, p. 154.
3. George Martine, *Reliquiae Divi Andreae*, p. 179.
4. Lamont-Brown, p. 154.
5. A.H. Miller, *Fife: Pictorial and Historical*, vol. 1, p. 272.
6. Lamont-Brown, p. 82.
7. *Ibid.*, pp. 99–100.
8. John Dowden, *The Bishops of Scotland*, pp. 13 and 18.
9. Lamont-Brown, p. 53.

Chapter 9

1. George Bruce, *Wrecks and Reminiscences of St Andrews Bay*, p. 55.
2. *Ibid.*, pp. 39–41.
3. *Ibid.*, p. 64.
4. *The Black Book of St Andrews*.
5. Bruce, p. 190.

Chapter 10

1. Alex R. MacEwen, *A History of the Church in Scotland*, vol. 1, pp. 126–7.
2. *Ibid.*, p. 129.
3. *Ibid.*, p. 140.
4. *Ibid.*, p. 141.
5. The *Scotichronicon*, vol. 8, 11 May 1410.
6. R.G. Cant, *The University of St Andrews*, p. 3.
7. *Ibid.*, p. 6
8. *Ibid.*, p. 6. *Bulla*: papal seal (usually of lead) placed at the foot of a document to attest authenticity.
9. John Dowden, *The Bishops of Scotland*, p. 216.
10. Cant, p. 7.
11. Annie I. Dunlop (ed.), *Acta Facultatis Artium Universitatis Sanctiandree 1413–1588*, vol. 1, xxxii. Cant, p. 8.
12. Cant, pp. 9–10.
13. *St Andrews University Calendar*, 1983–84.
14. *Ibid.*
15. Cant, p. 14.
16. *Ibid.*, p. 16.
17. *Ibid.*, p. 24.
18. *Ibid.*, p. 25.
19. Helen C. Rawson, *St Salvators Chapel*, p. 8.
20. *Ibid.*, p. 8.
21. Annie I Dunlop, *The Life and Times of James Kennedy*, p. 328.
22. James Graham, Marquis of Montrose, *My Dear and Only Love*.
23. *Roll of the Eminent Burgesses of Dundee*, pp. 33–4, 101–2.
24. Alex Cameron (ed.), *Patrick Hamilton: First Scottish Martyr of the Reformation*, passim.
25. John Herkless and Robert Kerr Hannay (eds), *The College of St Leonard*, passim. Cant, pp. 33ff.
26. *Ibid.*; R.G. Gant, 33ff.
27. D.R. Kerr, *St Andrews in 1645–46*, Ch. 4.

Chapter 11

1. R.G. Cant, *The University of St Andrews*, pp. 7–9.
2. *Ibid.*, p. 4. The prelate's name is sometimes spelled Lawrence. He was never Abbot of Lindores; but probably is so named after his birthplace.
3. *Ibid.*, p. 105.
4. *University Court of St Andrews*: Rectorial Elections, sequence 1925.
5. Janet Dunbar, *James Matthew Barrie: The Man Behind the Image*, p. 273.
6. James Matthew Barrie, *Courage*, p. 42.
7. *Ibid.*, pp. 42–3.
8. It is more likely that the bell was named after St Catherine of Alexandria, the martyr famed for the 'Catherine Wheel' of bonfire night and whose feast was celebrated on 25 November in medieval times.
9. Greg P. Twiss and Paul Chennell, *Famous Rectors of St Andrews*, pp. 59ff.
10. Burton J. Hendrick, *The Life of Andrew Carnegie*, vol. II, p. 21.
11. *Ibid.*, vol. II, p. 212.
12. Twiss and Chennell, p. 69.
13. Andrew Carnegie, *A League of Peace*, pp. 2, 43.
14. *Ibid.*, p. 45.
15. Douglas Young, *St Andrews: Town & Gown, Royal & Ancient*, p. 258.
16. Burton J. Hendrick, vol. VII, p. 214.
17. Simon Goodenough, *The Greatest Good Fortune: Andrew Carnegie's Gift for Today*, p. 80.
18. Andrew Carnegie, *Autobiography*, p. 272.
19. George Bruce, *Wrecks and Reminiscences of St Andrews Bay*, pp. 47–51.

Chapter 12

1. Frederick A. Pottle and Charles H. Bennett (eds), *Boswell's Journal of a Tour of the Hebrides with, Samuel Johnson*, p. 44. The priest they saw was the Rev. David Lindsay.
2. D.E. Easson, *Medieval Religious Houses of Scotland*, p.101.
3. *Ibid.*, p.113.
4. *Ibid.*
5. *Burgh Court Book of St Andrews*.
6. *All Saints Church St Andrews*.

7. T.T. Fordyce, *Hope Park Church*.
8. *Martyrs' Church, St Andrews: A Short History of the Congregation 1843–1993*.
9. *Martyrs' Church St Andrews: Stained Glass and Older Memorials*.
10. Glen L. Pride, *St Leonard's Parish Church, St Andrews*: Centenary History.
11. W.E. Rankine, *The Parish Church of the Holy Trinity St Andrews: Pre-Reformation*.
12. Raymond Lamont-Brown, *Fife in Legend and History*.
13. Murder record in Julia Buckroyd, *The Life of James Sharp, Archbishop of St Andrews 1618–1679*, Ch. 9, pp. 106ff.

Chapter 13

1. A. Bennett, *Robert Fergusson: An Eighteenth Century St Andrews Student*, p. 56.
2. John Thompson, *The Madras College 1833–1983*, p. 18.
3. *Ibid.*, p. 20.
4. J.S.A. Macaulay (ed.), *St Leonards School 1877–1977*, pp. 3, 6.
5. Julia M.Grant *et al.* (eds), *St Leonards School 1877–1927* and Macaulay.

Chapter 14

1. G.W.S. Barrow, *Robert Bruce and the Community of the Realm of Scotland*, p. 188.
2. Thomas Dickson, *Return of the Representative Members of the Parliaments and Conventions of Estates of Scotland*, p. 518.
3. Listing: Foster, *Members of Parliament: Scotland*.

Chapter 15

1. George Bruce, *Reminiscences of St Andrews Bay*, p. 73.
2. St Andrews Society of St Andrews, *Hugh Lyon Playfair (1786–1861)*.
3. Sir John Sinclair (ed.), *The Statistical Account of Scotland 1791–1799: Fife*, vol. X, p. 705 n.
4. J.G. Lockhart, *Cosmo Gordon Lang*, p. 6.
5. *The St Andrews Citizen*, Series 1877.
6. A.K.H. Boyd, *St Andrews and Elsewhere*, pp. 33–4.
7. R. McNair Wilson, *The Beloved Physician: Sir James Mackenzie*.

Chapter 16

1. R.F. Murray, *The Scarlet Gown and Other Poems*, p. 11.
2. For data on Open championships, see: Bobby Burnet, *The St Andrews Opens*.
3. Background information in: James K. Robertson, *St Andrews: Home of Golf*.
4. George Fullerton Carnegie. Collection *Golfiana*, 'Address to St Andrews', 1842.

Chapter 17

1. A.B. Paterson, *The Byre Theatre: Through the Years*.

Selected Reading List

Burgh

Boyd, A.K.H., *St Andrews and Elsewhere*, Longman Green, 1894.

Bruce, George, *Reminiscences of St Andrews Bay*, John Leng, 1884.

Buckroyd, Julia, *The Life of James Sharp: Archbishop of St Andrews, 1618–1679. A Political Biography*, John Donald, 1987.

Clark, Aylwin, *Queen Mary's House*, The Council of St Leonards School, 1977.

Frew, John (ed.), *Building for a New Age: The Architects of Victorian and Edwardian St Andrews*, Crawford Centre for the Arts, n.d.

Grant, Julia *et al.*, *St Leonards School 1877–1927*, Oxford University Press, 1927.

Kirk, Russell, *St Andrews*, B.T. Batsford, 1954.

Knight, Professor William, *Andreapolis: Being Writing in Praise of St Andrews*, David Douglas, 1903.

Lang, Andrew, *St Andrews*, W.C. Henderson, 1951.

Linskill, W T., *St Andrews Haunted Tower*, J. and G. Innes, 1958.

Lyon, Rev. C. J., *History of St Andrews, Episcopal, Monastic, Academic and Civil*, William Tait, 1843.

MacAdam, J.H.(ed.), *The Baxter Book of St Andrews: A Record of Three Centuries*, Scottish Association of Master Bakers, 1903.

MacAulay, J.S.A. (ed.), *St Leonards School 1877–1977*, St Leonards School, 1977.

Paterson, A.B., *History of the Byre Theatre*, Byre Theatre, 1983.

Pride, Glen L., *St Leonard's Parish Church: Centenary History*, Congregational Board of the Parish Church of St Leonard's, 2004.

Rains, M.J. and Hall, D.W. *et al.*, *Excavations in St Andrews 1980–89*, Tayside and Fife Archaeological Committee, 1997.

Rankine, W.E.K., *The Parish Church of the Holy Trinity St Andrews*, Oliver & Boyd, 1955.

Robertson, James K., *About St Andrews – And About*, Citizen Office, 1973.

Sinclair, David (ed.), *Martyrs' Church, St. Andrews: A Short History of the Congregation 1843–1993*, Martyrs' Church, 1993.

Smart, Veronica, *The Coins of St Andrews*, St Andrews University Library, 1991.

Thompson, John, *The Madras College 1833–1983*, Fife Educational Resources Centre, 1983.

Saint Andrews Society of Saint Andrews, *Hugh Lyon Playfair, 1786–1861*, 1986.

Young, Douglas, *St Andrews, Town & Gown, Royal & Ancient*, Cassell & Co., 1969.

University

Barrie, J.M., *Courage: St Andrews May 3rd 1922*, Hodder & Stoughton, 1922.

Bennett, A, *Robert Fergusson: An Eighteenth Century St Andrews Student*, St Andrews Citizen, n.d.

Cant, R.G., *The University of St Andrews*, Scottish Academic Press, 1970.

Dunlop, Annie, I., *The Life and Times of James Kennedy: Bishop of St Andrews*, Oliver & Boyd, 1950.

Dunlop, Annie I. (ed.), *Acta Facultatis Artium Universitatis Sanctiandree 1413–1588*, T. & A. Constable 1964.

Murray, R F., *The Scarlet Gown and Other Poems*, W.C. Henderson Ltd, 1954.

Rawson, Helen C., *St Salvator's Chapel: A History and Guide*, University of St Andrews, n.d.

Twiss, Greg P. and Chennell, Paul, *Famous Rectors of St Andrews*, Alvie Publications, 1982.

Cathedral, Priory and Castle

Baxter, James Houston (ed.), *Copiale Prioratus Sanctiandree: The Letter-Book of James Haldenstone, Prior of St Andrews 1418–1443*, Oxford University Press, 1930,

Dowden, John, *The Bishops of Scotland*, James Maclehose & Sons, 1912.

Easson, D.E., *Medieval Religious Houses: Scotland*, Longmans, Green & Co., 1957.

Fawcett, Richard, *St Andrews Castle*, Historic Scotland 1992.

Fleming, David Hay, *St Andrews Cathedral Museum*, Oliver and Boyd, 1931.

Hall, Ursula, *St Andrew and Scotland*, St Andrews University Library, 1994.

McRoberts, David (ed.), *The Medieval Church of St Andrews*, Burns 1976.

Martine, George, *Reliquiae Divi Andreae*, James Morison, 1797.

Sanderson, Margaret H.B., *Cardinal of Scotland: David Beaton c.1494–1546*, John Donald, 1986.

General

Andrews, William, *Bygone Church Life in Scotland*, William Andrews & Co., 1899.

Black, George F., *A Calendar of Cases of Witchcraft in Scotland 1510–1727*, New York Public Library and Arno Press Inc., 1971.

Bround, Dauvit and Clancy, Thomas Owen (eds), *Spes Scotorum: Hope of Scots*, T. & T. Clarke, 1999.

Burnett, Bobby, *The St Andrews Opens*, Sportsprint Publishing, 1990.

Fawcett, Richard and Oram, Richard, *Melrose Abbey*, Tempus, 2004.

Feachem, Richard, *The North Britons: The Prehistory of a Border People*, Hutchinson, 1965.

Fleming, David Hay, *Mary Queen of Scots: From Her Birth to Her Flight into England*, Hodder & Stoughton, 1897.

Keppie, Lawrence, *Scotland's Roman Remains*, John Donald, 1986.

Lamont-Brown, Raymond, *Fife in History & Legend*, John Donald, 2002.

Lamont-Brown, Raymond, *The Villages of Fife*, John Donald, 2002.

Mitchell, Alexander F., *The Scottish Reformation*, William Blackwood, 1900.

Reeves, William, Bishop of Down, *The Life of Saint Columba*, Dublin, 1857.

Robertson, James K., *St. Andrews: Home of Golf*, Macdonald Publishers, 1984.

Thomson, James, *The History of Dundee*, Walker, 1867.

Walker, Bruce and Ritchie, Graham, *Exploring Scotland's Heritage: Fife and Tayside*, Royal Commission on the Ancient and Historical Monuments of Scotland, 1987.

Index

BIRLINN LTD (incorporating John Donald and Polygon) is one of Scotland's leading publishers with over four hundred titles in print. Should you wish to be put on our catalogue mailing list **contact**:

Catalogue Request
Birlinn Ltd
West Newington House
10 Newington Road
Edinburgh EH9 1QS
Scotland, UK

Tel: + 44 (0) 131 668 4371
Fax: + 44 (0) 131 668 4466
e-mail: info@birlinn.co.uk

Postage and packing is free within the UK. For overseas orders, postage and packing (airmail) will be charged at 30% of the total order value.

For more information, or to order online, visit our website at **www.birlinn.co.uk**

Birlinn *Limited*
IMPRINTS: JOHN DONALD · POLYGON